# THE PALESTINIANS

## THE ROAD TO NATIONHOOD

**Minority Rights Group** is an international, non-governmental organization whose aims are to ensure justice for minority (and non-dominant majority) groups suffering discrimination by:

1. Researching and publishing the facts as widely as possible to raise public knowledge and awareness of minority issues worldwide.

2. Advocating on all aspects of human rights of minorities to aid the prevention of dangerous and destructive conflicts.

3. Educating through its schools programme on issues relating to prejudice, discrimination and group conflicts.

If you would like to know more about the work of Minority Rights Group, please contact Alan Phillips (Director), MRG, 379 Brixton Road, London SW9 7DE, United Kingdom.

## *m*

**Minority Rights Publications** is a series of books from Minority Rights Group. Through the series, we aim to make available to a wide audience reliable data on, and objective analyses of, specific minority issues. The series draws on the expertise and authority built up by Minority Rights Group over two decades of publishing. Further details on MRG's highly acclaimed series of reports can be found at the end of this book.

Other titles in the book series are:

*Armenia and Karabagh: The Struggle for Unity*
Edited by Christopher J. Walker (1991)

*The Kurds: A Nation Denied*
by David McDowall (1992)

*Refugees: Asylum in Europe?*
by Danièle Joly et al (1992)

*The Balkans: Minorities and States in Conflict*, 2nd Edition
by Hugh Poulton (1993)

*Polar Peoples – Self-Determination and Development*
by Beach, Creery, Korsmo, Nuttall, Vakhtin (1994)

*Cutting The Rose – Female Genital Mutilation*
by Efua Dorkenoo (1994)

# THE PALESTINIANS

## THE ROAD TO NATIONHOOD

by
David McDowall

Minority Rights Publications

© Minority Rights Group 1994

First published in the United Kingdom
in 1994 by
Minority Rights Publications
379 Brixton Road
London SW9 7DE

British Library Cataloguing in Publication Data
A CIP catalogue record of this book is available from the British Library.

ISBN 1 873194 70 6 hardback

Library of Congress Cataloguing in Publication Data
CIP Data available from the Library of Congress

Cover design by Wave Design
Typeset by Brixton Graphics in Stone Serif 9¼ pt
Printed on acid-free paper in the UK by Redwood Books

Cover photo of girls on the West Bank
©Marc Schlossman

# CONTENTS

LIST OF MAPS AND TABLES                                      vi
PREFACE AND ACKNOWLEDGEMENTS                                 vii
INTRODUCTION                                                 1

1    The Palestinians and early Zionism                      3

2    British rule: 1917–48                                   13

3    Partition and dispossession: 1947–9                     21

4    Deepening conflict: 1948–67                             33

5    The Palestinian Arabs inside Israel                     43

6    Exile and the rise of the national movement             63

7    Under Israeli occupation, 1967–87                       81

8    Resistance and the *intifada*                           93

9    The 1990s: Palestine lost or regained?                  107

10   A nation in the making: the Palestinians today          125

11   Palestine and Israel: in search of peace with justice   147

12   Palestinian rights: the international agenda             161

NOTES AND REFERENCES                                         167
SELECT BIBLIOGRAPHY                                          195
INDEX                                                        201

# MAPS & TABLES

*Maps*

1   United Nations 1947 partition plan for
    Palestine and the 1949 armistice
    demarcation line                                    22

2   Territories occupied by Israel since June 1967      39

3   Where the Palestinian Arabs inside
    Israel are concentrated                             42

4   Israel settlements established in the
    Occupied Territories, 1967-91                       85

5   One example of the West Bank cantonization
    that Palestinians fear                              121

6   Israel's expansion of Jerusalem's municipal
    boundary in 1967 and intended vast
    enlargement of 'Greater Jerusalem'                  153

*Tables*

1   Numbers and distribution of Palestinian
    refugees, 1948 and 1993                             64

2   Estimated current and projected
    Palestinian population                              126

# Preface and acknowledgements

The struggle of the Palestinian people to regain more than a few scraps of their original birthright is at a critical juncture, but I have tried to resist the temptation of predicting the future, while warning of the dangers of failing to achieve a modicum of justice now. The purpose of this book is to describe how and why the Palestinian people were dispossessed, the challenges they currently face and how the outside world can help them. If what I have written arouses indignation, not merely against the political ideology whereby they were dispossessed, but also against the behaviour of the West, so much the better. It is only the persistent expression of popular outrage at what has happened, and a demand for justice and respect for international law, that is likely to persuade the states involved that the real steps to peace have barely been begun.

I should give a short explanation of the terminology used in this book. I have used the term 'Palestine' to denote the area west of the river Jordan mandated to Britain by the League of Nations, except where it clearly has a political sense denoting the new Palestinian entity. I have used the term 'Eretz Yisrael' (the Land of Israel) to indicate Palestine as described in Zionist vocabulary. In 1919 the Zionists claimed within Eretz Yisrael the eastern escarpment of the river Jordan and a sizeable portion of southern Syria and Lebanon. Some Israelis still make this claim. By 'Palestinian' I mean the Arabic-speaking people of Palestine. Israeli Jews also have a right to be described as Palestinian, but I have refrained from this because few of them would welcome this description.

I owe an enormous debt indeed to those who kindly imparted their own knowledge and understanding while I was writing. These include Butros Abu Manneh, Khalid Amayreh, Mustafa Barghouti, Stephen Bowen, Peter Coleridge, Kais Firro, Rita Giacaman, Reema Hammami, Maria Holt, Jad Isaac, Tawfiq Jabariyin, Khayri Jamal, Najeh Jarrar, Hatim Kanaaneh, Mary Khass, Wendy Levitt-Kristianasen, Khalil Mahshi, Fadhil Na'ameh, Alex Pollock, Maha and Charles Shammas, and Raji Sourani. I am likewise indebted to those, some already importuned at the writing stage, who diligently commented on my first draft, pointing out numerous omissions as well as errors of fact or judgement: Peter Coleridge, Rita Giacaman, Nadia Hijab, Daniel Machover, Moshe Machover, Penny Maddrell, Nur Masalha, Ilan Pappé, Mouin Rabbani, Rosemary Sayigh, Yezid Sayigh, Patricia Sellick and Doug Soutar. For the use of material reproduced in the maps, I am grateful to Dr Clinton Bailey, the Council for the Advancement of Arab–British Understanding and the United Nations Cartographic Section. Finally, my thanks to Miles Litvinoff, who edited this book with skill, tact and forbearance.

David McDowall
London, October 1994

# INTRODUCTION

In 1918 Christian and Muslim Arabs still formed over 90 per cent of the population of Palestine. Within half a century they were not only a minority in their own land, but also bereft of political power or authority in any part of Palestine, and in the surrounding lands to which over half of them were condemned to live as refugees.

By June 1994, despite the Arafat–Rabin accord and autonomy agreement of September 1993, the status of the Palestinian people remained uncertain. Save for the absence of Israeli troops in Gaza town and camps, material conditions in Palestine had worsened. Although still more numerous than those who had displaced them, the Palestinians had discovered painfully that those world powers able to protect their few remaining rights were generally not disposed to do so, that Western public opinion was generally unsympathetic to Muslim Arabs, and that the very best they could foreseeably hope for was a recognized place probably in no more than one-sixth of their homeland, under conditions of guaranteed and institutionalized weakness.

This book sets out to explain how this state of affairs arose, the experience of the Palestinians as a result of dispossession, and the challenges they now face. Finally, the author expresses a personal view of the issues which must be faced to achieve a modicum of justice for the Palestinian people, and which may be essential to achieving long-term peace in Palestine/Israel.

# 1

# THE PALESTINIANS AND EARLY ZIONISM

## Palestine in history

*alestine* is a geographical term that has been in general usage since Roman times, if not earlier. But it is the name of a region without hard and fast borders, a part of greater Syria.[1] The definition applied by Britain from 1922 onwards referred to the land between Lebanon and Sinai, and excluded any land to the east of the river Jordan.

Today's Palestinians are almost certainly descended from the earliest recorded inhabitants of the area, who intermarried with later waves of conquerors. Among these were the Philistines (who gave the land its name), the Hebrews and the Arabs who conquered the region in the name of a new religion, Islam, 634–641 CE.

Because of its importance to Zionism, something should be said concerning ancient Jewish history. Hebrew tribes entered Palestine (or Canaan) at the end of the late Bronze Age, and were established by the twelfth century BCE, roughly the same time as the Philistines, one of several invading Sea Peoples. Both colonized and intermarried with the Canaanite population. The Hebrews were distinguished for their monotheism, and this may have been a factor in their century of ascendancy (tenth century BCE) under Kings David and Solomon. From the ninth century the Jewish kingdoms of Israel and Judaea were increasingly prisoners of more powerful neighbours, apparent in their payment of tribute, destruction, exile and reconstruction. Palestine came under Roman domination from 63 BCE, and the Temple in

Jerusalem was destroyed in 70 CE. The people of Judaea were subsequently dispersed or exterminated, while those of Galilee survived largely unscathed. By the fourth century Jews had probably begun to trickle back into Jerusalem. What marked out the Jews as unique was that, unlike other similar subject peoples of the period, they did not disappear but survived with their religious and cultural identity firmly established.

By the time of the Arab Muslim conquests the area was to a considerable extent Hellenized and Christianized, but this did not disguise the fact that Palestinian society had always been pluralist. Even during the short-lived Jewish apogee in the tenth century BCE, many non-Jewish groups lived in the region. Many Jews, no doubt, accepted Christianity and later, like most other Christians, accepted Islam. Ironically in the light of modern Zionism, therefore, many of the forebears of Palestinian Arab refugees today may well have been Jewish.

The Arab invasion, however, ushered in a new era, since, although the occupying Arab army cannot have been very large, it nevertheless imparted two unifying characteristics to the land: the Arabic language and the Muslim religion. Arabic probably became the functional language relatively quickly. Islam acquired more adherents as members of the two tolerated religions, Judaism and Christianity, sought to escape the tax and status applied to non-Muslims, some two or three centuries after the Arab conquest. By the nineteenth century 85 per cent of the population was Sunni Muslim, although a small number of Shiis and Druzes lived in the Galilee, in both cases the southernmost settlements of larger communities further north. The Christians were still at least 10 per cent of the population by 1900, mainly divided equally between the Orthodox and Greek Catholic traditions. Unlike the Muslims, half were town-dwellers and traders.

There was also a long-standing Jewish community, which towards the end of the nineteenth century numbered about 25,000, or approximately 6 per cent of the population. These Jews were concentrated in the four cities holy to Judaism: Jerusalem, Hebron, Safad and Tiberias. Many were from eastern Europe, but they were without political ambition, having come to pray and die in the Holy Land.

Palestine was governed as part of a wider area, first as part of the Islamic Empire, the capital of which had been first in Damascus, then in Baghdad. From the end of the twelfth until the beginning of the sixteenth centuries CE it had been generally governed from Egypt, first under the Ayyubids (Saladin's dynasty), and then under the Mamluks. In 1516 the Ottoman Turks wrested Palestine from the Mamluks and it remained in Ottoman hands until 1917. There was only one serious interruption to Muslim rule, the Crusades, which created in the Muslim mind much greater sensitivity regarding Jerusalem and its holy places than had existed hitherto.[2]

Palestine during the Ottoman period had never been a single administrative unit, although for most of the period it had been part of the *vilayet* or province of Syria. Palestine, as defined, was divided into three *sanjaks*, or districts, of Jerusalem (covering virtually all cultivable Palestine from Jaffa southwards); Nablus, which comprised a central area from the coast eastwards to the Jordan; and Acre, comprising Haifa eastward to Nazareth and Tiberias, and including Safad. A small portion of northern Palestine was part of the *sanjak* of Beirut. From 1887 the *sanjak* of Jerusalem ceased to be part of administrative Syria, and became directly responsible to the Ottoman capital, Istanbul. The following year the remaining *sanjaks* were incorporated in the new *vilayet* of Beirut. However, Palestine as a historic-geographical entity was understood and referred to by Ottoman officials to mean the area largely west of the river Jordan,[3] as indeed it was subsequently understood by British administrators and, more vaguely, by Arabs and Jews.

Palestinian society in the nineteenth century was far from homogeneous. The vast majority of the population (well over 80 per cent) was rural. Most of the peasantry lived in the same village as their forebears. Each village tended to be inhabited by one or two extended families (*hamulas*). Identity was governed essentially by village or religious affiliation. Nothing yet suggested a Palestinian identity. The other rural category was bedouin, practising their pastoralism on an increasingly sedentary rather than nomadic basis. Their main habitats by 1900 were the Naqab (Negev) desert, the Jordan valley and parts of the Galilee. Until the latter part of the nineteenth century[4] much of the most fertile land, along the coastal plain and the Plain of Jezreel, was uncultivated because of bedouin depredations and was only cultivated once the Ottomans drove them out, from the 1870s onwards. Wherever they have settled, their distinct cultural identity has persisted. The third category was the landowning families. Technically few people 'owned' land since in theory almost all belonged to the Sultan.[5] In practice those who collected taxes, for example, the local *mukhtar* (government appointed headman), the *shaykh* (the family or tribal head), money lender or local official, were well placed to acquire control of land and its inhabitants. Smaller landlords tended to live locally and to be involved in their village, but with the acquisition of larger estates many began to move to town. By 1900 peasant holdings were on average 50 dunums (1 dunum = quarter of an acre approximately) while larger landowners might have 9,000 dunums.[6]

Towns were small and tended to serve the locality. Even so, several towns had a reputation for particular products (and in some cases still do so): Nablus and Jaffa for soap, Hebron for glass, Gaza for rugs, Majdal for weaving and Jenin for charcoal. Jerusalem was different in character on account of the large number of Christians and Jews, the holy sites of all three religions and the stream of pilgrims these sites attracted. Towns had their own socio-economic make-up, with merchants and leading Muslim clerics, who formed an urban notable class, and traders of humbler status. Christians were increasingly prominent among the merchant class during the latter part of the nineteenth century, better placed to benefit from international trade.

During the nineteenth century Palestine began to change at an accelerating rate. A primary reason for this was European penetration. An increasing number of European visitors began to arrive in the Holy Land. Most came out of religious interest, and it was understandable, if absurd, that they should see nineteenth-century Palestine in terms of the Bible. Every scenic native, building or camel somehow validated holy scripture. It was but a small jump to conceiving of the country as one in which time stood still, the inhabitants a passive but colourful backdrop to those in search of biblical truth, particularly for Protestants with a strong Bible-reading tradition.

At the same time the missionary and political impulse of Europe made the Holy Land an area for competition. In the eighteenth century every orthodox sect had been rent with schism as one part was lured into union with the Catholic Church. In the nineteenth century the French (Catholic) and Russians (Orthodox) struggled for influence through the establishment of mission schools and protective rights over the Catholic and Orthodox communities.

At a political level, however, the Ottomans were under increasing pressure to reform their empire in conformity with European ideas. Since most Palestinians were peasants it was the changes in land registration which had greatest effect. The Land Code of 1858 and the Vilayet Law of 1864 had been intended to reassert government authority and eradicate abuses. Their effect, however, was to strengthen the grip of landholders to the detriment of the peasantry, and to confirm a local elite within the structure of the empire.[7] In 1871 the Land Registration Law further strengthened the magnate class. Since the authorities had two overriding intentions, the efficient collection of taxes and conscription of young men, the peasantry were anxious to avoid direct contact with government. So they sold the title to the land they customarily cultivated at nominal prices to magnates and notables to avoid registration themselves. Thus the landlord class expanded their landholdings dramatically. Large tracts of land were acquired by absentees, living in Beirut or elsewhere. Indeed, in 1867 foreigners (i.e. non-Ottomans) obtained the right to purchase land.[8] Even so, land registration was generally avoided so that 75 per cent of Palestine was still unregistered in 1925.[9]

In part as a result of Ottoman land measures but also as a result of European penetration, the socio-economic structure of Palestinian society began to change. The first intimation of serious change occurred in mid-century with regular steamship services, the import of European commodities, especially Manchester cotton goods (which rapidly destroyed the local textiles industry), and the export of wheat, sesame and citrus fruit to Europe. At the same time, there was a surge of interest in land, with bankers and merchants acquiring estates and their resident labour force. Thus the transformation from subsistence to a cash economy began to take place. Particularly along the coast of Palestine, peasants were transformed into sharecroppers and wage labourers, producing cash-crops, mainly citrus, for export. A fundamental change was now under way in labour relations and the economy. Far from being changeless, Palestine was being sucked into the vortex of modernization. It is easy to think of the people of Palestine, both then and subsequently, as passive before the maelstrom of events. It would be more true to say that, not yet constituting a conscious national community, the people of Palestine were profoundly weak on account of the geographic decentralization, social structure and absence of knowledge of the outside world.

**Early Zionism**

In 1881 Jewish settlers of a new kind, who had little in common with the old established communities, began to arrive in Palestine. They called themselves Hovevei Zion (Lovers of Zion). Unlike the existing religious communities, these new settlers were inspired by Jewish nationalism. They were driven by two challenges to Jewish survival in Europe: the growing barbarity of anti-semitic pogroms in eastern Europe, and the process of assimilation into a progressively secular culture in western Europe. They were seized with the ambition to regenerate Jewish identity and dignity away from such dangers, and they saw Palestine as the place in which to realize this. Albeit largely secularist, they were inspired by the Bible which gave historical and mystical authentication to their aims. Most lived in Jerusalem, Jaffa and in Tel Aviv (founded in 1909), but some were attracted to found agricultural colonies, first at Petah Tikva, outside Jaffa, and then elsewhere. The early settlers called on others to join them.

In Europe a Zionist movement began to attract young Jewish idealists. In 1897, under the leadership of Theodor Herzl, the first Zionist Congress adopted a formal programme for 'the establishment for the Jewish people of a home in Palestine secured by public law'. Implicit in this aim was the establishment of a Jewish state.[10] Publicly, however, this aim was denied to avoid conflict with the Ottoman government.[11]

How could a Jewish state be created? From the outset the Lovers of Zion were clear: 'We must be the majority. And when we are the majority, we will pick up arms and ensure our independence.'[12] One means to achieve this was through immigration of Jewish settlers, and the early Zionists lost no time in urging fellow Jews to realize their Jewishness in the fullest sense by returning to their ancestral land to create a model Jewish society. In fact the first Congress had advocated the 'promotion, on suitable lines, of the colonization of Palestine by Jewish agricultural and industrial workers.'[13] By 1914 the Jewish 'Yishuv', as the settlers were collectively known, had grown to 85,000, roughly 11 per cent of the then population, although only 12,000 of these lived outside cities.[14]

The second method was by the removal of the indigenous inhabitants. In the words of a new recruit to the movement, Rabbi Yitzhak Reelef of Meimel:

*'For the time being we are speaking of colonization and only colonization. This is our first objective. We speak about that and only about that. But it is obvious that "England is for the English, Egypt for the Egyptians, and Judaea for the Jews." In our country there is room for us. We will tell the Arabs: Move away. If they refuse, if they forcibly object, we will force them to move. We will hit them on their heads, and force them to move.'[15]*

In 1901 Herzl proposed to the Ottoman authorities that Jewish settlers should have the right to transfer the indigenous population.[16] The request was refused, but Herzl privately recorded his continuing aim 'to spirit the penniless population across the border by procuring employment in transit countries, while denying it any employment in our own [*sic*] country'.[17] This concept, 'transfer', became a recurring theme among Zionist leaders, was advocated across the political spectrum and came to fruition in 1948.[18]

Zionist leaders were thus well aware that Palestine was not an empty land. Israel Zangwill, for example, who adopted the phrase 'a land without a people for a people without a land', had already visited Palestine in 1897 and knew perfectly well that it was populated.[19] His view, however, echoed that of Herzl (who had also visited Palestine) that the natives were of little consequence. 'There is no particular reason for the Arabs to cling to these few kilometres', Zangwill pronounced in 1917; '"To fold their tents", and "silently steal away" is their proverbial habit: let them exemplify it now.'[20] The idea that the Arabs of Palestine could reasonably 'move over' to make room for a Jewish state became another recurrent theme of Zionist leaders, for example David Ben-Gurion, Israel's first Prime Minister, and Abba Eban, its persuasive Foreign Minister.[21] It was predicated on the idea that Arabs did not hold the land they inhabited in the same affection as the new settlers and that, in contrast to the Jews, they did not constitute a 'people'.

Other practical means adopted by the Zionists were economic. The first was called 'conquest of the land', in practice the acquisition of land for agricultural colonies. In fact it had a mystical aspect, the inalienability of the Land of Israel and the Jewish obligation to redeem it enjoined in Scripture, most specifically in Leviticus XXV, 5.[22] 'Redemption of the land' became a guiding principle of Zionism. By 1914 the Yishuv had acquired 420,000 dunums (94,000 acres), approximately 2 per cent of the cultivable land of Palestine. Most of the lands were purchased from absentee Arab landlords, some in Beirut or elsewhere outside Palestine. Of these perhaps the most notable was Ilyas Sursuq who sold a large tract of prime agricultural land around Fula and 'Afula in the Plain of Esdraelon in 1910.[23] In the period 1878–1907 only 6 per cent of the land sold was sold by local landlords or peasants.[24]

At first some of the peasantry, whose families had cultivated these lands for generations, were able to continue working the land as paid labour. But in 1901 the Jewish National Fund (JNF) was established with the aim of acquiring land not only for Jews, but also for the promotion of Jewish labour, the 'conquest of labour'.[25] Land acquired by the JNF became an inalienable part of the Jewish patrimony, and furthermore only Jews could work it. It was only a small progression to the idea that for any member of the Yishuv to employ non-Jews was to undermine the Zionist ideal. Thus the economic process, acquisition of land and denial of employment to its previous inhabitants meshed with the undeclared aim of getting rid of Palestine's indigenous population.

## The Palestinian response

Anyone following closely the utterances of Zionists in Europe would have deduced that systematic dispossession of the indigenous population was the clear intention. But the people of Palestine were, of course, in no position to learn the thinking of European Zionists. Their response was rooted in direct experience. That meant that few apart from those directly affected realized what was going on. Those who found themselves turfed off their ancestral lands because of a sale arranged, for example, in Beirut reacted violently. Between 1886 and 1914 at least eight of the forty or so Jewish colonies were attacked by local peasants.[26] Some peasants unsuccessfully tried to purchase their lands once they learnt that their landlord was negotiating with the JNF.[27]

Although the total number of peasants who thus lost their lands was still relatively small, and although the JNF also acquired uncultivated lands, the question of Jewish immigration and land acquisition had become the major political issue among the educated elite by 1914. The first protest had been sent by Arab notables in 1891 to the Grand Vizier in Istanbul asking him to prohibit European Jewish immigration, and to end land purchase by those already in Palestine.[28] Arab fears were well understood by the Ottoman government, which had tried to resist the progressive encroachment of the European Powers during the course of the century. It was characteristic of its own impotence that when it ruled that no more Jews could enter Palestine, the Great Powers acted together forcing it to limit the prohibition to immigrants *en masse*, rather than individuals, making the prohibition virtually worthless. They also thwarted Ottoman attempts to introduce a complete ban on European Jewish land purchase.[29] In 1902 the Syrian Muslim thinker and Arab nationalist Rashid Ridha warned in his Cairo-based journal *al-Manar* that the Jews sought national sovereignty in Palestine.[30]

The restitution of the 1876 constitution, following the Young Turk Revolution of 1908, allowed freedom of expression in Palestine, and anti-Zionism was one specific characteristic of the nascent Arab movement. A number of journals appeared, of which two in particular, *al-Karmil* (1908) and *Filastin* (1911), adopted a strongly anti-Zionist stance and spoke of Palestine as a distinct geographical entity.[31] Articles appeared opposing land sales, and criticizing would-be vendors. In 1914 a circular distributed and published in the press and entitled 'General Summons to Palestinians – Beware of the Zionist Danger' warned that 'The Zionists desire to settle in our country and expel us from it', and was signed anonymously by 'a Palestinian'.[32] Thus it could not be said that Palestinians were ignorant, passive or indifferent towards what was going on. But they were undeniably weak, because of the nature of land tenure and the decentralized nature of Palestinian society, and because government was under pressure from the European powers and was in the hands of Ottoman rather than a cohesive local leadership.

# 2

## BRITISH RULE:
## 1917–48

Palestine fell under British control during the First World War. In December 1917 British forces advancing from Egypt drove the Ottomans from Jerusalem, and in the next few weeks captured the rest of Palestine. The people of Palestine viewed these developments with considerable anxiety. On the one hand, the end of Turkish rule, with its recent but overt ethnic nationalism, was bound to be welcome to Arabs awakening to their own ethnic identity.[1] On the other, they felt apprehensive, confused by the conflicting undertakings Britain had made concerning the future of the captured Ottoman territories.[2] Of these the real bombshell came in November 1917, when the contents of a letter from the British Foreign Secretary, Arthur Balfour, to Lord Rothschild, drafted for publication, indicated that

*'His Majesty's Government view with favour the establishment in Palestine of a national home for the Jewish people, and will use their best endeavours to facilitate the achievement of this object, it being clearly understood that nothing shall be done which may prejudice the civil and religious rights of the existing non-Jewish communities in Palestine, or the rights and political status enjoyed by Jews in any other country.'*

Britain's motive in encouraging the colonization of an already inhabited land was to secure its political and strategic position in Palestine, and to undermine Russian and French interests provided for in the Sykes–Picot Agreement. Britain's desire for sole control of Palestine was to create a buffer between the Suez Canal, vital to the route to India, and any political entity (Muslim or European) further north.[3] The Declaration was also motivated by the strong Protestant Bible-reading ethic that prevailed in Britain's ruling establishment. The idea of assisting in the 'gathering in' of the Children of Israel resonated with a scriptural upbringing.

One year later, barely a week before the Armistice, Britain and France issued a joint declaration of their aim:

*'the complete and final liberation of the peoples who have for so long been oppressed by the Turks, and the setting up of national governments and administrations that shall derive their authority from the free exercise of the initiative and choice of the indigenous populations...'[4]*

It was a cynical and hypocritical statement. Neither Britain nor France harboured the slightest intention of allowing self-determination. Balfour certainly had no regard for 'the civil and religious rights of the existing non-Jewish communities', for in August 1919 he noted:

*'Zionism, be it right or wrong, good or bad, is rooted in age-long traditions, in present needs, in future hopes, of far profounder import than the desires and prejudices of the 700,000 Arabs who now inhabit that ancient land...as far as Palestine is concerned, the Powers have made no statement of fact which is not admittedly wrong, and no declaration of policy which, at least in the letter, they have not always intended to violate.'[5]*

It was impossible to pretend that a Jewish home might not ultimately lead to a Jewish state, or that Zionists were not crystal clear in their goals. As Israel Zangwill wrote in 1919, 'The Jews must possess Palestine as the Arabs possess Arabia, or the Poles Poland.'[6] Lord Curzon (who succeeded Balfour as Foreign Secretary) remarked of Chaim Weizmann, the chief Zionist spokesman, in January 1919: 'He contemplates a Jewish State, a Jewish nation, a subordinate population of Arabs, etc., ruled by Jews; the Jews in possession of the fat of the land, and directing the administration.'[7]

Weizmann, however, had one line for Palestinian consumption and quite another for Europe. In May 1918 he assured Palestinian leaders: 'It is not our objective to seize control of the higher policy of the province of Palestine.' Less than a year later he was demanding at the Peace Conference circumstances in which it would be

> *'possible to send into Palestine 70 to 80,000 Jews annually...*
> *Later on when the Jews formed a majority, they would be ripe to*
> *establish such a Government as would answer to the state of the*
> *development of the country and to their ideals.'*[8]

For the then 93 per cent of Palestine's population which was 'non-Jewish', the implications of the Balfour Declaration were devastating. It has often been assumed that in their opposition to Zionism, the Arabs of Palestine were anti-Jewish and anti-democratic. Yet they joined with other Arabs of Greater Syria calling for 'a democratic civil constitutional monarchy [under the Hashemite Amir Faysal] on broad decentralized principles, safeguarding the rights of minorities' and opposing the Zionist settlement of Palestine.[9] Zionism, and Britain's part in it, constituted a mortal attack.

Flowing from Britain's decision to encourage Jewish settlement, the Palestinians were further weakened by Britain's decision to follow previous Ottoman practice, and treat the Muslim and Christian communities as separate entities, in spite of the expressed Arab desire to be treated as a single community. Arabs could only construe it as a deliberate attempt to frustrate their unity. Then, when Britain was awarded the mandate for Palestine by the new League of Nations in 1922 (in disregard of its own Covenant)[10] the Palestinians learnt that it included the objective of the Balfour Declaration with the designation of a Jewish agency to assist the British authorities to develop Palestine economically.[11] The expectation that Jewish colonists would develop Palestine implied growing economic power in the country and it was not long before this expectation started to be fulfilled.[12]

Leading Palestinians failed to respond effectively to the challenge. In part this was because they had to challenge the legality of the actual mandate, its authorization of Jewish settlement, and its recognition of the Jewish Agency as the sole institution outside the British administration for economic development. Neither the League nor Britain had any intention of amending the mandate. They lacked the capital and skill resources to compete economically. Their failure was also to do with their unfamiliarity with the conduct of affairs in Britain. While Zionists like Weizmann were able to create powerful networks across the ruling establishment in Britain, the Palestinian Arabs had no foothold at all, and no easy route (unlike the Jewish community) whereby to achieve an easy familiarity with Britain's rulers. Possibly most damaging of all, the notable families of Palestine largely represented the religious, landowner and merchant elites of the land. They might form a discernible class, but as a class they tended to act in economic competition and rivalry with each other for prestige. Two broad factions existed around two leading Jerusalem families, the Husseinis and the Nashashibis. Decisions on how to respond to the acute challenge of Zionism were affected by inter-family rivalries, and the result was a failure to direct popular anger into an effective channel. Even had they been able to forge a unified programme, efficient mobilization of a highly decentralized population remained exceptionally difficult. In particular Palestine's leadership was damaged by the British decision (against the will of most leading Muslims) to appoint Hajj Amin al-Husseini as Mufti of Jerusalem, an appointment which implied primacy over Palestine's Muslims. Hajj Amin turned out to be a vacillating and poor tactician, though not the evil man that he has often been portrayed.[13]

As a result Palestinians tended to appear recalcitrant and negative. Because they viewed the mandate's provision for Jewish settlement as an illegal violation of the indigenous population's rights, they decided against any participation that might imply they accepted the mandate's legitimacy. Technically they may have been right. Practically they ruled themselves out of the game now in play, no longer one of preventing Jewish settlement, but one of seeking to limit and contain it by effective persuasive means. Thus both Christian and Muslim Arabs boycotted a Legislative Council proposed by the British to draw all communities into participation in the administration.[46] So the Palestinians abandoned the chance to moderate Jewish settlement, but proved too disunited to achieve the kind of total boycott of the British administration that might have force the mandatory's hand.[14]

By comparison the Zionist leadership was conciliatory, asserting that

> '*the absolute desire of the Jewish people is to live with the Arabs in conditions of unity and mutual honour and together with them to turn the common homeland into a flourishing land, the consolidation of which will ensure each of its peoples undisturbed national development.*'[16]

The failure of countless Arab delegations to modify British policy regarding Zionism meant that popular anger was expressed in violence. In 1920 a number of Jewish settlements were attacked. In 1921 a more serious outburst of anger by Arabs in Jaffa led to the deaths of nearly 200 Jews and 120 Arabs. What a commission of enquiry decided was a spontaneous outburst, was naturally interpreted by Jews as a pogrom similar in motive and kind to those from which they had escaped in eastern Europe. The Yishuv began to organize its military ability to defend itself.

Furthermore, leading Zionists felt freer to enunciate their long-standing views regarding Palestine. In the words of Dr Eder, a senior representative of the Zionist Organization: 'There can be only one national home in Palestine, and that is a Jewish one, and no equality in the partnership between Jews and Arabs, but a Jewish preponderance as soon as members of the race are sufficiently increased.'[17] Thus, before the end of 1921 Palestinian Arabs knew their fears to be thoroughly justified.

In 1929 Arabs massacred Jews in Jerusalem, Safad and most notably Hebron, three of the four cities of Palestine holy to the Jews. In all, 133 Jews died, 60 of them in Hebron.[18] Apart from the loss of life, the outrage was significant for two particular reasons. For the first time Arabs launched attacks on Jewish communities which pre-dated Zionism, and indicated that they no longer discriminated between Jews who merely lived in Palestine and those whose political programme threatened them. Secondly, the attacks had been made for religious reasons. Behind the attack lay the rising tension over control of the Western (Wailing)

Wall, sacred to Jews but abutting the Haram al-Sharif, the main Muslim shrine in Jerusalem, and legally under Muslim ownership since the twelfth century.[19] Hajj Amin al-Husseini, as Grand Mufti and President of the Supreme Muslim Council, skilfully used the Haram al-Sharif as a symbol of identity, one that was far more potent in the minds of ordinary Palestinian Muslims than abstract arguments concerning Zionism or that new-fangled notion, self-determination.[20] Thus the contest between Jew and Arab for Palestine spilled over into the religious domain, drawing in the wider Muslim world, and blurring the distinction between Zionist and non-Zionist Jews in Arab minds. The Haram al-Sharif and the Western Wall have lost none of their emotive appeal since that time.

While they remained a majority the Palestinian Arabs demanded representative national government, since this would enable them democratically to limit or end Zionist immigration and land purchase, but this was refused. Briefly Britain acceded to the demand to end Jewish immigration and ban land trans-fers, but the following year, 1931, retreated from these undertak-ings. Such vacillations merely heightened Jewish and Arab apprehensions concerning British policy.

In the meantime land purchases continued apace, now increasingly of cultivated land owned by local notables. As an official British report observed:

*'The result of the purchase of land by the Jewish National Fund has been that land has been extra-territorialized. It ceases to be land from which the Arab can gain any advantage either now or at any time in the future. Not only can he never hope to lease or cultivate it, but by the stringent provisions of the lease of the JNF he is deprived for ever from employment on that land.'[21]*

A growing number of peasants thus found themselves thrown off the land.

Finally, in 1936 the peasantry of Palestine rose in revolt in an attempt to drive out both their unwanted rulers and settlers. The revolt was most vigorous in those areas where new Jewish agri-cultural activity was greatest, and around Haifa and Jaffa to which much casual and evicted Arab labour had been attracted.[22]

It took British troops eighteen months to suppress the revolt and they only succeeded by using ruthless measures including the sacking of villages and the summary execution of suspects.

It was this popular outburst rather than the political efforts of notables which persuaded Britain to establish a Royal (Peel) Commission to investigate the causes of the revolt. For the first time the incompatibility of Britain's promises to Jews and Arabs was publicly admitted. In the light of this incompatibility the Peel Commission felt bound to recommend the partition of Palestine. It also recommended an 'exchange' of Jews and Arabs out of each area in order to remove dissident minorities. The recommendation perfectly stated the asymmetry implicit in population exchange: 225,000 Arabs to leave the coastal plain as against 1,250 Jews from Arab designated areas. In reality 'exchange' was clearly transfer, the idea which the Zionist leadership had been privately promoting for some years.[23] The fact that Britain had formally proposed the idea made it possible for Zionists to accept it publicly. As Ben-Gurion wrote at the time, 'as the British propose to give the Arabs part of the country they promised us, it is only fair that the Arabs in our state should be transferred to the Arab part',[24] a kind of 'heads I win, tails you lose' philosophy.

The 1937 Peel Report triggered a renewed outburst of Arab violence, and led to demands that Jewish immigration and land purchases be stopped, that Palestine should become an independent state like Iraq, linked to Britain by treaty, and that the total proportion of Jews to Arabs should not increase beyond 30 per cent. Palestinian leaders offered to safeguard Jewish civil and political rights under such a regime, with Hebrew as the second official language.[25]

Britain offered a fresh deal in its White Paper of 1939, proposing a single bi-national state, one less explicitly Arab that what the Arabs wanted, but including an undertaking that Jews would not constitute more than one-third of the total population. It proposed to restrict Jewish immigration to 75,000 over five years. It also proposed to form a Palestine government as soon as conditions allowed.

The Zionists were angrily opposed to any such proposals, not only on principle but now because of what was beginning to happen to the Jews of central Europe. The Palestinian Arab leadership rejected the White Paper too, not because it did not go far enough concerning control of Jewish immigration, but because it did not include an explicit and cast-iron commitment to Palestinian independence at the end of a transitional period (now clearly defined by oncoming war between Britain and Germany). Undoubtedly this rejection was a bad miscalculation of Palestinian popular feeling, let alone the political situation.

However, it is doubtful whether, had the Palestinians accepted the White Paper, it would really have made any difference. World war and the Holocaust in Europe changed the situation entirely, and neither the Palestinians, nor indeed Britain, were able to resist its implications. To the very end of the Palestine mandate, however, Britain wavered between partition and its preferred solution of maintaining the integrity of Palestine, under some kind of trusteeship.[26]

# 3

## PARTITION AND DISPOSSESSION:
### 1947–9

At the end of the war Britain was exhausted economically at home and in Palestine found itself engaged in a fruitless endeavour to maintain security against a skilful and deadly campaign by Zionist groups and, more importantly, against the psychological impact of the Holocaust. In 1947 it decided it could no longer fulfil the promises it had made 30 years earlier and asked the United Nations, as heir to the League of Nations, to terminate the mandate and take whatever steps it felt necessary to resolve the question of Palestine.[1]

### Partition

By 1947 the Palestinians were in a much weaker state than they had been before the war. Whatever capacity they had for guerrilla war had been largely smashed in the rebellion of 1936–8. They also now faced a highly organized Jewish fighting force, based upon the defence force the British had helped to train during the 1936 rebellion, and the Jewish brigades which had served in the British army during the war, and they faced Jewish terror organizations whose ability for violence far surpassed their own, both in quality and in quantity.[2] Furthermore, the extermination of European Jews had driven its survivors in desperate search of refuge to Palestine. Hitler's genocide wracked Europe and the USA with guilt and with a desire to provide a safe haven for the survivors. That guilt was turned to popular disgust by British government atttempts to limit Jewish immigration by turning back illegal immigrant ships.

MAP 1

## United Nations 1947 partition plan for Palestine (*left*), *and the* 1949 armistice demarcation (*right*)

Based on D. Watkins, *The Exceptional Conflict: British Political Parties and the Arab-Israeli Conflict*, Council for Advancement of Arab–British Understanding, London, 1984

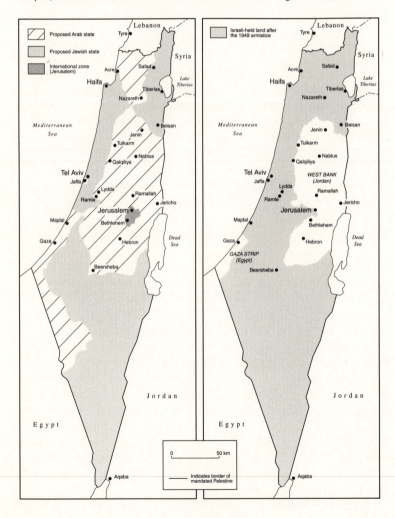

Most importantly, however, the traditional Palestinian leadership was both marginalized, as a result of the 1936–9 revolt, and fragmented. The leadership of the Yishuv was able to forge a consensus, and to plan a strategy for the oncoming test. In contrast, Palestinians found themselves dependent on neighbouring Arab states for military and political support, because of the weakness of the Palestinian political leadership and because these states could act as members of the UN. However, each of these Arab states had its own vital and conflicting interests to pursue.[3]

The basic Arab argument was that 'the future constitution and government of Palestine should be based upon the free consent of the people of that country and must be shaped along democratic lines'.[4] This was a restatement of the repeated Arab demand for self-determination and democracy, expressed in 1919 (for all Greater Syria), and by representative Palestinian Arab bodies in 1928, and again in 1939.[5] The maintenance of the geographical integrity of Palestine, and the establishment of a secular democratic state, one in which the existence of the Arab majority could be assured, were and remained the guiding political principles of the Palestine Arabs. But the manner in which the Arabs made their case was unfortunate, to say the least.[6]

The UN Special Committee on Palestine (UNSCOP), established to decide what should be done with the territory, favoured partition,[7] with proposed Jewish and Arab states and an international zone. UNSCOP was composed of lesser UN members all of which knew that the two superpowers favoured partition, and most of which were profoundly ignorant about Palestine.[8] Once again, the Palestinians boycotted UNSCOP and thereby forfeited the chance to minimize the damage. Partition was confirmed by General Assembly Resolution (UNGAR) 181 of 29 November 1947. In order to secure a majority in favour of partition, the United States applied pressure on a number of member states.[9] Predictably the Palestinians rejected the UN decision, while the Jewish Agency accepted it (see Map 1).

It is worth explaining why each party responded as it did. The Jewish side, led by Ben-Gurion, decided to accept the partition proposal because it provided for international recognition of a sovereign Jewish state in part of Palestine. This gain outweighed the fact that the proposed Jewish portion fell short of Zionist claims. Ben-Gurion knew that the Yishuv was much stronger than the Palestine Arabs politically, militarily and economically. He urged fellow Jews to accept the partition plan, pointing out that arrangements are never final, 'not with regard to the regime, not with regard to borders, and not with regard to international agreements'.[10] Indeed, he probably greeted partition in the same light as the Peel partition proposal ten years earlier: 'I see in the realisation of this plan practically the decisive stage in the beginning of full redemption and the most wonderful lever for the gradual conquest of Palestine.'[11] So when his Minister of Justice designate suggested in May that Israel's declaration of independence should specify the borders of the new state, Ben-Gurion kept his options open: 'Anything is possible. If we decide here that there's to be no mention of borders, then we won't mention them. Nothing is *a priori*.'[12]

The Arab leadership had equally clear reasons for rejecting the partition. On principle it objected to a Jewish state in Palestine, for it was a foreign and colonialist intrusion. Furthermore, the partition plan awarded 54 per cent of the land area to the proposed Jewish state, even though Jews constituted less than one-third of the population. It was manifestly unjust (and arguably absurd) in its demographic division, since it proposed a Jewish state that would be virtually 50 per cent Arab,[13] but an Arab state that would be no less than 98.7 per cent Arab.

The real failure of the Arabs, Palestinians and neighbouring governments was not one of principle but of procedure. They failed almost totally to prepare a coherent diplomatic strategy, or to prepare a practical plan to safeguard as much of Palestine as possible.[14]

The Jewish Agency had counted on partition from 1937, but was convinced it would only be workable if the vast majority of Arabs were removed from the Jewish state. It therefore created a Population Transfer Committee the same year. Josef Weitz, director of the JNF's Land Department, became the committee's most dynamic member. In 1940, when 'ethnic cleansing' was in full swing in central Europe, he advised a colleague:

*'Among ourselves it must be clear that there is no room for both peoples in this country...and the only solution is the Land of Israel, or at least the Western Land of Israel [Palestine], without Arabs. There is no room for compromise on this point...Not a single village or a single tribe must be left.'[15]*

Transfer remained a central issue. In November 1947, on the eve of the General Assembly vote, the Jewish Agency Executive met and a consensus emerged that it should deny Israeli citizenship to as many Arabs as possible, since with Israel citizenship, 'it would only be possible to imprison them, and it would be better to expel them than imprison them'.[16] A few days after the partition vote Ben-Gurion warned:

*'Together with the Jews of Jerusalem, the total population of the Jewish state at the time of its establishment, will be about a million, including almost 40 per cent non-Jews. Such a composition does not provide a stable basis for a Jewish state. This fact must be viewed in all its clarity and acuteness. With such a composition, there cannot even be absolute certainty that control will remain in the hands of the Jewish majority.'[17]*

As a result of UNGAR 181 Palestine slid towards communal war. The overwhelming majority of Palestinians took no part in the conflict. Very few exercised violence against Jews but those who did so, such as members of the irregular Arab Liberation Army (ALA), demonstrated yet again that they confronted Jewish skill with disunity and incompetence. An honest assessment would have persuaded the Arabs they could not possibly win a war.

Conflict with the Palestinians provided a golden opportunity to create a viable Jewish state. In mid-December 1947 Ben-Gurion noted: 'We adopt the system of aggressive defence; with every Arab attack we must respond with a decisive blow: the destruction of the place or the expulsion of the residents along with the seizure of the place.'[18] This was the prevailing counsel of Ben-Gurion's advisers also. One advised him that 'a high rate of casualties to the Arabs would increase Arab fear, and would render external Arab intervention ineffective',[19] while another urged:

*'we need cruel and brutal retaliating policy; we have to be accurate*

*in time, place and number of dead. If we know that a family is
guilty, we should be merciless, and kill the women and children as
well, otherwise the reaction is useless. While the forces are in
action, there is no room for checking who is guilty and who is not.*[20]

Such advice won the day.

Fighting began to intensify. The Haganah, the main Jewish
force, had foreseen the military struggle and was prepared for it.
In December it already boasted 27,000 Second World War veter-
ans. Against this there were only irregulars, 8,000 in the ALA,
and not more than 4,000 locally assembled Palestinians ready to
fight. By April 1948 the Jewish army was 52,000 strong, of whom
22,500 were trained regulars.[21] In short, neither in manpower,
weaponry, skills nor commitment was there any contest.[22]

The Zionist 'Plan Dalet', adopted in March 1948 but in fact
evolved four years earlier, aimed to consolidate control of Jewish
areas and to seize strategic areas allotted to the proposed Arab
state before Britain withdrew on 15 May. Not only were Jewish
forces ordered to expel Arab inhabitants wherever they resisted,
but 'In internal discussion, in instructions to his men, the Old
Man [Ben-Gurion] demonstrated a clear position: it would be
better that as few a number as possible of Arabs would remain in
the territory of the [Jewish] state.'[23] By the time Britain withdrew,
and the first Arab regular troops entered Palestine, the civil war
phase was over, approximately 300,000 Arabs had already been
rendered homeless and the Haganah had captured substantial
areas allotted to the putative Arab state. As important, Plan Dalet
provided for the takeover of state institutions. By 15 May the
Yishuv was ready to operate the machinery of state, while the
Arabs remained wholly unprepared.[24]

The task of the new Jewish state, Israel, was made a good deal
easier by the disunity and mutual suspicion existing between the
adjoining Arab states. Much of this arose from the secret collusion between King Abdallah of Transjordan and the Jewish
Agency to divide Palestine between them, and thereby prevent
the emergence of a Palestinian state.[25] Both Egypt and Syria,
apprehensive of Abdallah's wider regional ambitions, wished to
frustrate him in Palestine. When they intervened, therefore, Arab

unity of purpose, let alone of action, was a fiction. Disunited, Arab regular forces were both untried and locally outnumbered by Jewish forces. To cap it all, they had the disadvantage of operating on exterior lines.[26]

During subsequent fighting against Arab regular forces, Israel gained on every front, only effectively constrained by Transjordan's small Arab Legion[27] and by the fear that if it seized too much territory it might find itself in confrontation with Britain (which had treaties with Transjordan and Egypt).[28] By the time an armistice was agreed in 1949 Israel controlled 73 per cent of Palestine.

## Into the wilderness: fled or driven?

By the time hostilities ended, approximately 725,000 Arabs found that they were refugees, forbidden to return home to the 400 or so villages they had in many cases been forced to leave.[29] The United Nations tried to negotiate their return almost immediately after Britain's withdrawal, but the Israeli leadership had already decided against allowing any back, and on 16 June 1948 the Israeli Cabinet adopted this position formally. In the words of Moshe Sharett, Israel's Foreign Minister, 'they will not return. That is our policy. They are not returning.'[30] Count Bernadotte, the UN mediator later murdered by Yitzhak Shamir's LEHI (also known as the Stern Gang), found Sharett 'as hard as rock'.[31] The Israeli position was pragmatic and simple: they would not readmit so many Arabs into the Jewish state, and they needed Arab lands for the absorption of the large numbers of Jewish immigrants now expected.

This, however, was not the view of the international community, which considered the refugees had certain inviolable fundamental rights, regardless of the political or military situation. In December 1948 the United Nations General Assembly affirmed (UNGAR 194) that regardless of how they left, the refugees were entitled to return:

*'the refugees wishing to return to their homes to live at peace with their neighbours should be permitted to do so at the earliest practicable date, and that compensation should be paid for the property of*

*those not choosing to return and for the loss or damage to property which, under principles of international law or in equity, should be made good by the Governments or authorities responsible.'*[32]

Israel, however, had already argued that, having voluntarily 'abandoned' their land and dwellings, the Arabs no longer had a claim on them, and it had proceeded to bulldoze most of the Arab villages to make sure there could be no going back.[33]

How the Palestinian Arabs became refugees, whether they fled of their own free will or were driven, has been hotly debated ever since. Chaim Weizmann, Israel's first President, described the refugee situation as 'a miraculous clearing of the land; the miraculous simplification of Israel's task'.

To be sure, about 70,000 had indeed voluntarily left Palestine by the end of January 1948, before the serious fighting had really started. These were the mainly urban elite, in a sense leaving Palestinian society leaderless. Had they stayed, others might have tried to stay too. But they represented only one-tenth of the total, which exceeded 700,000.[34] Far from being a miracle, Weizmann himself was well aware that the removal of the Arab inhabitants had been a long-standing aim since Herzl's first utterances on the subject almost fifty years earlier, formalized since 1937 under the aegis of the Transfer Committee.[35] As Arab peasant families were already either being killed or expelled under Plan Dalet, or fleeing for fear of getting caught up in the fighting or being massacred, Ben-Gurion stated his unsurprising expectation, 'I believe that war will also bring in its wake a great change in the distribution of the Arab population.'[36] Five days before Britain formally withdrew, a leading member of the leftist Mapam party protested:

*'There is reason to assume that what is being done...[is being done] out of certain political aims and not only out of military necessity...In fact what is called a "transfer" of the Arabs out of the area of the Jewish state is what is being done.'*[37]

It is difficult to believe that the vast majority of Palestinians would have fled if they had for a moment imagined it would be anything but temporary.[38] The reality is that they were largely defenceless, and sought to avoid getting caught in the fighting. But there was a significant proportion of the population terrorized into leaving. At first this was the result of threats, intimidation and acts of terror, in cities like Jaffa and Jerusalem, carried out by two Jewish terror organizations, IZL (Irgun Zvai Leumi) and LEHI (Lohamei Herut Israel). Of such acts the most notorious occurred on 9 April at the village of Deir Yassin on the western side of Jerusalem, when 254 villagers were killed, some in a terrible manner.[39] Deir Yassin had a devastating impact on Arab civilian morale, in the words of Israeli military intelligence, 'a decisive accelerating factor [to flight]'.[40] Menachem Begin, whose Irgun forces carried out the massacre, commented: 'Arabs throughout the country, induced to believe wild tales of "Irgun butchery", were seized with limitless panic and started to flee for their lives. This mass flight soon developed into a maddened, uncontrollable stampede.'[41] Deir Yassin has always been considered as an Irgun outrage, but it now seems that destruction of the village was approved by the Haganah.[42]

There were also deliberate efforts to force the Arabs to leave their homes. During the summer months a decision was taken to prevent Arab villagers, both in the forward battle area and behind Jewish lines, from harvesting their summer and winter crops in 1948, an act which

> '*effectively deepened the psychological and physical separation of the Arab fellah [peasant] and tenant farmer from his lands and home, reinforcing his sense of, and existence as, an exile. In the Negev, still largely in Arab hands, the prevention by fire and sword of Arab harvesting was one direct cause of the Palestinian exodus.*'[43]

Others were directly expelled. In July Israeli forces resolved to seize the two Arab towns of Lydda and Ramla, both designated for the putative Arab state. From the start, the operations against the two towns were designed to induce civilian panic and flight, and at least one of the four Israeli brigades was told: 'Flight from the town of Ramle of women, the old and children is to be facilitated. The males are to be detained.'[44] In Lydda fear led to panic, and many were shot down in what 'amounted to a large-scale massacre' of probably 250–300 men, women and children after the town had surrendered.[45] When General Allon asked: '"What shall we do with the Arabs?" Ben-Gurion made a dismissive, energetic gesture with his hand and said: "Expel them."'[46] Approximately 70,000 inhabitants of the two towns were then driven out, almost 10 per cent of the refugee total. They were forced to march to Arab Legion lines in the foothills to the east through the heat of the day. Many, possibly hundreds, died on that march.[47]

Expulsions, sometimes accompanied by atrocities, became increasingly frequent in the mopping-up operations from late summer onwards, and increased the fearfulness of the Arab population.[48] As one refugee from Beit Jibrin recalled:

*'I was twelve in 1948 when the Jews drove us out. We fled from the village when the soldiers came and started shooting people. My grandparents did not want to leave their home; they hid in a cave near the village and the soldiers found them and shot them.'*[49]

We shall never know precisely how many atrocities actually took place, but they were on a sufficient scale for Israel's troubled Minister of Agriculture, Aharon Zisling, to say, 'Now Jews too have behaved like Nazis and my entire being has been shaken.'[50]

In the course of his research the Israeli scholar Benny Morris found an Israeli intelligence report that estimated that 70 per cent of those who fled in the decisive period up to 1 June did so as a result of direct or nearby Jewish military or paramilitary action. In other words, they fled either because they were expelled or because they thought their lives were in immediate danger, not because they voluntarily 'abandoned' their homes.[51] Although there may not have been any general written order to expel the Arab population, we now know there were explicit orders at least in certain cases. Furthermore, it was widely understood what was intended, and it took place under 'a coalition government whose policy, albeit undeclared and indirect, was to reduce as much as possible the Arab minority which would be left in the country and to make sure that as few refugees as possible would return'.[52]

Israel continued to claim that the Arab flight was 'a tactic of war on the part of the Arabs who directed the war against the Jews'.[53] This version, cooked up by none other than the Transfer

Committee in its report of November 1948,

> *'formulated the main line and arguments of Israeli propaganda in the following decades. It denied any Israeli culpability or responsibility for the Arab exodus – denied, in fact, its own members' roles in various areas and contexts. It also strongly advised against any return of the refugees.'*[54]

Thus Israel's case was as mendacious as it was misleading, but the Israeli public and many of Israel's friends abroad continued to believe it. Even after the armistice agreements of 1949, Israel continued to expel or coerce thousands of Palestinians into leaving, notably from the 'Little Triangle', a strip of West Bank land ceded by Transjordan during negotiations, and in the south from Majdal (now Ashkelon) on the coast, to Faluja and Beersheba, the environs of Hebron, and from the demilitarized zone east and north of the Sea of Galilee.[55] In 1953 it expelled another 7,000 bedouin.[56] Only 17 per cent of the Arab population, approximately 160,000, remained in what became Israel. What had really taken place was the second major case of 'ethnic cleansing' in the post-war world.[57]

We do not know what might have happened if the Arabs had prevailed in this first Arab–Israeli war. Bearing in mind that they, too, had committed atrocities against Jews, one may speculate that they would have acted in a similar fashion. If Israel's regular forces were unable to respect the rules of war, it is unlikely that irregulars would have done so. Moreover, it is difficult to imagine a victorious Arab force allowing a mass of Jewish refugees to return. Like the Jews, they wanted to be rid of the demographic threat to their own community.

However, the international community, responsible for the partition of Palestine, bore a heavy obligation for the protection of the victims of this war, whether they turned out to be Jews or Arabs. Thus it laid down the conditional[58] right of Palestine's indigenous people to return to their homes, and Israel's responsibility to facilitate this at the earliest practicable date. It is in regard to this commitment that the United States' willingness to assist Israel settle Jews from Russia and elsewhere, while leaving the people of Palestine languishing in refugee camps and in a state of semi-permanent insecurity for over forty years, is a clear dereliction of a prior duty.

The United Nations attempted to tackle the refugee question by establishing a Palestine Conciliation Commission (PCC). Its call to Israel to facilitate repatriation was an affirmation of the human rights of the situation, but did not reflect pragmatic expectation. Attempts were made to persuade Israel to accept a proportion of the refugees. In May 1949 Israel offered to take over the Gaza Strip together with its refugee and indigenous population,[59] but retracted it when it discovered that there were 280,000 Arabs in Gaza, not just over 100,000 as it had thought. Under US pressure it made a second offer to accept 100,000 returnees in July 1949 but this collapsed in a storm of protest inside Israel and repudiation by Arab states which pointed out that, if Israel could absorb hundreds of thousands of European Jews, it could most certainly take back the indigenous inhabitants of Palestine.

If Israel was not going to budge, the only apparent alternative was resettlement. Syria's leader, Husni Za'im, secretly offered to resettle 300,000 refugees as part of a comprehensive peace. Israel rejected the offer.[60] Transjordan indicated that the more land Israel was willing to cede, the more refugees it would be willing to absorb.[61] Egypt also made tentative offers.[62] But in every case, for both Israel and the Arab states, settling the refugee question was a political question, not an ethical one. As the Israeli representative to the PCC remarked, the refugees had become 'a scapegoat. No one pays attention to them, no one listens to their demands, explanations and suggestions. But...all use their problem for purposes which have almost no connection with the aspirations of the refugees themselves.'[63]

The refugees themselves formed a delegation to represent their views, but were ignored not only by Israel but by the Arab governments. Their plea was essentially humanitarian and non-political, offering 'to accept Israel as it existed on the condition that each refugee be allowed to return to his home, whether it was under Arab or Israeli jurisdiction'.[64] No one was willing to provide the muscle necessary to fulfil this utterly reasonable humanitarian request.

# 4

## DEEPENING CONFLICT:
## 1948–67

**From 1948 to 1967**

With the conclusion of an armistice between Israel and its neighbours, Palestine ceased to exist in international consciousness, and Palestinians were thought of only as refugees. Egypt was left in control of the town Gaza and a small strip of land, 45 km long by 6–10 km wide. The Gaza Strip remained notorious for deprivation and overcrowding, the area's indigenous population of 80,000 (and their identity) being swamped by some 200,000 refugees, a proportion of 70 per cent that remained constant as the total population inexorably climbed over the next 44 years to exceed one million. Egypt administered the territory through a military government, but it did not annex it.

However, in the truncated hinterlands of Jerusalem, Nablus and Hebron, now known as the West Bank, King Abdallah moved quickly to legitimize his hold. With his troops actually holding the area, the local notables bowed to the inevitable and gave him their support in December 1948. Here, the refugee population was proportionately lower than in Gaza, approximately 55 per cent (falling to 44 per cent in 1967). In 1950 the West Bank was formally annexed into the renamed Hashemite Kingdom of Jordan. Thus the new state's population of 450,00 was almost trebled to 1,280,000 citizens, of whom just over half a million were refugees.

Whatever the Hashemite monarchy gained in territory and power it lost in stability. It was correctly suspected of having reached a cynical understanding with Israel[1] and that, as a result, it had not defended Palestine as it could have done. There was great bitterness over the loss of Lydda and Ramla, which the overstretched Arab Legion had not attempted to defend. The sense of betrayal was increased when the term 'Palestine' was removed from all Jordanian maps and official statements in 1950.[2]

In order to retain economic and political power, the Hashemite regime reduced the administrative importance of Jerusalem, and the civil governors appointed to the three new governorates, Nablus, Jerusalem and Hebron, were usually East Bank Jordanians. Popular participation even in local government was limited by direct control from Amman, and by the small number of eligible voters. The Hashemites rewarded those notables willing to incorporate themselves into the establishment, thus achieving a grip on the socio-economic structure of the West Bank, with the exception of the refugees.[3] It also deliberately favoured the economic development of the East rather than the West Bank, to allow the latter to become a backwater.[4] As a result, there was little love lost between the Hashemite monarchy and the majority of Palestinians who mourned the loss of their identity and the advent of yet another set of imposed rulers, and pro-British ones at that.[5] Palestinian frustration found expression in the growth of radical ideas in the refugee camps both sides of the Jordan, and in the assassination of Abdallah in Jerusalem in July 1951. For the next few years Jordan was in serious ferment as the monarchy came under repeated threat from Arab nationalists and democrats demanding a constitutional monarchy. By the end of the decade, however, King Hussein, Abdallah's grandson, had suppressed nationalist expression.

Even during the 1948 war the terms of the conflict had been rapidly redefined from a communal Arab–Jewish conflict inside Palestine to an *interstate* Arab–Israeli conflict that now affected a wider region. Following the 1949 armistice, when it was perfectly clear that Israel was stronger militarily than all its neighbours put together, Israel made clear it would not brook any trouble on its borders. On the whole Israel's neighbours, fearful of losing more territory, took that warning seriously, but talked of a 'second round' once they were ready to settle the account. With such talk, with long borders to defend and local people and junior commanders in the border areas incensed by the injustice they felt, the Arab governments found it almost impossible to prevent border incidents, though there is no doubt that for at least five years they generally did their best to do so.[6]

The central problem was what was termed 'infiltration'. The vast majority of those who infiltrated were peasants trying to slip home, either to return, or to see relatives or to harvest crops either on account of acute hunger or out of deep attachment. Large numbers of refugees lived either within sight of their homesteads, or within three hours walk or so. In 1952, the peak year, there were over 16,000 detected cases of infiltration.[7] Occasionally these infiltrators robbed or murdered Jews, a personal vengeance for their misfortunes. Up to the mid-1950s such infiltrators were responsible for the deaths of about 40 Jewish civilians annually.[8] Such incidents, and the danger of refugees resettling themselves quietly inside Israel, made the latter react vigorously, accusing its neighbours of deliberately fomenting trouble. But Glubb Pasha, commanding the Arab Legion, believed it was

> *'some deep psychological urge which impels a peasant to cling to and die on his land. A great many of these wretched people are killed now, picking their own oranges and olives just beyond the [armistice] line. The value of the fruit is often negligible. If the Jewish patrols see him he is shot dead on the spot, without any questions. But they will persist in returning to their farms and gardens.'*[9]

On the whole, Glubb's assessment seemed true. Infiltrators, regardless of age or sex, tended to be shot without compunction, including those wounded. The IDF took relatively few prisoners.[10] Between 1949 and 1956 between 3,000 and 5,000 infiltrators were killed, the vast majority unarmed.[1193] The Israeli army also carried out round-ups in Arab villages, and expelled those it decided were 'illegals'. In the Negev, for example, Israel expelled close to 17,000 bedouin in the years 1949–53, most being alleged infiltrators.[11] Such expulsions were often conducted with brutality. One *kibbutz* woman wrote anonymously of seeing such 'infiltrators', men, women and children, blindfolded, being trucked out:

> *'Those of us standing nearby had witnessed no bad behaviour on the part of the Arabs, who sat frightened, almost one on top of the other. But the soldiers were quick to teach us what they meant by "order". "The expert" jumped up and began to...hit [the Arabs] across their blindfolded eyes and when he had finished, he stamped on all of them and then, in the end, laughed uproariously and with satisfaction at his heroism. We were shocked by this despicable act. I ask, does this not remind us exactly of the Nazi acts towards the Jews?'*[13]

Having studied what happened, Benny Morris concludes that the Israel Defence Forces' (IDF) killing of unarmed civilians

> *'reflected a pervasive attitude among the Israeli public that Arab life was cheap (or, alternatively, that only Jewish life was sacred)...The overall attitude, at least down to 1953, seemed to signal to the defence forces' rank and file that killing, torturing, beating and raping Arab infiltrators was, if not permitted, at least not particularly reprehensible and might well go unpunished.'*[14]

As Morris notes, sadists exist in all armies. The issue is how vigorously senior commanders of an army enforce discipline and punish offenders, and what orders are actually given. Clearly the IDF's record contradicted its publicly professed ethic of 'the purity of arms'.

It is hardly surprising that, since peasants were refused the right of return and were treated so harshly as infiltrators, and since many wanted revenge, infiltration began to give way by 1953 to armed bands crossing the border, intent on killing as many Jews as possible. In some cases local Arab border commanders turned a blind eye out of sympathy. The Israeli public was profoundly shocked by the brutal killing of Jewish civilians. As Israel hit back frequently at innocent targets in order to achieve surprise, and to deter Arab governments from the much vaunted 'second round', pressure mounted on these governments to stand by the refugees.

Thus Egypt, Jordan and Syria increasingly found themselves pursuing a contradictory policy of trying to limit violations of the border from their side,[15] but also allowing or even encouraging a small number of *fidayi* (or guerrilla) raids into Israel from 1955.[16] Notorious *fidayi* raids included the ambush of a bus at Maale Akrabim in 1954 in which eleven were killed, and the Ramat Rachel attack by a lone Jordanian soldier in which four were killed.

Israel made it a policy always to strike back much harder. Of such raids the most notorious were on Qibya in the West Bank, in 1953 when 69 civilians, mostly women and children, were killed and their homes blown up, and the Gaza raid of February 1955 which seemed directed against Cairo, and seems to have persuaded Nasser that Israel had no interest in peace.[17] Now Egypt started in earnest, encouraging Palestinian *fidayin* to launch attacks mainly from the Gaza Strip, and a year later so too did Jordan. Palestinians, now with official blessing, and the IDF traded raids and killings.

In 1956 killings between Jew and Arab reached a new climax in Israel's Sinai/Suez operation, carried out in collusion with Britain and France, both determined to deal with the imagined threat to their interests presented by Egypt's President Nasser. Israeli forces in Gaza summarily executed all *fidayin* that they captured, and in addition carried out two massacres, one in Khan Yunis where the UN reported 275 victims, and another in Rafah where between 50 and 100 residents were shot. In all, the UN reckoned 500 civilians perished during Israel's seizure of Gaza.[18] Israel only withdrew after the United States threatened UN sanctions in February 1957. Where it had the will the United States could, indeed, ensure that Israel conformed with international norms of behaviour.

## The 1967 war

Until the 1967 war it had been generally hoped in the West that the Arab–Israeli conflict would quietly wither, with the refugees bowing to the inevitable and integrating themselves into their host countries, and Arab governments accepting Israel. But this hope foundered. Syria, Jordan and Egypt found it impossible to make peace with a neighbour that increasingly acted as an instrument of Western domination, and which pursued a policy of border belligerence, a policy of humiliating them publicly. They found themselves driven by the need to validate the rhetoric they used to assuage popular indignation with Israel.[19] By its acts against the Palestinian people Israel also laid a sure foundation for the resistance movement that burgeoned after 1967.

During 1966 tension grew between Israel and Syria, partly because the latter was following the former's example in exploiting the Jordan headwaters unilaterally and partly because it was allowing Palestinian guerrillas to operate from its territory. Israeli threats resulted in a pact between Syria and Egypt, making it almost inevitable that war between Israel and Syria would bring Egypt onto the battlefield. Following a major Israeli reprisal on the West Bank village of Samu in late 1966 and the consequent rise in tension, Jordan too felt compelled to join Egypt in a mutual defence pact. On both the Arab and Israeli sides belligerent counsels rapidly eclipsed more pacific ones. Finally, Egyptian sabre-rattling, and its closure of the Straits of Tiran,[20] provided Israel with the pretext for attack.

Israel routed the opposing Arab armies, seizing the rest of Palestine (both the West Bank and the Gaza Strip) and Sinai from Egypt before moving on to take the Golan from Syria in a total of six days (see Map 2).

Israel's Six Day War proved almost as great a disaster for the Palestinians as the 1948 war had been. Large numbers of Palestinians fled or were expelled from villages or refugee camps, particularly those on the floor of the Jordan valley where they could flee across the river. Altogether 355,000 crossed to the East Bank, of whom 210,000 had not previously been refugees and were now described as 'displaced'. Of those displaced either during the 1967 war or immediately after it, only 15,000 were allowed to return, less than 5 per cent of the total.[21] Furthermore, those given permission tended to be elderly, and many did not take up the offer since it meant family separation. Israel did not want back Palestinians young enough to procreate. By 1994 the dis-

MAP 2

**Territories occupied by Israel since June 1967**

Based on United Nations map no. 3243, rev. 2, June 1991

placed of 1967 numbered an estimated 800,000.[22] Once again, as in the period after the 1948 war, it seems that Israeli troops routinely shot civilians trying to slip back home.[23]

The Israeli cabinet hoped that even more Palestinians would leave. Within a fortnight of victory it met to consider the demographic implication of its conquests. Two cabinet members favoured demolition of all the refugee camps and resettlement in Sinai. Two others favoured resettlement of these refugees in Syria and Iraq.[24] A resettlement plan was adopted and a special unit charged with 'encouraging' the departure of Palestinians.[25] When Yitzhak Rabin became Prime Minister for his first term in 1974 he hoped to 'create in the course of the next ten or twenty years conditions which would attract natural and voluntary migration of the refugees from the Gaza Strip and the West Bank of Jordan'.[26] But his hopes remained unfulfilled.

The 1967 war finally persuaded the international community that, far from disappearing, the Arab–Israeli conflict was deepening and its resolution was more urgent than ever. In November 1967 the Security Council passed Resolution 242 which emphasized 'the inadmissibility of the acquisition of territory by war and the need to work for a just and lasting peace in which every state in the area can live in security'. It called for

> '(i) Withdrawal of Israeli armed forces from territories of recent conflict; (ii) Termination of all claims or states of belligerency and respect for and acknowledgement of the sovereignty, territorial integrity and political independence of every state in the area and their right to live in peace within secure and recognized boundaries free from threats or acts of force.'

To achieve these two objectives, the resolution also affirmed the necessity

> '(a) For guaranteeing freedom of navigation through international waterways in the area [i.e. the Straits of Tiran]; (b) For achieving a just settlement of the refugee problem; (c) For guaranteeing the territorial inviolability and political independence of every state in the area, through measures including the establishment of demilitarized zones.'

In their humiliation, the Arab states had already decided on four guiding principles: no peace with Israel, no recognition of Israel, no negotiations with Israel and action to safeguard the Palestinian people's right to their homeland. Now Jordan and Egypt accepted UNSCR 242. Syria refused, accepting it by implication only when it accepted UN Security Council Resolution 338 following the 1973 war.

It was not until 1970 that Israel accepted UNSCR 242, doing so only under pressure from the USA. In spite of the resolution's preamble, Israel made it clear it would not withdraw from all the territory it had captured. Indeed, it had integrated the Arab and Jewish sectors of Jerusalem within weeks of its capture. It had no intention of handing back East Jerusalem, or of returning other territory that it decided it needed. Here there was an ambiguity between claims on the whole Land of Israel (Eretz Yisrael) and claims on land needed for strategic security. Either way, Israel seemed bent upon taking yet more land from the Palestinian people. Nor was it willing to construe 'a just settlement of the refugee problem' as a confirmation of the terms of Resolution 194. It regarded Palestine's refugees as part of a population exchange in return for those Jews who had left Arab countries to settle in Israel.

MAP 3

**Where the Palestinian Arabs inside Israel are concentrated**

# 5

# THE PALESTINIAN ARABS
# INSIDE ISRAEL

When the armistice was signed in 1949 there were approximately 160,000 Palestinians inside the borders of the Jewish state. Almost all lived in the countryside, since the vast majority of the urban Arab population had fled or been expelled. The highest concentration was in the Galilee, particularly around Nazareth.[1] Altogether 25 per cent of Israel's Palestinians were forbidden to live in their homes, and became internally displaced. The other two main concentrations were in the 'Little Triangle', the strip of land running adjacent to the West Bank from Qalqiliya to Umm al-Fahm, ceded by Jordan in the armistice negotiations, and in the northern part of the Negev, where by 1953 the remaining 11,000 of the pre-war 92,000 bedouin inhabitants, were now congregated (see Map 3).

## Unequal and inferior: legal discrimination and military government

Israel's declaration of independence promised that it would 'maintain complete equality of social and political rights for all citizens, without distinction of creed, race or sex'. But both legal and practical discrimination reduced the Palestinian community to political, social and economic impotence.

Various laws ensured preferential treatment for Jews, to the detriment of Arabs. The Law of Return (1950) accorded any Jew the automatic right to settle in Israel, contrasting with the refusal given to the refugees and internally displaced who had so recently inhabited the land. The Entrance to Israel Law (1952) granted citizenship to non-Jews on a discretionary basis. The Law of Citizenship (1952) accorded automatic citizenship to any Jewish immigrant, while Palestinians still living in what had become Israel were denied this automatic right but had to apply for citizenship, and in many cases were refused it,[2] though allowed to 'reside'. Another law revealed the demographic competition. The National Insurance Law (1953) was enacted to encourage families to procreate with the promise of generous child benefits. When it became apparent that Arabs, on account of their higher fertility, benefited disproportionately, the law was repealed. In 1970 the Discharged Soldiers Act (1949) was amended to entitle soldiers' families to special benefits, including welfare grants, kindergarten, housing and job training entitlements. Since most Arabs were disqualified from military service they were also disqualified from these benefits. In the words of one Knesset member, 'the intention is to encourage births among one part of the population of Israel and to effect the opposite among the other part'.[3] In practice beneficiaries included Jews who had not served in the forces: 'Service in the army was...used to distinguish, crudely but seemingly innocently, between Jews and Arabs, since it rewarded Jews who had not served in the army at all.'[4]

The World Zionist Organization and the Jewish Agency (Status) Law (1952) charged these two organizations with functions normally carried out by government such as land administration, housing and infrastructural development. By their respective constitutions both are charged with providing benefits solely to Jews.

Finally, the Basic Law: The Knesset (Amendment 9) (1985) defined Israel as 'the State of the Jewish people', a definition which embraces all Jews wherever they might be and by implication relegates non-Jewish citizens of Israel to lesser status. It also prohibits any party from participating in the political process which challenges this definition of the state. Advocacy of full equality between Jews and Arabs in Israel, redefining Israel as the state of all its citizens, constitutes a rejection of Zionism, and therefore breaches this law. It is difficult, consequently, to understand how Zionism and democracy are compatible.[5]

Thus, the Israeli government, without ever once mentioning 'Arabs' or 'Palestinians', established legal mechanisms whereby the Palestinians of Israel would remain on the periphery of national life, systematically excluded from essential benefits of being an Israeli.

From the outset Palestinians were not wanted. As Foreign Minister, Moshe Sharett, one of Israel's more dovish leaders, declared in 1950: 'If there is a possibility of inducing the Arab minority...to leave the country, to send them on their way by peaceful means – this must be done.'[6] This is how Israel's Palestinians found Israel's declared 'complete equality' to be.

As already noted, Israel selectively expelled more Arabs following the armistice agreements. In the early 1950s it drew up a plan for the 'voluntary transfer' of Galilee Arab farmers to South America,[7] but never implemented it. The Sinai campaign of 1956 was seen as a potential opportunity for further expulsions. Moshe Dayan, the Chief of Staff, had already informed the ruling party, Mapai, that he favoured the transfer of all Arabs out of Israel in 1950.[8] Now a plan, entitled Operation Hafarfaret, was drawn up for the expulsion of the 35,000 Arabs from the border villages of the Little Triangle, into the West Bank in the event of war with Jordan.[9] Both as Prime Minister and as Dayan's mentor, Ben-Gurion almost certainly had approved the plan. Jordan gave Israel no pretext for action and these expulsions did not happen (but see p. 49, regarding Kafr Qasim). Further north, however, General Rabin exploited the Sinai campaign to expel between 2,000 and 5,000 Arabs south of Lake Hula into Syria.[10]

It was agreed in the leadership that the land, particularly the borders and the areas where Arabs were concentrated, had to be controlled by a physical Jewish presence, to guard against the alien threat without and within. This was achieved through the strategic settlement of thousands of the new Jewish immigrants who needed land for the agriculture and industry that would sustain them.

Regardless, therefore, of the high moral tone of Israel's independence declaration, Palestinian Israelis were placed under tight military control until 1966. The military government established in the Arab-populated areas enjoyed almost absolute powers, able to restrict freedom of movement, detain or expel inhabitants, designate any lands required for military or other purposes as 'closed areas', and control the issue of travel permits, essential to employment outside the village.[11] In theory these restrictions applied to all those living in certain areas, but in practice they were applied only to Arabs.[12]

## Land seizure and control mechanisms

It will be recalled that Jews held title to only 6 per cent of the land area of Palestine prior to 1948. The state now set about 'redeeming' the land by the transfer of most Arab land to state (i.e. Jewish) control, in order to weaken the Arab community economically, provide living-space and resources for new immigrants, and to enlarge *kibbutzim* and *moshavim*. The process of land expropriations was legitimized under more than thirty different laws of which the most notable was the Absentee Property Law (1950). This legitimized the transfer of land not only from those driven out of the Jewish state, but also from those thousands who were displaced internally. The total quantity of 'absentee property' amounted to some 300 emptied or semi-emptied villages, over 16 million dunums (4 million acres) of land.[13] Israeli Palestinians lost 40 per cent of their land under the Absentee Property Law.[14] Many internally displaced found their ancestral villages 'closed military areas'. Certain whole villages were emptied of their inhabitants, the two most notorious cases being the Christian border villages of Iqrit and Kafr Bir'im.[15] Under the Land Acquisition (Validation of Acts and Compensation) Law[15] (1953) land could be expropriated from any landowner who was not in actual possession of the land, for example those denied access by the army declaring the land a closed military area.

Israel also required of its Arab citizens proof of ownership in the form of land deeds issued by the British mandatory authority. Since landownership registration had never been completed, Israel was able to declare most of the remaining Arab-held lands to be state land. In the case of the Negev bedouin usually the only documentation held was in the form of inter-tribal agreements regarding grazing and recognized tribal rights. These were ignored. In other cases farmers were denied access to their lands by various administrative and legal instruments so that they were unable to cultivate their fields. Under an old Ottoman law, lands uncultivated for three successive years could be confiscated.[17] All in all, Arab villages probably lost over half their land during the period of military government.

Israel also gave administrative responsibility for virtually all these lands to the JNF. Thus in reality the land ceased to be state land, for these lands were wittingly passed to an agency which by definition would deny their use to Arabs.[18] The JNF administers over 90 per cent of the land area of Israel.[19]

The National Planning and Building Law (1965) omitted a hundred Arab communities from its accompanying maps, and these were retroactively declared illegal, and their lands state property, even though they pre-dated the foundation of the state. Those unrecognized communities which survive remain under threat, denied basic services (water, electricity, waste disposal, telephones, paved roads).[20]

The state also confiscated the assets of the Muslim *waqf*, endowments of land and property belonging to the Islamic community. *Waqf* property accounted for one-tenth of all land in Palestine before 1948, and 70 per cent of all shops in some Arab cities, besides urban estate, houses and businesses, which was now put at the disposal of the Jewish community.[21] This seizure was a severe blow to any hopes the surviving Arab community may have had of a relatively autonomous economic sector of its own.

Apart from land confiscation, Israel resorted to a variety of methods of control to ensure that Israel's Palestinians remained largely quiescent. It deliberately exploited the divisions that already existed in Palestinian society. Both the Druzes and the bedouin had, traditionally, an uneasy relationship with Sunni Muslims and peasantry respectively. Offered separate status and benefits, the Druzes, guided by their leadership, opted for automatic (male) conscription from 1956. The Druzes subsequently acquired a reputation for ruthlessness in their treatment of Palestinians in the Occupied Territories. The following year they were recognized formally as a separate community. In 1961 their nationality was changed on their identity cards from 'Arab' to 'Druze'. In 1967 separate government departments were created to deal with Druze affairs. In 1976 Druze education was hived off from Arab education 'to emphasize Druze tradition and history' – in other words their distinctiveness from other Palestinians. This, however, did not protect the Druzes from land seizures almost on the same scale as other Palestinians.

Israel also reinforced the cultural and geographical separation of the bedouin from sedentary Palestinians. Most of the Negev bedouin were temporarily relocated near Beersheba, but given assurances that their ancestral lands would be safeguarded for them. This temporary situation is now permanent. They were segrated from each other also. Under the military government members of one tribe were forbidden to visit another, or attend market day in Beersheba without permission.[22] In this way the state was able to destroy the old political solidarity that had existed between the different tribes all of which belonged to the Tiyaha confederation, and also keep them separate from the rest of Israel's Arabs.[23] By removing them from the 2 million dunums they had cultivated prior to 1948 Israel turned them from an economically independent community into one dependent on wage labour and meagre livestock. Today the bedouin number approximately 140,000, of whom 95,000 are in the Negev and the remainder in the Galilee.

Israel adopted a policy of leasing a limited amount of state land to the bedouin and other Palestinians under highly restrictive terms. All applicants are vetted; plots are never leased to the original landowner, nor to the same person for more than nine months; trees may not be planted. On so short a cycle there is no motivation to nurture the soil, and soil impoverishment is inevitable. By contrast, Jewish farms in the Negev may hold land on a 49-year lease. In effect Jews may hold the same land for most or all their working life.

Among the sedentary population, as among the bedouin, Israel revived and manipulated traditional structures, each village being organized along the lines of the *hamula*, or extended patrilineal family. By 1948 the *hamula* system was in decay. By reorganizing village representation on the basis of *hamulas*, by the provision (or withholding) of permits through *hamula* heads, it was easy to play off one *hamula* against another. Furthermore, by the promise of work, travel or housing permits, and university education the military government could easily co-opt people. Political parties still try to secure votes through the *hamula* system, with the promise of personal or group benefits.

The Israeli state did not want Arabs and Jews to fraternize, so it kept Arabs separate, socially, politically and administratively. The only areas where Jews and Arabs were likely to rub shoulders were in mixed towns. Under normal conditions of modernization a proportion of the peasant population would drift to town. In the case of Israeli Palestinians, the proportion who were town-dwellers fell from 12 per cent in 1948 to 9 per cent by 1976. In Acre, to give a stark example, it remained official policy to reduce the city's Arab population from 25 per cent to 6 per cent.[24] Even in mixed cities Jews and Arabs were destined to live in distinct and separate quarters. Palestinians still find that housing companies are reluctant to sell or rent apartments to Arabs, a large number because they are administered by the Jewish Agency and therefore debar Arabs.[25]

In the administrative field, the government established separate departments in most ministries, so that Arabs could be treated differently from Jews. The heads of Arab departments were almost invariably Jews. Overarching these Arab departments is the Office for Arab Affairs attached to the Prime Minister's office. It is, quite simply, a system of separate development.

Israel has always felt able to use direct force, to uproot or repress. The bedouin in particular became familiar with the brutal manner in which they were treated when grazing their livestock on ancestral pastures designated 'unauthorized areas', or were forcibly moved away from their lands to a resettlement area. But cases occurred elsewhere.

In October 1956 border guards under IDF command committed a major massacre at the village of Kafr Qasim, a border village in the Little Triangle, probably within the context of Operation Hafarfaret.[26] Forty-nine villagers, including fifteen women and eleven children, were lined up and shot for breaking a curfew (of which they had not been informed). An enquiry was instituted, and those responsible court-martialled. But where sentences were passed they were progressively reduced and within three years all the perpetrators of this mass killing were out of gaol. Both the original act, and state leniency towards the perpetrators, showed Palestinian Arabs that in the official view their lives were of little importance. This was not the last time that troops shot and killed fellow citizens. Over the years individual shootings occurred, for example while an 'unauthorized' bedouin encampment was being evicted. On 30 March 1976, troops shot dead six demonstrators protesting state sequestration of Arab lands, an outrage commemorated as Land Day thereafter. Land Day proved a decisive milestone in the political consciousness and self-confidence of the Arab community, which began to build institutions to support and protect itself from state discrimination. On 27 February 1994 Jewish troops shot dead a bedouin protesting against the massacre in Hebron two days earlier. No Jewish protesters have ever been shot dead by Israeli troops. The conclusion that the security forces are willing to shoot to kill Arab but not Jewish Israelis is inescapable.

In order to control its Arab population by extra-legal means, the state also employs the defunct[27] British mandate Defence (Emergency) Regulations of 1945, to detain at home, in their home town or in prison those it views as a danger to security. These regulations effectively strip individuals of all their basic freedoms without any need either to bring them to court, or for explanation. By 1986 one Israeli Arab, Salih Baransi, who had a long record of non-violent opposition to the state, had enjoyed only two years of freedom since 1948. Shortly after the British had enacted these regulations in 1945, the Jewish Lawyers' Association demanded their repeal. One eminent Jewish lawyer in Palestine, Ya'acov Shapira, exclaimed:

*'there were no such laws even in Nazi Germany...It is our duty to tell the whole world that the Defence Laws passed by the British Mandatory Government in Palestine destroy the very foundations of justice in this land...No government has the right to pass such laws.'[28]*

Once he became Israel's Attorney General, Shapira modified his view, noting: 'It is one thing for the military to use someone else's law. It is quite another for the Knesset to enact as its own a preventive detention law.'[29] In fact the first Knesset in 1951 expressed dismay that the government treated these regulations as having legal validity: 'The Defence Laws (State of Emergency) 1945 which have existed since the time of British rule, are incompatible with the principles of a democratic state.'[30] It called on the government to renounce them but this never happened.

## Continuing exclusion

When Israel abandoned military government in 1966 many Arabs hoped to play a fuller and freer part in the state. But this was to misunderstand a driving economic reason for its abandonment, the need to fill low-paid and unskilled jobs being vacated by African and Asian Jewish immigrants now moving into skilled or semi-skilled employment. The free movement of Arabs was an economic imperative; but they were expected to return to their villages at night, and virtually all of them did. Very few successfully rented accommodation closer to work, partly because of the difficulty of renting as non-Jews and partly because of neighbourhood hostility that had quasi-official sanction. In 1986, for example, the Chief Rabbi, Mordechai Eliyahu, declared, 'In the Land of Israel it is forbidden to sell apartments to Gentiles.'[31] Consequently the majority of the Arab labour force became used to long hours spent travelling to and from work, obliged to treat their homes as hotels, as some bitterly call them.

One might have expected Israel to relax its policy towards its Arab population after its overwhelming victory in 1967. In fact it became more anxious regarding the danger of Palestinian irredentism inside Israel, resulting from contact with the inhabitants of the West Bank, particularly since most of them lived in areas allocated by the UN partition to the Arab state. Thus a new drive was begun to 'Judaize' predominantly Arab areas, and within a decade the average loss of Arab village land had increased from one half to more than two-thirds.[32] The process continues.[33]

Since half the bedouin live in 'unrecognized' locations they are particularly vulnerable. In 1992 the government finally took action to remove the Galilee bedouin settlement of Ramiya, which had been notified of liability to removal in 1976 when the new Jewish town of Carmiel was being established. The 1992 removal was to allow room for Russian Jewish immigrants.

If illegal Jewish settlements in the Occupied Territories are evacuated, Israeli Palestinians fear they will be relocated on their own lands, in an effort to consolidate Jewish control of Arab population areas. That may mean seizure of most of the land remaining in Palestinian hands.

Given this extensive loss of land, but a fourfold population increase by the mid-1980s, Palestinians have been rapidly transformed from a peasantry to a rural proletariat. In some cases sequestered land for Jewish development was deliberately carved out of cultivable lands in order to reduce the already modest Arab agricultural base.[34] The government found the bedouin resistant to land seizures. In 1976 it offered them what it described as a compromise:

> 'Of the lands they could prove they owned [itself a notoriously difficult task], they could keep 20%. They would receive 65% of the "market value" of a further 30% of the land. The remaining 50% would be taken by the government without compensation. The offer was not accepted and the bedouin have fought a losing battle in the courts since then.'[35]

Three years later, following Israel's withdrawal from Sinai, the government confiscated Tal al-Malah, a 130-year-old bedouin site, 80 per cent of which was under cultivation, for use as an airbase. The bedouin were denied substitute farmland, and their treatment contrasted unfavourably with that offered to the Jewish settlers of Yamit. As the chief Israeli planner for the Negev said at the time, 'the bedouin can't have *moshavim* [co-operative villages] – we need them to work in our new industries in the Negev'; while another senior official reportedly remarked: 'I'm not giving good Jewish [sic] land and water to Arabs.'[36] In the case of the bedouin of Ramat Hovave, they were resettled around the perimeter of Israel's only toxic waste dump, itself sited on bedouin land.[37]

A substantial number of those Palestinians who still worked on their ancestral lands did so as wage labourers for their new Jewish possessors, but the numbers progressively dwindled because of JNF efforts to prevent them working on its lands. Agriculture accounted for 39 per cent of the Arab labour force in 1966, but this had fallen to only 9 per cent by 1984.[38] Even where Palestinians practise agriculture they are disadvantaged in two vital areas. 'Planned settlements' – virtually the whole of the Jewish sector of *kibbutzim* (collectives) and *moshavim* (semi-co-operatives) are not subject to the same pricing scheme for water as 'other users', i.e. Arabs. Arab farmers in the Negev cannot obtain water for agriculture at all. So, while accounting for 18 per cent of land allotted to field crops and fruit and 23 per cent of land allotted to vegetables, Palestinians consume only 2.72 per cent of water used for agriculture.[39] The other reason is that marketing is strictly controlled,[40] and permits are required for production. Even where Palestinians account for 25 per cent of crop production, they are only nominally represented on marketing boards. They remain unrepresented in branches with more lucrative export crops.

The majority, thrown off the land, now work in the Jewish economic sector, mainly in unskilled jobs in construction and service industries, in the jobs most susceptible to booms and slumps. Palestinian unemployment therefore tends to be about twice the national average except in boom periods. It was easy for Jewish Israelis to assume that the absence of an Arab industrial sector was due to the inability of Israel's Arabs to adjust to modern economic challenges; but this ignored the fact that before 1947 Palestinian Arab industry and business were the most advanced in the Arab world. Centred on Haifa, Jaffa and Acre, both were lost in 1948 when the business or managerial class fled in its entirety. Half a century later, however, this no longer explains the absence of an autonomous Palestinian economy.

From 1948 the Israeli state deliberately eschewed Arab areas in locating new industries. The Histadrut (General Labour Federation), which controls a quarter of the state's productive capacity, did not establish a single factory or firm in Arab population areas. This was essentially a political rather an economic choice. The state did not want the Arab community to wield any autonomous economic power. It was for this reason, too, that virtually no Jewish or Arab entrepreneur would invest in the Arab sector except for ideological reasons, since it was well understood that Arab enterprise was more likely to encounter bureaucratic or other obstacles than Jewish enterprise.[41] There is now growing concern that Arab locations are being deliberately chosen for polluting industries.[42]

Furthermore, Palestinians found themselves excluded from virtually every imaginable avenue to economic advancement. Many employers require applicants to be ex-soldiers, effectively a means of saying 'no Arab need apply'. Quite apart from the reluctance to employ Arabs except for menial or unskilled work, regulations were enacted to debar Arabs from working in any defence-related industry. In so highly militarized a society, even working in a food-processing plant was forbidden if any of its produce was used by the IDF. Obtaining a good education therefore had little to do with economic advancement.

The state also exercises systematic discrimination against the Palestinian Israelis in almost every area of state finance, services and permits. Under its Law for the Encouragement of Capital Investments, it divided the country into three zones, two of which qualify for development assistance. Generous incentives regarding rent, low interest loans and grants are offered in priority areas, 'Zone A', for industrial projects. Similar incentives at significantly lower rates are available for 'Zone B'. Zone A includes upper and eastern Galilee, areas of Jewish numerical preponderance, but excludes western Galilee where Palestinians are more numerous. Parts of western Galilee are defined as Zone B, but here the line has been drawn to include Nazareth Illit (Jewish), Tiberias, Carmiel and Ma'alot but to exclude adjoining Arab Nazareth and other Arab towns and villages. These do not qualify for any development incentives, even though per capita income is substantially lower in Palestinian population areas and unemployment twice the national average. In the south, Zone A includes all the Negev except the area immediately around Beer-sheba where the bedouin have been settled, which is designated Zone B.[43]

In 1987 the government produced an economic development plan for the Northern District up to the year 2000.[44] At the time there were 150,000 Palestinians in 24 settlements in western Galilee, compared with only 28,000 Jews in 45 settlements. The plan proposed fresh incentives for Jews to settle in the Galilee, including land expropriation, euphemistically described as 'an adjustment in land ownership', and an industrial development programme. The Palestinian sector was almost completely ignored even though Arab Nazareth had the highest unemployment rate in the country.[45]

The government also discriminates regarding grants and loans to Jewish and Arab local councils. In 1973 the Jerisi Commission established in great detail that Arab localities received per capita between one-quarter and one-eighth of allocations to Jewish localities. Since then there has been a vigorous campaign to make funding more equitable. With regard to local plannning and civic status, only four Palestinian towns have municipal status, two of which, Nazareth and Shafa Amr, already enjoyed this status in 1948. A third, Umm al-Fahm, was given municipal status only in 1985 when it already had 25,000 inhabitants, and Tayba obtained it only when its population exceeded 22,000 in 1991. Theoretically municipal status qualifies a locality for economic and government support. Only Nazareth and Shafa Amr, however, have central sewage systems. All of the other 137 Arab towns and villages are without a sewage system.[46] The average Arab village contains approximately 5,000 inhabitants, although many have populations in excess of 7,000. Raw sewage is therefore a common sight on the streets of these locations. By contrast virtually every Jewish settlement with more than 5,000 inhabitants (and many smaller ones) has a proper sewage system.[47]

Thus the vast majority of Palestinian Arabs live in what are officially described as 'urbanized' villages, which are denied the basic characteristics of urbanization. Take, for example, the contrast between Rahat, a bedouin resettlement town, and Arad, a Jewish development town nearby. Both have a population of approximately 18,000. Arad has its own local authority, a sewage system, sidewalks, five public parks, two swimming pools, two sports grounds, a cultural centre and a museum. Rahat has none of these appurtenances of a civic culture.[48]

In 1987 only 56 out of 137 Arab locations had their own elect-ed authority. Only since then has this proportion risen to two-thirds. The remainder have no local or municipal services. Many are administered by government appointees. In 1965 the state required all local authorities to produce a master plan for devel-oping their area. Approval, provided to all Jewish councils, empowers a local council to issue building permits according to the master plan without further reference to central government. In its absence a council must apply to central government on a case-by-case basis for all construction. Despite the submission of master plans over the past twenty years, barely a single Palestin-ian local authority has received approval for its plan. The gov-ernment is reluctant to grant approval for several reasons. It disputes the status of much of the land involved in these plans; it wishes to keep its options open on further land confiscations; and through the provision or denial of building permits, it can exert power over the Palestinian community, rewarding the co-operative and punishing the recalcitrant.[49]

All recognized localities are 'zoned', in other words, land is des-ignated either as land for housing/construction or for agriculture. Palestinians retain control of tightly delimited zones for their own habitation, but their agricultural lands are usually under the control of a (Jewish-controlled) regional council. The three vil-lages of Sakhnin, 'Araba and Deir Hanna, for example, are limited to administering 12,000 dunums on behalf of 20,000 inhabitants (i.e. 0.6 dunums per person). Misgav Regional Council, which controls their agricultural lands, controls 450,000 dunums on behalf of only 5,000 people (i.e. 90 dunums per person).

Regional councils refuse to allocate more land for housing, despite the needs of a population that has increased fivefold since 1948, so thousands of new dwellings have been built ille-gally. Some are torn down by the authorities. Those rendered homeless are charged with the cost of demolition, including policing the operation. The Markovitch Report of 1987 recom-mended the immediate destruction of 500 out of 2,332 illegal dwellings, and scores of hamlets in the Galilee and Negev.[50]

Palestinian accommodation remains severely overcrowded. A

survey in the early 1980s concluded that 72 per cent of Arabs compared with only 22 per cent of Jews suffered overcrowding. In 1983, 29 per cent of Arabs lived three or more to a room, compared with 1.2 per cent of Jews.[51] In 1989 some discharged Druze servicemen from the village of Jatt requested permission to live in the deserted Jewish settlement of Gitta, built on land previously confiscated from Jatt. They were refused on the grounds that 'the Jewish Agency is in charge of these "look-out" settlements and the Druzes are not Jews'.[52]

Similar disparities exist in the field of health and education. Apart from three small and inadequate charitable hospitals in Nazareth, all other hospitals are located in exclusively or predominantly Jewish areas. Emergency cases must make long journeys to the nearest hospital. In education, arguably the most serious area of neglect, Palestinian children on average benefit from only one-third of the national average per capita allocation. In 1988 the Committee on Arab Education concluded that 'if standards of education in the Jewish sector were applied to the Arab establishments, then the latter would be in need of 11,740 teachers rather than the 7,600 present today'.[53] Despite this teacher shortfall, the government halved training vacancies for Arabs between 1975 and the early 1980s, although there were only two training institutes for Arabic secondary schools compared with forty-two for Hebrew education. There is a sharp discrepancy between the aims of history teaching in the Jewish and Arab sectors. In the former the aim is 'to instill a Jewish national consciousness' and 'the feeling of a common Jewish destiny' while for Arabs the aim is 'to value correctly [*sic*] the part played by Jews and Arabs in the culture of mankind'.[54]

## Palestinian reactions

It is hardly surprising that, after many years of military government, Palestinian Israelis hardly felt reconciled to the Zionist state. Whatever they really felt, however, their behaviour in successive elections reflected their ambivalent situation. Throughout the 1950s and 1960s Mapai (Labour) was able to command a majority of Arab votes.[55] Although the proportion voting for

Zionist parties declined, Labour, and to a lesser extent other Zionist parties, hung onto a significant slice of the Arab vote. This was partly the result of granting favours to *hamulas* which co-operate, but it also resulted from the knowledge that any party perceived as 'representing the Arabs' would be excluded from functional power. In the struggle between Labour and Likud during the 1980s and early 1990s, Labour was able to portray itself as the party more likely to secure peace for the Occupied Territories. There was, therefore, a pragmatic reason for supporting it.

Many Palestinians, however, turned to the party of 'loyal dissent', the Communist Party (Rakah) and its successor, Hadash (Front for Peace and Equality). Since 1965 it has tended to win between three and five seats, insufficient to have much impact on the political scene. But it has done much at the local level, resisting land expropriation, improving employment prospects, fighting for higher wages and council budgets, and organizing the campaign for economic and political rights.

Two bodies in particular emerged with strong Communist support: the Committee for the Defence of Arab Lands, which has campaigned effectively to inhibit (but not entirely to prevent) further land seizures; and the Committee of the Heads of Local Councils, which has become the chief vehicle for Palestinian political expression inside Israel. The Committee of the Heads of Local Councils has campaigned effectively for a more reasonable share of the budget. Two other parties have competed for the vote of Palestinians: the Progressive List for Peace which flourished in the 1980s, and the pro-Labour Arab Democratic Party led by an ex-Labour politician, Abd al-Wahhab Darawsha.[56] But there has always been a dilemma over which party to vote for. In 1992 a slight majority of Palestinian voters supported Zionist parties, mainly Labour, presumably in the hope it would negotiate peace. It is widely understood within the Palestinian community that parties which depend on the Arab vote will not be invited to join any coalition government.[57] In 1992, for the first time, a Labour administration depended on the Arab members of the Knesset (MKs) to support it in the Knesset, though without inviting them into government. Thus, in the sphere of political representation, Israel's claim to democracy is vitally diminished for its Palestinian minority.

Since half the Palestinian population is aged under 15 (a much younger community than Israeli Jews) its voting power remains masked (about 13 per cent of the electorate while 19 cent of the population). In the long run the Arab vote, if united on a single issue or a coherent group of issues, could account for one-fifth of the Israeli vote, a formidable bloc on the national scene.

Beyond the parties of 'loyal dissent' are those Palestinians who reject the legitimacy of the Israeli state. Two main groups exist: the secular Abna al-Balad (Sons of the Land), and the Muslim al-Harakat al-Islamiya (the Islamic Movement). Abna al-Balad emerged in the mid-1970s, the creature of young nationalist radicals. It explicitly rejected the legitimacy of the Israeli state, supported the PLO, and advocated a single democratic state in Palestine. After initial success in the 1970s and early 1980s it failed to expand its base further and has remained marginal.[58] The Islamic Movement is more formidable. It began to attract notice only in the late 1980s but has become a major factor in mobilizing Palestinians. In 1983, for example, only one of fifty Arab mayors or heads of local councils belonged to the Islamic Movement. In 1989 this number had increased to five, including the head of the important town of Umm al-Fahm. It has yet to take a clear position regarding national elections, but may become a potent challenger to Jewish rule in the fullness of time.

Palestinian mobilization has been more significant through local government councils. The Committee of the Heads of Local Councils is now the most important instrument of Palestinian mobilization in Israel, partly because it is the only forum for Palestinians denied participation in national politics, partly because it is the main vehicle for the campaign for a fairer slice of state services, and also because it is a main employer in the Arab sector. The committee now campaigns on both local and national issues. Its achievements are substantial. In the 1970s the average ratio between a Jewish locality's budget and an Arab one was 13 to 1; this improved substantially to 2.5 to 1 in the 1980s. Yet in view of the lack of infrastructure in Arab localities this ratio would have to be reversed for some years in order to achieve an equitable standard of services between Jews and Arabs.

Palestinians have also formed voluntary groups in other fields. The Arab Association for Human Rights, based in Nazareth, promotes awareness of discriminatory practices; the Galilee Society for Health Research and Services has drawn attention to the serious environmental degradation and absence of public health facilities in Arab areas, and undertakes health projects of its own; the Galilee Center for Social Research promotes study of the Arab community. All these activities reflect Palestinian challenges to the status quo that would hardly have been dared a generation ago.

Palestinian Israelis feel profoundly alienated from a state which continues to treat them as third-rate and unwanted citizens. By 1980 over two-thirds felt they could not be equal citizens, and believed Zionism was racist or at least immoral.[59] Ninety per cent favoured repeal of the Jewish Law of Return or an amendment (implicitly to allow Palestine refugees to return). Yet at the same time they acknowledge that the *Israeli* element in their cultural identity has increased; they function easily in Hebrew and tend to read it as much as, or more than, Arabic. Their political identity is nevertheless cast increasingly in Palestinian terms.[60] Despite government co-optation among both the bedouin and the Druze (now 80,000 strong), there is now a growing sense of solidarity among the younger generation of both groups with the rest of the Palestinian people. State-inspired divisions seem to be in decline.

Contacts between Palestinians across the armistice line remain limited. Solidarity unquestionably increased as a result, first, of the 'reunification' of Palestine in the 1967 war, and then of the *intifada* of 1987. The 1993 Declaration of Principles (DoP) had a mixed impact. On the one hand, there was acute disappointment at the meagre fruits offered to fellow Palestinians in the Occupied Territories; on the other, they felt able to be more assertive concerning their own Palestinian identity, and that they could now get on with their own struggle for equality. The DoP also sparked hopes of normalization in their relations with Jews. But it has also created unease that Israel and the PLO may, for example, strike a deal that involves the transfer of Arabs from the Triangle in return for dismantling Jewish settlements in the Occupied Territories.

Since the mid-1970s there has been a growing consensus among Israeli Palestinians that they should be recognized as a national minority with political and cultural rights. They are acutely aware, however, of the danger that they might be offered a form of geographical autonomy that would exclude them formally from mainstream national life.

Demographically, in spite of ex-Soviet Jewish immigration, the Palestinians are almost certainly bound to increase as a proportion of the Israeli population, on account of their higher birth rate. Their younger population promises continued demographic change unless their birth rate falls dramatically or the Jewish rate increases. The Arab birth rate is falling but probably not fast enough to avoid substantial demographic change. While Palestinians (including those of East Jerusalem) are only 19 per cent of the population of Israel, they already constitute 25 per cent of Israelis under the age of 20. The other important factor is their location. Palestinians are concentrated in areas close to the West Bank, in the Little Triangle, the Galilee and north of Beersheba. Repeated attempts to settle Jews among them tend to succeed temporarily before the government perceives another demographic crisis, particularly in the Galilee. Behind overt attempts to Judaize Arab areas lies the real dilemma for the Jews of Israel; are they ready to embrace Palestinians as equal citizens and share functional power? After almost half a century, all the indications are that Israel remains committed to denying them not only equality but even status as a national minority.

# 6

## EXILE AND THE RISE OF THE NATIONAL MOVEMENT

### The fate of the refugees

The refugees of 1948 fled with whatever they could carry. Altogether they numbered approximately 725,000 according to UN estimates.[1] Over four and a half decades their numbers have almost quadrupled in the following countries where they took refuge. The figures in Table 1 (p. 64) represent those defined as refugees by the United Nations, namely those resident in Palestine for the two years prior to the 1948 war who lost both their homes and their means of livelihood as a result of the conflict, and their descendants. This definition excludes, for example, those in border areas who lost either home or lands but not both, those outside Palestine, for example studying in Beirut, and those who moved beyond the area of operations of the UN Relief and Works Agency for Palestine Refugees in the Near East (UNRWA).

The refugees were vulnerable, removed from their habitat, disoriented, without political rights, and dependent on the goodwill of their neighbours and the local authority. The vast majority were peasant farmers, few of whom had travelled beyond their neighbourhood before. They found a mixed reception; there was some sympathy, but they also faced the difficulties arising from the practical strain on the host communities absorbing such large numbers and from the impact their arrival had on the social composition on the receiving countries.

In the case of Lebanon, the refugees constituted a tenth of the total population (equivalent to Britain receiving 5 million

TABLE 1

**Numbers and distribution of Palestinian refugees, 1948 and 1993**

| Country | 1948[a] | 1993[b] |
|---|---|---|
| Lebanon | 100,000 | 328,176 |
| Syria | 75,000 | 314,039[c] |
| Jordan (East Bank) | 70,000 | 1,072,561[c] |
| West Bank | 280,000 | 479,023 |
| Gaza Strip | 200,000 | 603,380 |
| Total | 725,000 | 2,797,179[d] |

NOTES

[a] UN estimate.
[b] UNRWA figures for 30 June 1993.
[c] These figures include 482,082 refugees (and descendants) displaced to Jordan from the West Bank and Gaza and 32,236 refugees displaced to Syria as a result of the 1967 war. Including *non-refugees* displaced in 1967 (to Jordan 210,000 and to Syria 125,000), one may assume the total non-refugee displaced to Jordan and Syria (including descendants) is now about 600,000.
[d] This excludes 45,800 people (and their descendants) who, although still inside Israel, lost both their homes and livelihoods during the 1948 war and who, as refugees, were the responsibility of UNRWA until June 1952 when Israel assumed responsibility for them and they lost their refugee status.

....................................................................................................................................

refugees), and inevitably they were perceived to threaten the delicate confessional balance on which the Lebanese political system operated, in particular the dominant position of the Maronite Christian community. In the West Bank of what became Jordan, the refugees doubled the population and, with annexation of the West Bank, Jordan became predominantly Palestinian. Here, too, the massive influx of Palestinians into the East Bank threatened to transform the Hashemite monarchy, whose power base rested primarily among the southern tribes of the country. In Syria, too, although proportionately small, the refugee presence presented a political danger to successive narrowly based regimes, since it was a constant public reminder of Arab failure. The Gaza Strip, the truncated remains of Gaza District, received the biggest proportionate influx. Its 80,000 or so population was swamped by 200,000 refugees. Furthermore over half the resident Gazans had no income since the lands they cultivated had been lost to the Jews. Circumstances such as these, quite apart from refugee hopes of a return, belied Israeli accusations about a cynical refusal on the part of the Arab states to resettle the refugees.

If one has not been a refugee it is almost impossible to imagine its psychological impact. In the Palestinian case, a widespread sense of shame and worthlessness numbed many of them. They had to get used both to pity and to jibes from the host population.[2] Like other refugees, they had to get used to a loss of identity; where formerly they had been known as of such-and-such a family in a particular village or town, and had a recognized position within a community, in exile they became faceless people bereft of all status and identity, except to be Palestinian refugees.

At first the refugees were scattered in many places, sheltering on the edge of villages, or wherever they could.[3] The haste in which people had left led to separation. Some were forbidden to travel from one country to another in order to be reunited with their families. The fragmentations of society were exaggerated, for those with education and means, particularly the urban middle class, tended to disappear into the towns and cities of the region where they rebuilt their lives. For the peasantry it was different. Without land, they found themselves seeking casual agricultural labour, or anything else on offer. Since the host countries themselves had a surfeit of unskilled labour this often led to competition with local people.

Each country adopted its own policy towards the refugees. Jordan went for headlong integration, officially banning the term 'Palestine' and conferring full citizenship.[4] Syria extended equal rights to the refugees, allowed them to maintain their Palestinian identity and even join the army or enter government service. But it must be remembered that the influx added only 2 per cent or so to the Syrian population. Lebanon was a good deal less hospitable, placing the refugees in an indeterminate category, neither foreigners nor nationals. It also issued work and travel permits sparingly, leaving many refugees in acute crisis. Most worked without permits, in menial unskilled employment. In every country the refugees were carefully watched by the security services, and those suspected of political activity were liable to be arrested, beaten or imprisoned. Significantly, the Arab states opposed the inclusion of UNRWA-registered refugees within the competence of the United Nations High Commission for Refugees (UNHCR).[5] While this appeared as a repudiation of the idea that the refugees would not return to their homes, it had the practical effect of preventing any form of international legal or physical protection being granted to them. In these two respects the refugees remained the wards of the governments within whose jurisdiction they fell.

## UNRWA: political stability or humanitarian concern?

Once it was clear that there would be no early solution, the United Nations established its Relief and Works Agency for Palestine Refugees in the Near East, UNRWA, at the close of 1949 to provide essential services to the refugee population.[6] It has remained in operation ever since. Its first task was to provide food aid, and help refugees move from tented to cinderblock shelters. Throughout the region permanent camps sprang up, although some refugees were still under canvas in the late 1950s. Although only a third of the refugees ever lived in these camps they became symbolic of their plight.

UNRWA's most important contribution has been in the fields of health and education. In the former UNRWA has faced the serious challenge of epidemics from overcrowding and difficult sanitation conditions, but it triumphed over extremely adverse circumstances.[7] In the longer term its most significant achievement has been in the field of education and vocational training. UNRWA established a system that provided for the first nine years of education, the last three being provided in host government schools. It helped change traditional attitudes regarding the value and propriety of educating girls.[8] From the early 1950s UNRWA-educated or vocationally trained refugees made a significant contribution to the development of the oil industry in the Gulf. By 1986, 33,000 artisans, technicians and professionals were contributing not only to the economy of the region but, as importantly, to the well-being of their family in camp or slum. At moments of crisis, notably in Jordan in June 1967, and during the *intifada* of 1987–92, UNRWA did much to assist refugees in adverse circumstances. Except in moments of crisis, UNRWA's operation has been hampered by an inadequate budget, since it is dependent on voluntary contributions from UN member states which have proved unwilling either to ensure implementation of UNGAR 194 or, alternatively, to provide for adequate refugee services.

Apart from its budgetary constraints, the UNRWA operation has been problematic in other ways. Directed by an international cadre, the Palestine refugees have effectively been denied any real control over the relief of their own predicament. It is a modest measure of UNRWA's own recognition of this dilemma that since about 1990 it has made serious efforts to encourage refugee communities to development themselves economically and socially.

The other serious problem relates to UNRWA's purpose. Was it truly there for humanitarian or pragmatic purposes? As one US Assistant Secretary of State informed Congress in 1950:

> 'The political loss of the Middle East would be a major disaster... the political strategic position of the Soviet Union would be immeasurably strengthened by the attainment of its objectives in the Near East...Against this background, our solicitude for the Palestine refugees, partly [sic] based on humanitarian consideration, has additional justification. As long as the refugee problem remains unsolved...the refugees will continue to serve as a focal point for exploitation by communist disruptive elements which neither we nor the Near Eastern governments can afford to ignore.'[9]

At times it seemed to the refugees that the desire to keep them quiescent overrode all other considerations.

It was generally assumed that once the refugees got over their anger, they could indeed be gradually resettled. In the mid-1950s

UNRWA sought the implementation of two major resettlement schemes, a Yarmuk–Jordan Valley development proposal in collaboration with Jordan to irrigate 500,000 dunums, and another in Sinai in collaboration with Egypt.[10] In both cases it was the refugees themselves who most vehemently repudiated resettlement, and insisted on 'the right of return', a right with which the Arab masses themselves strongly sympathized. Thus, while Arab governments undoubtedly sought to exploit the refugee situation for their own political purposes, Israel's charge that the Arab states themselves were the obstacle to resolving the refugee problem was at best only partially true. The real obstacle to resettlement lay with the refugees' insistence on their right to return, Israel's refusal to grant it, and the international community's inadequate resolve to ensure implementation of UN General Assembly Resolution 194.

## The growth of national identity

At first the expectation that they would return home and the immediate imperatives of survival prevented the refugees from organizing themselves for a long exile. However, alongside the effect of dispersal and fragmentation, exile accelerated the emergence of a Palestinian national identity. Wherever they went, the refugees were now known simply by their status as Palestinian refugees, differentiating them from the host community. As Fawaz Turki wrote:

> *'If I was not a Palestinian when I left Haifa as a child, I am one now. Living in Beirut as a stateless person from most of my growing up years, many of them in a refugee camp, I did not feel I was living among my "Arab brothers"...I was a Palestinian.'*[11]

While refugees tended to be concentrated in camps and certain urban quarters by their host governments, another dispersal was taking place as those refugees with even modest skills sought employment elsewhere. A growing number, particularly from Jordan, went to Kuwait and other oil-rich Arab countries. Palestinians became the backbone of much Arab world development in the 1950s and 1960s, particularly in Kuwait where they pervaded and almost ran Kuwaiti institutions. They had relative freedom to develop their own institutions, as long as the stability of the countries they were in did not seem threatened.

As it slowly became apparent that no return was in sight, the refugees began to organize and act with a growing sense of their Palestinian identity. Thus they organized demonstrations and protests against state or UN-sponsored resettlement schemes. But they also began to organize in social fields. The General Union of Palestinian Students (GUPS) was established in 1959, the League of Palestinian Women in 1962 and the General Union of Palestinian Workers in 1963. It was no accident that all these were founded in Egypt where the refugees were less than 0.01 per cent of the population and therefore presented no problem for the government.

By the late 1950s there was growing Palestinian national feeling among the refugee communities. Jordan and Lebanon were inclined to suppress any expression of this feeling, but the Arab League, dominated by the United Arab Republic (the shortlived union of Egypt and Syria), favoured helping the Palestinians to organize themselves to participate in the liberation of Palestine. In 1960, to Jordan's intense displeasure, the Palestine Liberation Army (PLA) was founded. In 1964 the Palestine Liberation Organization (PLO) was established by leading and traditional notables with encouragement from the Arab League. It was essentially a political structure, with no intention of engaging in guerrilla activity. Liberation would come by conventional war, Palestinians fighting under the direction of the Arab armies. It was officered and partly financed by Palestinians. Yet it was questionable how much freedom the Arab states, particularly Jordan, wished the PLO to have.[12]

Defeat of the Arab states in 1967 changed all that. A growing number of Palestinians had already concluded that only Palestinians would put Palestine first, and thereby recover it. The most important group was Fatah (Conquest) a reverse acronym for its full title, Harakat Tahrir Filastin (Palestine Liberation Movement). It had been founded in 1959 and was led by young engineer, Yasir Arafat.[13] Its basic idea of subordinating political disagreement to the issue of 'return' had immense appeal to the refugees, and made Fatah a broad church able to withstand considerable internal disagreements. Fatah took care neither to oppose the PLO (associated with the defeated Arab regimes), nor to allow itself to become identified with it. Its first guerrilla raid was made in 1965.

After the 1967 war, however, Fatah began to grow, and following a heroic stand against a major Israeli reprisal on the East Bank village of Karama in 1968 it could barely cope with the tidal wave of recruits anxious to play their part in the recovery of Palestine. Because of this success, the old conservatives of the PLO were swept away and Fatah acquired control of the Executive Committee of the PLO in 1969. Arafat was elected Chairman, a position he continued to hold thereafter. Fatah remained the dominant component of the transformed PLO.

It was one thing to dominate the new PLO, quite another to control and co-ordinate it. The challenges Fatah faced were formidable, from managing and directing its own rapidly expanding forces, to providing overall guidance to other newly constituent members, as well as maintaining relations with these other members, and with the Arab states, both those that acted as hosts, notably Jordan and Lebanon, and those that provided substantial funding, like the Gulf states. It also faced the problem of how to win over those countries outside the region most able to influence the course of events in Palestine.

Fatah was faced by several groups with a radically different view of things. The most formidable was the Popular Front for the Liberation of Palestine (PFLP), which was Arab nationalist in inspiration. It saw Palestine as an integral part of the Arab world, and viewed the struggle against Zionism, imperialism and Arab reaction as one. It therefore preached social revolution in the Arab world as a precondition to the liberation of Palestine. This had immediate and threatening implications for 'reactionary' Jordan, which in 1957 had cracked down on many radical politicians including George Habash, the PFLP's founder. The PFLP remained committed to the Arab nationalist movement's ideal of revolutionary change. 'The only weapon left in the hands of the people...is revolutionary violence,' it proclaimed.[14] Because of its disagreements with Fatah, the PFLP only intermittently held seats on the PLO Executive Committee. On account of its more ideologically visionary approach, which, in the words of one critic, 'allows for the continued misinterpretation of reality', the PFLP was particularly susceptible to schism. In 1968 a splinter broke away under the leadership of Ahmad Jibril to form the PFLP-General Command (PFLP-GC). A year later, another splinter broke away under the leadership of Naif Hawatma to form the Democratic Front for the Liberation of Palestine (DFLP).[15]

These groups, and others sponsored by Arab states – for example, the Syrian-controlled al-Sa'iqa (The Thunderbolt) and the Iraqi-controlled Arab Liberation Front – had a substantial following of their own. Much as he may have wished to, therefore, Arafat was unable to concentrate political and military leadership in his own hands and thus achieve unity of command and action. The resistance movement was too fragmented. So the PLO became an umbrella organization. It was better than nothing, for it provided an arena for co-ordination, but it paid a heavy penalty, repeatedly drawn into conflict with host countries, with the West and between its constituent members.

In spite of Fatah's principle of non-intervention in the internal affairs of Arab states, the presence of large numbers of *fidayin* was bound to affect relations with the host governments. Of these Jordan and Lebanon were the most vulnerable, Jordan on account of its large Palestinian population, and Lebanon because of its political fragility. In both countries Arafat tried to avoid clashes, but Fatah's neutrality was compromised by more aggressively political groups and indiscipline within its own ranks. In the mid-1950s Palestinians had already been prominent in a radical movement that sought to reduce the Hashemite monarchy to constitutional rule and to align with the Arab nationalists elsewhere. That movement had been crushed. Now the monarchy found itself under far greater threat, as virtually all Palestinians gave spontaneous support to the guerrilla movement. A Palestinian revolutionary movement would in all probability sweep the monarchy away. When mounting tensions finally provoked a showdown, Jordanian troops, fiercely loyal to the Crown, drove the *fidayin* out of the country in 1970–1. Perhaps 3,000 Palestinians, military and civilian, died in the struggle.[16]

Jordan permanently closed all the civil and social institutions associated with the Palestinian national movement. Most of the *fidayin*, the politically active and their families made their way to Lebanon, where once again conflict with elements of the Lebanese state became virtually inevitable.

In Lebanon the Palestinian movement initially enjoyed popularity with the downtrodden, the Shii villagers of south Lebanon and the large Sunni and Shii population of Beirut and other towns, notably those living in low-income and slum areas. They shared a sense of deprivation on the margins of an increasingly prosperous society. In addition the Palestinians were the particular target of Deuxième Bureau harassment. In September 1969, as the new resistance movement gathered force, refugees in the camps had thrown the Deuxième Bureau and its network of informers out of the camps.

After the arrival of the defeated PLO from Jordan large tracts of south Lebanon, quite apart from the camps, came under its informal control. In November 1969 a formal agreement was reached in Cairo between the Lebanese government and the PLO, whereby the latter was granted autonomous control of the refugee camps, and permitted to continue its liberation struggle against Israel from Lebanese territory.

The PLO also started to build civil institutions in Beirut. The Palestine Red Crescent Society, originally founded in Jordan, provided a health network, with an emphasis on hospitals and curative services. The PLO also established SAMED, which ran production workshops for clothing, embroidery, metalwork and other 'cottage' industries. This gave gainful employment to many refugees, and a modest source of income to assist the families of 'martyrs'. Such institutions demonstrated the will, ability and energy of Palestinians to build their own civic society in exile.

There had been considerable sympathy for the Palestinian struggle among those Lebanese who also responded to Arab nationalist ideas. However, many saw this struggle as an act of recklessness that threatened to destroy Lebanon's delicate political fabric and bring their country into open conflict with Israel. These critics belonged most notably to the dominant Maronite Christian community.

Developments soon justified these fears. Israel began to respond to *fidayi* raids by deliberately destroying Shii villages, at first those from which the *fidayin* were believed to launch their attacks, but then more generally to indicate that the Shia could not expect a quiet life if they permitted the *fidayin* to operate freely. Neither the Lebanese army nor the Shia themselves were strong enough to control the Palestinians. The PLO became increasingly unpopular because of Israel's deliberate reprisals against the civil population.

Then the Palestinian national movement's presence in Lebanon began to act as a catalyst in the delicate confessional (Muslim–Christian) balance of the country.[17] The dominant Maronite Christian community felt increasingly threatened by the Arab nationalist/Muslim challenge, spearheaded by the large Palestinian *fidayin* presence. As the country slid towards civil war in early 1975, Palestinian *fidayin* were inexorably drawn into the conflict to assist the Arab nationalists who had previously supported them.

Internationally, however, the PLO was carried forward on a wave of success, acknowledged in October 1974 at an Arab League summit as 'the sole legitimate representative of the Palestinian people', and the following month represented by Arafat on the UN General Assembly podium itself. Here Arafat sought to soften the harsh terms of the Palestine National Charter.[18] 'When we speak of our common hopes for the Palestine of the future,' he told his audience, 'we include in our perspective all Jews now living in Palestine who choose to live with us there in peace and without discrimination...that we might live together in a framework of a just peace in our democratic Palestine.'

Away from the media hype, however, the PLO's plans were beginning to go seriously awry. While the civil war in Lebanon was a major distraction from its fundamental objective of regaining Palestine, it still continued to attack Israel from south Lebanon. In early 1978 a PLO attack on Israel's coastal highway left 37 civilians dead. Israel responded by invading Lebanon. During its operation some 700 were killed, 250,000 people displaced and many homes destroyed. Israel was forced to withdraw under pressure from US President Carter. UN Security Council

Resolution 425 required Israel's immediate and unconditional withdrawal from Lebanon, and provided for the UN Interim Force in Lebanon (UNIFIL) to be deployed to prevent border violations from either side. Israel thwarted the UN intention by maintaining a surrogate Lebanese Christian militia force in the border area.[19]

The PLO's acceptance of UNIFIL's role was significant as its first implicit acceptance of a ceasefire with Israel.[20] In July 1981 after a particularly heavy air raid on Beirut in which over 200 civilians died, the PLO engaged in another ceasefire, this time brokered by the USA. The PLO was aware that Israel had intended to drive it out of the south during its 1978 operation, and that it might seek next time to corner and destroy it between its own forces and the PLO's adversaries in Lebanon, the Christian Phalange and Lebanese in East Beirut.

In June 1982 an assassination attempt on Israel's Ambassador in London by Abu Nidal's Fatah Revolutionary Council[21] gave Israel the pretext it sought. Within days a massive force had broken through UNIFIL lines and was racing up the coastline, sealing off and pounding refugee camps as it progressed. It surrounded, besieged and bombarded West Beirut with its air, land and sea forces for twelve weeks. But it dared not risk the heavy casualties necessary to storm the city. Under acute local pressure, and deserted by those Arab governments that might have used their diplomatic and economic influence in Washington, the PLO withdrew in late August to relocate in Tunis, under firm guarantees from the United States of its safe withdrawal, and of US protection for Palestinian civilians left behind. These undertakings were not adhered to, and US Marines were withdrawn prematurely. On 3 September Israel began to violate its undertaking not to enter the city, moving its troops forward. These entered the city on 15 September following the assassination of Lebanese President-elect (and Israel's ally) Bashir Gemayel. The following day Israel's Chief of Staff, Rafael Eitan, sent the Phalangists to deal with 'terrorists' in Sabra/Shatila camp 'with their own methods'.[22] Those methods were notorious.[23] There the Phalangists massacred 1,300 or more men, women and children.[24] Israeli troops provided illumination to help them work through the night. It was barely conceivable that Israeli commanders did not anticipate what would happen.[25]

The massacre of Sabra/Shatila became, like Deir Yassin, symbolic of the Palestinian ordeal. It was also a blow to the credibility of the PLO leadership, since it had trusted US assurances.[26] Many *fidayin* lost their families in the massacre, and lost faith in Arafat's leadership. Israel's invasion of Lebanon left 19,000 dead,[27] of whom fewer than 5,000 were combatants, and a massive legacy of destruction.

The following year the PLO was finally run out of Lebanon by pro-Syrian Palestinian groups. Now that it had lost its military option, the PLO had no choice but to pursue diplomacy. It had been attempting diplomatic contacts with the United States since the late 1970s, but its use of violence gave the United States the pretext it wanted for rejecting such overtures.

**Failure of the PLO**

From the outset the PLO had had difficulties over what it stood for. It was easy to say that it stood for the recovery of Palestine, but of how much? And how would it treat the Jews? By the early 1970s guerrilla attacks were clearly failing to recover any of Palestine. There was profound ambiguity in the words and actions of the PLO and other Palestinian groups which gave ample ground for those hostile to Palestinian claims to reject the PLO's advances. Some inside the PLO argued that, despite the unpromising result of guerrilla activity, they must keep their sights on the liberation of all Palestine, as proposed in the Palestine National Charter. A growing number, however, wanted to limit their immediate objective to the recovery of part or all of the territories captured by Israel in 1967. Fatah discussed the matter in 1973, deciding that 'the best for us is that the West Bank and Gaza should be a Palestinian state'.[28] But the DFLP was the first to call publicly for a two-state solution, in early 1974. Later that year the Palestine National Council (PNC) affirmed: 'The PLO will struggle...to establish...sovereignty on every part of Palestinian land to be liberated', an indication of its willingness to compromise, and to negotiate a two-state solution.[29]

Why did the PLO fail? There were several reasons. Foremost, it was thwarted by Israel's absolute opposition to a two-state solution, or to recognition of any Palestinian legitimacy whatsoever in Eretz Yisrael. In view of random Palestinian acts of violence against Jews and others, it was not difficult for Israel to defend its hard line, and to warn of serious destabilization if Palestinian demands were acceded to. In 1970 the PFLP leader, George Habash, had stated: 'We believe that to kill a Jew far away from the battlefield has more effect than killing a hundred of them in battle: it attracts more attention.'[29] That year the PFLP had hijacked and destroyed three civil airliners in Jordan. It was perceived as an attack on world order. Two years later, Black September (a Fatah splinter) infiltrated the Olympic village in Munich and killed eleven Israeli athletes. In 1974, within weeks of its call for a Palestinian state merely in the Occupied Territories, the DFLP carried out an attack on Ma'alot in which 24 Israelis, mainly children, were killed.

Alongside its acts of violence, some Palestinians believe the PLO also failed to understand the diplomatic essentials required for progress with the Western powers. It could not refrain from contradictory utterances, which were quickly pounced on as evidence of its insincerity. Its National Charter (Art. 15) demanded 'the elimination of Zionism in Palestine', an apparent shorthand for the destruction of Israel, echoing unsubstantiated Zionist claims of previous calls to 'drive the Jews into the sea'. The world easily forgot that in reality Israel had driven the Arabs of Palestine into the desert. In addition the PLO had refused to join the international consensus on UNSCR 242, on the grounds that it failed to recognize a Palestinian right to self-determination. By opposing UNSCR 242 the PLO dealt itself out of the diplomatic process. Clearly it believed that, in time, the world would still have to recognize it, mainly because of the influence it was beginning to attract in the Occupied Territories (see Chapter 7), but it paid a heavy price for its decision.

In mainstream Western opinion the Palestinian struggle became synonymous with terrorism. Only a tiny minority who knew the story of Palestine recalled that Israelis were equally, if not more, proficient in the execution of atrocities. The great majority saw Palestinian outrages as blind hatred for the Jewish people, part of the seamless fabric of anti-semitism. Thus the PLO attracted wave after wave of public revulsion in the West. This made it much easier for the United States to explain its opposition to Palestinian self-determination. In reality this opposition was based upon its strategic struggle against the Soviet Union, and its perception of Israel and Jordan as its allies, and Syria and the PLO as linked to its adversary. In pursuit of that strategy it applied pressure where it could to dissuade other Arab states from supporting the PLO. Disqualifying the PLO on grounds of its terrorism conveniently masked its real motive.

Terrorist acts made it easy to outlaw and demonize the PLO, and this policy was readily consumed by a public that preferred to perceive the struggle as one between the forces of light and an 'evil empire' (the Soviet Union) and its acolytes. This state of mind reached a climax during the Reagan presidency in the 1980s, and was given sharp focus by the *Achille Lauro* affair in 1985, when a disabled American Jew, Leon Klinghoffer, was shot by Palestinian hijackers and dumped in the sea. The incident served to confirm every prejudice about Palestinians in particular, and Muslim Arabs in general. One American was moved to write an opera, *Klinghoffer*. No one in the West felt sufficiently moved to create a similar artistic work to commemorate the 14,000 or more civilians slain by Israel when it had invaded Lebanon three years previously. They remained faceless victims of a distant war.

During the 1980s the PLO was also weakened by the splits in its own ranks over Arafat's leadership. In 1983 Fatah rebels critical of Arafat formed the National Salvation Front under Syrian sponsorship. Another group, the Democratic Alliance (DFLP and Palestine Communist Party), criticized Arafat for his unilateral actions and called for greater democracy but rejected Syrian involvement. Despite such substantial opposition, Arafat obtained a mandate from the PNC to explore a proposal by King Hussein for a joint Palestinian/Jordanian initiative based on UNSCR 242. Negotiations produced a framework for co-operation in early 1985, omitting mention of the armed struggle, calling for an international conference and pledging acceptance of *all* UN resolutions, specifically Security Council ones. Implicitly this included UNSCR 242, but Israel and the United States both rejected the initiative, arguing that there was no question of Palestinian statehood or of direct PLO participation in any peace talks. Instead the United States Congress, always prejudiced in Israel's favour, detailed three conditions necessary before the USA could negotiate with the PLO; it must recognize Israel's *right* to exist (something quite different from recognition of existence), accept UNSCR 242 and formally renounce terror. The *Achille Lauro* incident in 1985 destroyed any last chance of progress for the Jordan–PLO initiative.[31] Then Jordan and the PLO quarrelled bitterly, Jordan accusing the PLO of unreasonableness regarding UNSCR 242 and recognition of Israel, while the PLO suspected that Jordan's reluctance to concede the Palestinian right to self-determination was a ploy to regain the West Bank for itself.

Meanwhile the PLO's expulsion from Lebanon in 1982–3 left the remaining refugee population highly vulnerable. Ordinary Palestinians hoped they would now be left in peace. It was not to be. After the arrests, tortures and killings inflicted by the rightist government installed by Israel, Palestinians now became victims of the Shiite militia Amal's growing ambition to dominate all of West Beirut. Amal enjoyed the support of Syria and the predominantly Shii Lebanese 6th Army Brigade. All three were determined to eliminate potential elements of defiance to the new order they hoped to impose on Lebanon. A number of refugee camps lie in predominantly Shii areas: Rashidiya, Bass and Burj al-Shamali camps around Tyre abutting the Shii heartlands of Jabal Amil, and Sabra/Shatila and Burj al-Barajna camps which pre-dated the massive settlement of the southern suburbs of Beirut by Shii migrant workers in the 1960s and 1970s. All these camps were subject to Amal's efforts to control them.[32]

The epic siege of Sabra/Shatila camp in 1985 captured worldwide attention.[33] The camp's inhabitants underwent an ordeal that rivalled the climactic nightmare of September 1982. On the first day of the holy month of Ramadan (19 May), Amal launched a massive surprise attack on Sabra/Shatila, using artillery, tanks and infantry. Taken totally by surprise, the refugees put up a desperate and successful defence. Amal lifted its siege at the end of the month, venting its anger by killing hundreds of Palestinians who fell into its hands either in the course of the fighting or rounded up in other parts of Beirut. A year later Amal launched another month-long attack in May and June 1986. Again it was repulsed. In November, Amal made a third attempt to destroy the camp. For five months through the winter the Palestinians defended the heaps of rubble to which the camp had been reduced. For long periods men, women and children lived in flooded dugouts and trenches, on the point of starvation as they eked out their meagre supplies. On 6 April 1987 Amal lifted its siege, defeated militarily by the stubborn and skilful resistance it had encountered, and politically by rising international pressure on Syria to restrain it. During the 'battle of the camps' probably 2,500 Palestinians had died. Hundreds of others had been maimed by sniper fire and shelling.

The end of the siege did not lead to normalization. Amal made its peace, but Syrian troops took over the checkpoints. Palestinian men found they were still unable to move freely. And for over a year the inhabitants of the remains of Shatila were forbidden to rebuild. Then in 1988 Syrian artillery reduced the camp yet again to rubble to expel Fatah fighters. By now the Palestinians no longer had the support of any of the major political or confessional groups of Lebanon. Most of the social, economic and educational institutions so painstakingly built up had been destroyed. Only a handful of Lebanese-registered charities were able to continue operating.

Meanwhile the PLO stood impotently on the sidelines, trying to jump on the back of various Arab peace initiatives, but absolutely excluded from the fora of international power. By 1987 it seemed to many Western observers that the PLO was finished. Then the *intifada* broke out at the end of that year, and it slowly became clear to Israel and the United States that peace without the PLO was no longer credible.

# 7

## UNDER ISRAELI OCCUPATION, 1967–87

It took just over twenty years before Palestinians in every part of the Occupied Territories took to the streets in open and spontaneous revolt in December 1987. Before then there had been countless protest shutdowns and demonstrations and periods of coherent resistance of which the most notable was the Gaza resistance of 1969–72. Yet the more remarkable feature of the occupation was the comparative docility of the subject people.

This docility was no accident. Israel decided to establish a strong but relatively invisible grip that would create an impression of normality. Military forces were deployed along the Jordan valley floor, but generally kept away from Palestinian population concentrations. The Israeli authorities decided to control the population less visibly, through a pervasive bureaucratic system, through Arabic-speaking and mainly Druze border guards, and through a network of informers operated by Shabak (the General Security Service). In this it was greatly helped by the capture of Jordan's West Bank internal security files, and an exchange of information with Jordan. It negotiated an 'open bridge' to Jordan, a safety valve whereby the inhabitants could still go to Amman to sell their agricultural produce. But the 'open bridge' did not allow the 300,000 or so displaced in 1967 to return; and, as after 1948, some Israeli troops routinely shot 'infiltrators'.[1] Instead, Israel allowed 100,000 'summer visitors' to cross each year and maintain contact with their families. Furthermore, it decided to govern through the traditional elite which had served the Jordanian government, who were allowed to travel freely to

Amman to 'confer', creating the illusion of normality. Permission to cross the bridge (exercised by both Jordan and Israel) was a useful means of reward and punishment. Searches on the return journey tended to be gratuitously humiliating.[2]

It was not long before Israel was consciously working towards the physical integration and economic dependency of the Occupied Territories, and also the frustration of Palestinian communal solidarity. In order to achieve such ends, however, it had to violate international law.

## The law

Israel's occupation of captured territories is circumscribed by international law as framed in the Hague Regulations of 1907 and the Fourth Geneva Convention of 1949 (relative to the Protection of Civilian Persons in Time of War). Eventually Israel reluctantly accepted the applicability of the Regulations, but not of the Convention, of which it made a unique interpretation.[3] Israel had a practical reason for rejecting the Convention, for it expressly prohibited key elements in the state's subsequent policy: collective punishments (e.g. curfews except strictly for security purposes and the demolition of homes); the transfer and settlement of people from the occupier's own territory; the expulsion of inhabitants from the area; sequestrating private or public property; changing the corpus of law already in operation in the territories (except for permissible military regulations regarding security); the improper conduct of regular trials; and suspension of the provision and system of education.[4]

Israel later argued that only customary law and not treaty law (i.e. the Convention) was binding. In the Palestinian view, Israel applied the Hague Regulations selectively to protect its troops and Jewish civilians, while it ignored or breached other provisions in order to strip Palestinians of their rights and to dispossess the inhabitants by quasi-legal means. Thus Israel created a system based upon laws applied by the Ottoman Empire, the British mandate, Jordanian law and Egyptian administrative orders (Gaza) and military orders of the Israeli occupation. By 1994 Israel's military authority had issued over 1,100 orders in the West Bank and over 900 in Gaza, thus effectively changing the body of Jordanian and Egyptian law previously exercised in the Occupied Territories.[5]

The Israeli government introduced a sophisticated machinery for legal repression. It allowed local (Jordanian or Egyptian) courts continued jurisdiction in certain civil matters, but only for resident Palestinians and not for Jewish settlers. In the words of one leading lawyer, 'inefficiency and corruption continue to characterize the state of local courts'.[6] Appointments in these courts are made on political grounds, thus destroying any notion of the independence of the judiciary.[7] Israel also established Israeli civil courts for Jewish settlers, thereby illegally transferring its domestic law to occupied territory. Additionally it established military courts and tribunals which, unlike local courts, enjoy the assured co-operation of the police. Under international law military courts may be established to try cases which involve the security of the occupying power. The farcical nature of these courts is graphically described by David Grossman in his remarkable essay on life in the West Bank, *The Yellow Wind*.[8] Israel extended the jurisdiction of these courts to include land cases, and they are empowered to define what is 'state land', land which then passes out of indigenous control and effectively becomes part of the Jewish patrimony.[9] Plaintiffs have no court of appeal, only an Objections Committee, which is also composed of military officers able to recommend but without jurisdictional authority.[10] Palestinians do have recourse to the Israeli High Court in some cases, but the expectation of success is so low, and the anticipated costs are so high, that few resort to it.[11]

Israel has also used measures which required no semblance of legal process, nor even allegations of breaches of criminal law. These include administrative detention (on a six-monthly but in practice an indefinitely renewable basis), deportation of political leaders or activists, and punishments like the demolition of homes, without the need for a suspect to be charged, let alone tried, and without regard to a suspect's family, which is also penalized by the reduction of its home to rubble. In other words, a family may have its home demolished for unspecified and unknown crimes against the state.[12] In order to execute such measures without appearing to enact laws making such repressive measures legal, Israel resuscitated the defunct Defence (Emergency) Regulations of 1945 (see p. 50) in the West Bank and Gaza Strip. Apart from the fact that these regulations were rescinded for all Palestine in May 1948, they never formed part of Jordanian law and therefore contravene the Fourth Geneva Convention. They also contravene the Convention by the inhumanity of their provisions.

In the last resort Israel used direct force to keep people in subjection. After the suppression of the Gaza resistance of 1969–72, renewed Palestinian defiance was periodically expressed in demonstrations, shutdowns and stone-throwing. Many shootings occurred during demonstrations, even though this is strictly forbidden. Children were frequent victims. Such shooting was not confined to the IDF. Israel armed its illegal settlers, who believed the land to be theirs and viewed the indigenous population as there purely on sufferance. Predictably, settlers, like soldiers, used violence with virtual impunity, shooting people dead and beating up others.[13]

Arrested Palestinians were exposed to beatings and torture. Although men were the most frequent target, women were not excepted.[14] The 1987 Landau Commission conceded in its report that Shabak routinely tortured detainees, and had regularly committed perjury in court for years. It recommended against prosecution of those who had committed either offence, and accepted the legitimacy of 'a moderate amount of force' and 'non-violent psychological pressure' when seeking to obtain information.

### Road, land and water

Israel set out to integrate the territories it had captured while marginalizing its inhabitants. This was most graphically demonstrated by the road system it set about creating, one which made it increasingly easy to drive from Israel direct to the new Jewish settlements in the West Bank or Gaza without passing through Arab population centres. By the 1990s the road system reflected the needs of the Israeli state and its settler population,[15] by-passing even such major Arab towns as Nablus and al-Bira-Ramallah.

MAP 4

## Israeli settlements established in the Occupied Territories, 1967–91

Based on United Nations map no. 3651, September 1991

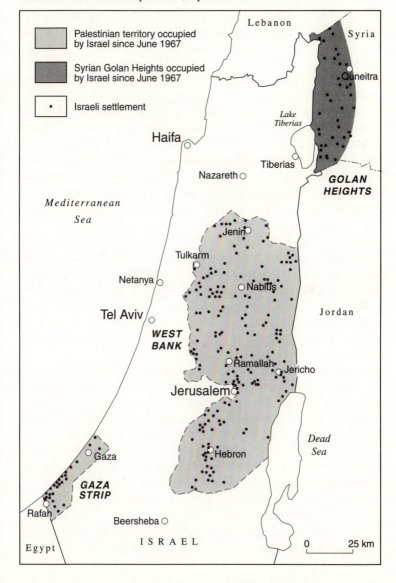

While marginalizing the Palestinian population, Israel wanted to take control of two vital assets, land and water. Land seizures attracted particular attention, for it was determined to incorporate as much as possible of the territories not captured in 1948. By the early 1990s Israel had acquired well over 60 per cent of the West Bank and 35 per cent of the Gaza Strip for Jewish use (see Map 4). Initially most was sequestered for 'military purposes' before being handed over to settlers in violation of the Geneva Convention. Later, when discussing a limited form of Palestinian autonomy in 1978, the Likud government redefined vast tracts as 'state land' in order to reserve it for exclusive Jewish use.[16] Land was also acquired by private purchase, mainly through coercion, intimidation or corrupt dealings.[17] Arab East Jerusalem was ringed with residential blocks with both the function and appearance of fortresses, to prevent reunification of the city with the rest of the West Bank. Illegal Jewish settlers in Arab Jerusalem are now numerically equal to the 150,000 Jerusalem Palestinians, but a major government programme, supported by US government finance, is currently under way to achieve demographic 'victory' there. By 1992 another 101,000 settlers lived outside East Jerusalem in the West Bank and Gaza Strip. Here the settlements follow distinct phases of integration. The first was Labour's system of strategic defence, along the Jordan valley floor and along the watershed of the central uplands; then came a wider scheme under Likud from 1977 onwards to recover the whole of Eretz Yisrael.

The discriminatory system exercised by Israel is seen at its extreme in the sequestration of land in Gaza for sole use by Jews. By 1992 sixteen Jewish settlements, inhabited by 3,500 people, occupied 22,250 dunums of land, while eight refugee camps, with a population of approximately 300,000 people, were confined to 5,500 dunums. By 1992 there were 128 illegal settlements in the West Bank, most of them in close proximity to high-density Arab populations.

As the prospect of Arab self-administration became an increasing possibility in the 1980s, Israeli settlement policy aimed at containment and segmentation of Arab population areas so as to break up the territories into pockets of Arab population concentration. Thus it would appear that Israel may intend to retain effective sovereignty over most of the West Bank, even if it delegates partial control of the territory of Gaza.

The Jews who decided to settle the Occupied Territories fell into two broad categories. The first came out of ideological conviction that the land belonged to Jews and must be repossessed. Most notable of these organizations was Gush Emunim (Bloc of the Faithful). However, from the later 1970s many more were attracted essentially by subsidized housing in pleasant surroundings within easy commuter distance of Jerusalem and the coastal towns. Today, excluding settlers in Arab East Jerusalem, about 40 per cent are probably ideologically motivated, and the remainder motivated by convenience.

By 1992 there were 97,500 settlers in the West Bank and 3,500 in the Gaza Strip, as well as 150,000 in those parts of the West Bank within the enlarged Jerusalem area.[18] Overall, they represent almost 11 per cent of the population of the Occupied Territories. Apart from in East Jerusalem, the actual number of settlers is likely to increase as a proportion only very slowly, and may well decline.[19] They have enjoyed preferential treatment amounting to gross discrimination in terms of the provision of space, construction, water provision (see below) and grants. It has been a deliberate policy to constrict Arab areas of construction, leaving Palestinians, in the infamous words of former Chief of Staff and current Tzomet leader Raphael Eitan, like 'drugged cockroaches in a bottle'.[20] As Palestinians pay taxes based upon Israel's own domestic tax system, one might expect them to be entitled to comparable government grants. However, in per capita terms Jews receive fifty times more grants than Palestinians. Put another way, of government aid spent in the Territories, 96.5 per cent is spent on Jewish settlers, and 3.5 per cent on the 90 per cent Palestinian population.[21]

Besides the illegal and discriminatory nature of the Jewish settler presence, Palestinians found themselves defenceless while the settlers were all armed and allowed to kill Palestinians 'in self-defence'. Moreover, it emerged following the massacre of over thirty Muslim worshippers in Hebron in February 1994 that the army had orders not to shoot settlers, even if they were shooting Palestinians. For Palestinians the message is simple: Jewish life is sacred,[22] Arab life is not.

After 1967 Israel quickly took control of all the water resources of the Territories and began to integrate them into its own national grid system. Twenty-five per cent of its own water consumption originated in the West Bank, so Israel was intent on guaranteeing its own water security. The government immediately froze Palestinian water consumption to prevent any increase until 2010.[23] No such limits were placed on Jewish settlers, who consume per capita almost three times as much as Palestinians for domestic purposes, and thirteenfold in the West Bank and sevenfold in Gaza for agricultural irrigation.[24] By 1990 the amount of water available for thirty Jewish agricultural settlements was only one-third less than that available for 400 Palestinian villages.

Overall, including both domestic and agricultural use, a Jewish settler enjoys approximately seven times as much water as a Palestinian.

## The Palestinian economy

The loss of vast tracts of land, the deliberate restriction of water use to 1967 levels and restricted markets were three principal reasons for the inability of Palestinians to expand their agriculture.[25] But it was not merely the resources of the Occupied Territories that Israel sought. It also intended to reduce Palestinian agricultural ability so as to remove competition and create a rural proletariat dependent on the Israeli economy for employment. In 1984 a military order made it possible for Palestinians to plant a new or replacement fruit tree only with a permit. These permits were hard to obtain, sometimes taking five years or more. The immediate target was the citriculture of Gaza, a natural competitor for Israel's own citrus sector. Citriculture had accounted for 50 per cent of Gaza's agricultural output and 70 per cent of its exports in the mid-1970s. Unable to replace low yield or dead trees, Gaza's production went into long-term decline.

Marketing was another area in which Palestinians were deliberately restricted. Before 1967 Gaza had exported its citrus to

Europe, but after 1967 Israel stopped this competition with its own produce. West Bank produce was allowed across the bridge as a part of 'normality', but ultimately fell victim to a combination of Israeli restrictions and enlarged agricultural productivity on the East Bank.[26] While Israeli goods were universally and unrestrictedly sold in the Occupied Territories, the authorities introduced strict production quotas in 1984 to prevent Palestinian farmers exporting to Israel. Finally, even in the domestic market, Palestinians had to compete with an Israeli agriculture that was heavily subsidized by the government. It was no surprise therefore that the Palestinian agricultural sector declined in productivity and in the number of people it supported.

The Occupied Territories' industrial sector went into decline after 1967, and by 1986 accounted for only 7 and 10 per cent of the West Bank and Gazan GDPs respectively. It remained backward and small scale, the average West Bank enterprise employing only four people, and 90 per cent of enterprises in Gaza employing fewer than eight people.[27] Most of these enterprises were engaged in processing agricultural products such as olive oil, soap, fruit, tobacco and liquid margarine. Other significant areas of production include furniture, textiles, leather and the provision of building materials for Israeli construction firms. As with the agricultural sector, Palestinian manufacturers found themselves frustrated by Israeli constraints devised to prevent any competition, including severe limitations on credit facilities. Israel wanted Palestinians to depend on Israeli banks, which could easily be controlled as instruments of government policy. These banks offered loans subject to the approval of the military government, subject to Israeli law (in spite of taking place outside the jurisdiction of Israeli law) and subject to protracted procedures.[28] Attempts to export into Israel's markets were deliberately thwarted.[29] Only after the European Community put pressure on Israel in the late 1980s were Palestinians able to export to western Europe. But they still had to do so through Israeli ports, and it was not long before the obstacles involved reduced such exports to a trickle.

The restriction of the Palestinian economy made the labour force dependent on the Israeli economy. In practice, Israel operated an apartheid system without having to formalize it, for the Palestinians had separate geographical and political status. All it required was for Israel to forbid Arabs of the Occupied Territories to sleep overnight inside Israel,[30] and to issue work permits to control the flow of cheap labour eager enough to do the menial tasks few Jews were willing to do. By the late 1980s one-third of the Palestinian labour force of about 300,000 were working in Israel, and several thousand more worked in the construction and maintenance of Jewish settlements in the Occupied Territories. It was a measure of their predicament that Arab labourers found themselves accomplices in the process of their own dispossession. In practice less than half the 120,000 or so workers crossing into Israel daily were registered with the authorities. Even those so registered were ineligible for Histadrut membership, and thus had no labour organization to represent them. Palestinian labourers could expect to earn on average about half the wages of their Jewish counterparts.

As with Israeli Palestinians, skilled Arabs in the Territories found it harder to find work commensurate with their skills or qualifications. Probably half or more were compelled to work outside their profession, usually as unskilled workers, or to migrate in search of suitable employment. Many others were forced to find work abroad. Their predicament suited Israel, since it ensured financial remittances which helped maintain civil quiescence, while removing potential leaders from the scene. During the 1970s approximately one-third of the labour force sought a better life in the Gulf states. All these migrant workers had to return once every three years in order not to forfeit their right to live in the land of their forebears. From 1983, however, the Gulf economies started to contract and retrench,[31] and an increasing number of Palestinians lost their jobs and returned. The 1990–1 Gulf crisis destroyed the Palestinian presence in Kuwait, wiping out virtually all the remittances which had helped maintain the standard of living in the Territories (see p. 108).

Alongside Israel's political and physical programme of incorporation, it had become clear by the mid-1980s that the occupation had become profitable in economic terms. By 1986 its exports to the West Bank alone amounted to $40 million annually, totalling possibly $700 million since 1967, with a similar story in Gaza, making the Territories Israel's second largest market after the United States.[32] Even ignoring the strategic and ideological considerations, then, it was unlikely that Israel would willingly relinquish a profitable captive market.

# 8

## RESISTANCE AND
## THE *INTIFADA*

At first it was only the Jeremiahs who warned that Israel intended to retain and colonize what it had conquered. The general expectation was that the superpowers would persuade Israel and Jordan to negotiate terms for the return of the West Bank to Hashemite rule in exchange for peace. So Jordan was relieved that Israel kept the old elite in place to provide municipal services.

Based on this expectation, the notables who now effectively represented the West Bank population trimmed their sails accordingly, allowed by Israel to travel to Amman frequently. Israel and Jordan shared a common aim of thwarting the emergence of a leadership outside their control.[1] Most people followed the lead of the notable class, shunning the efforts of Fatah to build a local resistance base. The PFLP had more success in the Gaza Strip where Egypt had previously encouraged *fidayin* activity, but its cells were smashed by 1972.[2]

### Resistance evolves, 1967–87

For the first four or five years, it seemed as if Israel and Jordan would together deny the PLO a following in the Occupied Territories. The 1972 municipal elections confirmed Israeli expectations, returning the old pro-Hashemite elite to their municipal office. By now, however, its experience of suppression in Jordan persuaded the PLO that its future depended on successfully challenging Jordan in the West Bank, and it began to collaborate with the Patriotic Front, a network of Communists in the West

Bank.[3] In the period 1973–5 the PLO's influence swept through the Territories, enhanced by the formal recognition the PLO won from the Arab states and the United Nations in 1974.

Underestimating PLO progress, Israel confidently ordered new municipal elections in 1976. The result was a shattering rebuttal of its 'normalization' policy, for nationalist candidates openly supportive of the PLO were swept to office. Israel never tried municipal elections again. It was less clear, however, that the PLO had convincingly defeated Jordanian interests. Although the new mayors were professionals, they still came from notable families and still found themselves co-operating with Amman to ensure that their municipalities continued to receive financial aid and access to Jordanian markets.

In 1978 Egypt, Israel and the United States reached agreement at Camp David on, *inter alia*, an autonomy plan for the Occupied Territories. The plan excluded the PLO and denied the Palestinian people the choice of their own representatives. Furthermore, Israel's Likud government, which signed the accord, was ideologically committed to retaining sovereignty of the Territories and integrating them into the Israeli state and, to this end, was taking numerous measures, including widening the illegal settlements policy initiated by Labour.[4] The vast majority of the Territories' inhabitants saw the plan as a means to thwart the demand for self-determination, to remove the legal protection of the Fourth Geneva Convention and of UNSCR 242, and to integrate the Territories while giving the inhabitants limited self-administration. The scale of their protest demonstrations in the towns and camps of the Territories persuaded the PLO, which might otherwise have explored the plan, to follow suit, amid fears that the people might otherwise opt for local leadership. Local protest was encouraged by the PFLP, by the DFLP and to some extent by the mayors themselves, who formed a new National Guidance Committee.[5] While loyal to the PLO, they were critical of its leadership.

The PLO now demonstrated the external power it could bring to bear on the people of the Territories. Following the Camp David Accords the Arab states had established a 'steadfastness fund' to assist the people of the West Bank and Gaza Strip. Control of the fund was put into the joint hands of Jordan (technically still maintaining its claim to sovereignty over the West Bank) and the PLO (as legitimate representative of the Palestinian people). Their Joint Committee used this immense financial power to strengthen those institutions and individuals well disposed to them, and to withhold such funds from leftists, radicals and independently minded institutions. Jordan and the PLO extended their patronage through a network of co-operative associations, limiting agricultural export through Jordan to 'loyal elements'.

Israel was happy to assist in crushing the National Guidance Committee in late 1981. It expelled several mayors and detained others, some of whom had already been severely maimed as a result of car bombs placed by militant settler groups. It now abandoned any thought of co-operation with Jordan and unsuccessfully attempted to establish a local quisling regime, known as the Village Leagues.[6] Then it turned its attention to trying to liquidate the PLO itself by its massive assault in Lebanon in 1982. The PLO's defence of West Beirut against overwhelming Israeli firepower greatly heightened its standing.

One by one, however, the outside contenders, even the PLO, had found that the inhabitants of the Territories had a will of their own, and this was not to be thwarted. This stubbornness tempered the natural loyalty felt for the PLO. Many inhabitants watched uneasily as the PLO and Jordan unsuccessfully attempted a joint initiative to rescue the Territories between 1984 and 1986. The majority simply no longer wanted Jordan to have any hand in their future, and hoped the PLO would stand firm on the essentials of self-determination.

## The popular movement[7]

While the political leadership of the different Palestinian factions operated covertly inside the Territories, each had its own overt social or professional associations intended to mobilize and maintain people within its orbit. Each faction had its own coded names for such associations – the Shabiba (Youth) indicated Fatah; 'Progressives', the Communists (or Palestine People's Party as they were renamed in 1990); 'Unity', the DFLP; and the 'Action Front', the PFLP. These tended to operate on instructions from above and from outside, competing to gain control of student bodies, professional associations, and cultural and sports clubs.

Nothing was more important to liberation than the creation of effective bonds across a society which in 1967 was still far from homogeneous. Indeed, after 1967 Israel and Jordan had both backed the old notable class against the newly emergent professionals, and the traders. The latter had turned to the national movement. As late as 1981 it was still possible to distinguish between urban merchants, traders, labour contractors and professionals among whom national activism was common, and a rural population which was still to a great extent preoccupied with more immediate matters. As one sociologist was able to say: 'peasant consciousness remains the main force among the Palestinians employed in Israel'.[8]

It was in such circumstances that the popular movement came into being. At a theoretical level one could argue that what the Palestinians began in the late 1970s was, to use Gramsci's phrase, a 'war of position', an attempt to mobilize the masses, and to detach as far as possible from the occupier, displacing Israeli institutions with their own. In practice, different professionals began to look at their various sectors and recognize how Israeli institutional control, traditional social attitudes and also foreign remittances (from the PLO, from the Gulf and from well-intentioned foreign voluntary agencies) all reinforced a sense of dependency.

Women were perhaps the most obvious category that was kept in a state of dependence. In the late 1970s a number of university-educated women formed 'women's working committees' with revolutionary intent. Women's associations had a long history. In 1919 the first groups had formed in Jaffa, Haifa and Jerusalem. In 1929 an Arab Women's Association (AWA) had brought these groups together. The AWA was innovative but remained a largely upper- and middle-class urban network.[9] One activist, Samiha Khalil, led the formation of the new Union of Arab Women in 1956 and established Jami'at In'ash al-Usra (the Family Revival Society) in 1965. Both organizations, dedicated to vocational training for women so that they could earn a living, were town-based and helped individual people only.

The new women's movement eschewed the patronage implicit in such traditional charitable associations and was concerned with mobilizing women across the social spectrum. It was rapidly realized that women were so preoccupied with their daily problems that real mobilization would be possible only through co-operative action. That meant the formation of women's committees in refugee camps and villages across the Territories. These identified their priorities and received support in achieving their aims: the provision of day-care centres for children so that mothers could go to work; literacy classes, because a large proportion of adult women were illiterate; sewing workshops and domestic food-processing. These seem modest activities. Intrinsically perhaps they were, but they were vehicles whereby women discovered the power they could acquire by organizing themselves, the revolutionary implications of operating these committees on a democratic basis, the chance of playing a fuller part in society and, possibly most important of all, a political self-confidence (with regard to gender) scarcely dreamt of before.

In the field of health a small handful of professionals recognized in 1979 that the Israeli-administered and highly inadequate health system ensured dependence and control. Consequently they formed an entirely new system based upon the principle that 'the real measure of development is the ability of a people to build its own comprehensive and complementary and independent infrastructure that is capable of dealing with its own problems, needs and aspirations'.[10] Thus the Union of Palestinian Medical Relief Committees (UPMRC) began to offer health services to villages and refugee communities, but expected these to organize their own health committees to decide what health issues concerned them most, and to provide local support for a UPMRC clinic. To provide the service, UPMRC recruited health professionals to offer part of their free time voluntarily to serving these communities. The effect was electric. From barely ten such professionals in 1979, there were over 700 health professionals serving 50,000 patients by 1988. Much more important in terms of national development, the approach of UPMRC helped ordinary people discover the power of democracy and organization at the grass-roots level.

Similar developments occurred in the field of agriculture and the provision of voluntary labour. Locally formed committees sought ways to achieve co-operative action, sometimes to defeat landlords and commission agents rather than the effects of the occupation. The trade union movement, which was never strong, moved away from ideas of class struggle towards the question of national liberation, especially in the early 1980s when younger cadres replaced the old guard. In Gaza, particularly, unions defied Israeli government prohibitions on their activities.

In many respects what took place was a transformation of Palestinian society and of the national movement. Power undoubtedly shifted during the 1980s to the popular movement, yet the national issue was also the popular movement's Achilles' heel. There was a natural dilemma as to whether to place social or national issues at the top of the agenda. With the growing tension between the different external constituents of the national movement, particularly following the Camp David Accords, the women's committees fragmented into four networks, reflecting the thinking of the DFLP (adherents of which had led the women's committee movement from the outset), the PFLP, the Communists and Fatah.[11] An enormous amount of energy was expended in rivalry and feuds. Likewise, new health networks sprang up reflecting the different parties, because the UPMRC was popularly identified with the Communists;[12] and the trade union movement, too, became bitterly fragmented. All these divisions continued throughout the 1980s, and were particularly severe during the period of Jordanian–PLO negotiations in 1984–6. However, in April 1987 the reconciliation of PLO factions at the Eighteenth Palestinian National Council (the PLO's assembly) in Algiers allowed a new spirit of co-operation. Although largely ignored by the outside world, the popular movement (and the 1987 reconciliation) prepared the ground for the people under occupation to take their destiny into their own hands.

## The *intifada*

By 1986 the people of the Occupied Territories had found themselves surrounded by powerful forces that seemed intent on eroding their will to resist. The current United States government, more anti-PLO than its predecessors, set about destroying local solidarity through a much vaunted 'quality-of-life' aid programme that would offer financial help through Jordanian and Israeli channels. Jordan announced a $1.2 billion development plan, its own ploy to undermine the PLO. Israel co-operated with Jordan, appointing jointly selected mayors for Hebron, Ramallah and al-Bira, and permitting an Amman-based bank to open a branch in Nablus. The intention, clearly, was to offer material advantage and external patronage in return for political tranquillity. Such inducements coincided with the toughest crackdown in the Territories since the Gaza operations of 1969–72. Prime Minister Peres presided over an unprecendented phase of repression, arrests, expulsions and house demolitions.[13]

Meanwhile the PLO seemed both down and out, largely written off by the West as a spent force, and deliberately ignored in the Arab world.[14] As 1987 drew to a close, it was clear to the people of the Occupied Territories that they could look for deliverance to nobody but themselves.

This sense of growing despair finally exploded on 9 December 1987, in reaction to an incident in which an Israeli truck driver had hit a car and killed four Palestinians in Gaza. Within hours there were riots and demonstrations from one end of the Occupied Territories to the other. It was the moment that political activists had been waiting for. Through the popular movement, in its many facets, it was possible to mobilize the entire population within days. For many months afterwards Palestinian stone-throwing youths defied Israeli military firepower on the streets. It was a defining moment for the Palestinian people.

For the first time all the people of the Territories acted as a nation. Prime Minister Shamir claimed that the Israeli army was making strenuous efforts to avoid bloodshed, stating: 'Terrorists and hooligans who attack our security forces are not heroes. But these criminals know that the army is trying not to wound or kill them, so they become more impudent. No one wants blood-shed.'[15] But his Defence Minister, Yitzhak Rabin, ordered the army to use 'might, power and beatings' to restore order,[16] while a government official argued that 'if the troops break his [a stone-thrower's] hand, he won't be able to throw stones for a month and a half'.[17]

The number of fatalities began to soar. In April 1988 a Jewish settler shot dead three Palestinians during an affray in which a Jewish settler had accidentally shot and killed a Jewish girl.[18] This marked an intensification of conflict between Palestinians armed with stones, and sometimes molotov cocktails, and armed set-tlers. In September 1988 Rabin introduced plastic bullets, saying, 'It is our intention to wound as many of them as possible... inflicting injuries is precisely the aim of using plastic bullets.'[19] Those captured were dealt with brutally. One leftist journal reported

*'systematic beatings on kidneys, stomach, testicles, women's breasts, hands, soles of feet, burns, beatings and illnesses exacer-bated by prisoners being drenched by water or forced to stand for days in the scorching sun, their heads covered by stinking sacks. Dozens of women miscarried, some during and after interroga-tion, most from the after effect of anti-riot gas.'[20]*

The popular health networks found themselves working around the clock to treat the injured. The UPMRC established a computerized blood donor data base which rapidly attracted 50,000 names. Through this data base it was able to bring appro-priate donors to the injured at short notice, saving many lives. Through such humble means those not demonstrating on the streets could play their part. A nation was rapidly coming of age.

Scenes of Israelis beating and breaking the bones of defence-less Palestinians, recorded by television crews, aroused world-wide condemnation. But no state brought pressure to bear on Israel to conform with international law. By the end of 1991 more than 1,000 Palestinians had been killed, mainly by shoot-ing but over 100 by beatings, tear gas or some other non-bullet death. Furthermore, over a quarter of those who had died were under 16 years of age. Another 100,000 had also suffered serious injuries, while over 15,000 had been held without trial for at least six months. More than 300 dwellings and other buildings, mainly those of 'security suspects', had been sealed or demolished, rendering over 2,000 people homeless. Israel closed down virtually every Palestinian educational institution, even kindergartens, in the name of security – a breach of international law and convention, whose effect was collectively to punish the youth of Palestine by denying it education for two or three years.

The Palestinians had rapidly developed their own clandestine leadership, the Unified National Leadership of the Uprising (UNLU) which was composed of local representatives of Fatah, the PFLP, the DFLP, the Palestine Communist Party and, temporarily, Islamic Jihad. UNLU put out regular communiqués in order to guide and co-ordinate strikes, demonstrations and other forms of resistance.[21]

A particularly important element was in the socio-economic field. For a long time it had been recognized that the Palestinian consumer market and labour force were both highly profitable to Israel. There was now a concerted attempt to withdraw custom, labour and the payment of taxes. In many localities popular committees, a natural extension of the popular movement, were established not only to arrange local resistance but more importantly to co-ordinate self-help and domestic production. Many Palestinians began to produce as much food as possible. Voluntary medical teams and teachers sought to provide informal services. Many Gazans, in particular could not survive without working in Israel, and labour there only fell by 40 per cent. As both sides tried to inflict greater damage on the other, the authorities began to destroy Palestinian agriculture. During the summer of 1988, 8,000 olive and fruit trees and thousands of dunums of wheat were burnt. Palestinians responded in kind, burning woodland.[22] It was reckoned that the monthly cost of the *intifada* to Israel was $120 million for security forces and $38 million in indirect, economic costs.[23]

For the first year or so, it seemed as if the *intifada* might succeed in its aim of throwing off the Israeli yoke. But a war of attrition quickly set in. As more and more leaders – those who co-ordinated efforts with the PLO – were arrested, so UNLU and local popular committees lost control of the uprising to the *shabab*, the youths who actually did battle with Israeli troops on the streets and in the refugee camps. They were unable to restrain the level of street fighting, co-ordinate strikes and shutdowns, or bring discipline or direction to the movement. The PLO also found itself unable to channel or discipline the *shabab*. Perhaps the most damaging aspect was the *shabab*'s predilection for punishing collaborators, which in practice meant indiscriminate extra-judicial killings not only of known or proven informers, but also of suspects, criminals and women of 'compromised virtue'. Perhaps as many as 700 so-called collaborators were killed.

Yet, according to some in the popular movement, the PLO bore some of the blame for what happened. It had been taken by surprise by the *intifada* and, failing to understand the popular movement, had sought to militarize the uprising. This contributed to the loss of popular participation and to the disintegration of the bond of principles that had held people together.

In the economic sphere Israel gradually forced localities to pay their taxes and water dues by coercive means. Those who failed to pay their taxes had all their possessions removed, most notably in virtually every household in Beit Suhur, near Bethlehem, in late 1989.

Thus the *intifada* slowly lost momentum. While it failed to shake off Israeli rule, however, it brought substantial achievements. Inside the Israeli establishment the debate shifted dramatically. No longer could the Territories and their inhabitants be considered an economic asset. The policing required to keep the Palestinians quiescent had now turned the Territories into a liability. Right- and left-wing policy makers seriously differed only over how to retain control of the Territories while allowing their inhabitants to govern themselves. Furthermore, at a time when the international community had dismissed Palestine as 'yesterday's problem', the *intifada* brought it back to the centre of the long-term Middle East agenda, despite the 1990–1 Gulf crisis (see p. 107).

In November 1988, at considerable cost to itself, the PLO publicly accepted UN Resolution 242, renounced terrorism and recognized the right of Israel to exist, in words dictated by the

United States. It was a major climb-down for the PLO, which now relied on the *intifada* as its sole bargaining chip. It was modestly rewarded by the United States with an agreement for contacts between the US Ambassador in Tunis and PLO headquarters. Formal recognition, however, was withheld; and when a PLO commando (presumably seeking to undermine Arafat's position) attempted an attack on Tel Aviv's beach in 1990, even these minimalist contacts were suspended. Once again the world seemed to lose interest in the Palestinian predicament.

## The Zealous Ones: Islamic revival[24]

By now the PLO faced not only an impasse internationally but growing opposition inside the Occupied Territories. For the preceding twenty years its main internal opponents had been radical and secular leftist groups. Now, however, the challenge came from a new direction, the Muslim Brotherhood or Ikhwan al-Muslimin.[25] Fatah's founder members traditionally had had close contact with the Ikhwan, which had established a strong foothold among the poor and the refugees in the Gaza Strip. But the Ikhwan was committed to a revival of both individual and social commitment to Islam. *Jihad* (holy war) could come later. It was in this spirit that social, cultural, health and educational societies were established throughout the Territories. People grew to respect such societies for the quality of service offered, and open Islamic expression began to revive from 1978 onwards. These societies were usually located in the rapidly growing number of mosques built during the 1980s. Funding for these mosques and the activities in them came from conservative Arab states.

The most important of these organizations, al-Mujamma' al-Islami (the Islamic Association), was established in Gaza in 1973, and had a rapidly centralizing influence on the Ikhwan movement. The reluctance of al-Mujamma' al-Islami (as the Ikhwan became known in Gaza from 1973 onwards) to take political or military action left the field clear for the PLO, which criticized al-Mujamma' for failing to join the *jihad*. Its leader, Shaykh Yasin, however, stuck to the Quranic precept, 'Prepare before you fight', as justification for promoting a spiritual revival prior to *jihad*. Only one faction which split away from the Ikhwan in the 1960s, the Islamic Jihad, actually commenced attacks on Israeli targets in the mid-1980s, and most of its operatives were captured before the *intifada* erupted. Meanwhile, amid increasing disillusionment with the PLO, and a new proliferation of mosques, al-Mujamma' widened and deepened its following.

The *intifada* presented al-Mujamma' with a challenge. Could it afford to continue standing aside once virtually the whole populace had taken to the streets? Its response was immediate. On 14 December 1987 al-Mujamma' issued a call to the people to confront the occupation. In January 1988 a separate organization sponsored by al-Mujamma', al-Harakat al-Muqawama al-Islamiya, known by the acronym Hamas (in Arabic, zeal) joined the *intifada*.

Hamas, which quickly established branches across the Occupied Territories, had financial support from the Ikhwan in Jordan, with which there had been long-standing links.[26] It soon showed itself reluctant to accept the discipline of UNLU. It frequently ignored UNLU communiqués, or contradicted them in its own leaflet campaigns. Such was its success and appeal that it was not long before Hamas had eclipsed al-Mujamma' and itself became synonymous with the Ikhwan. Hamas soon commanded possibly one-third of Gaza's population and was rapidly building a similar following in the West Bank. The PLO became seriously worried by this challenge and invited Hamas to join it, but could not accept the terms Hamas demanded: 40 per cent of the seats on the Palestine National Council.

Hamas's relations with the PLO sharply deteriorated after the latter's recognition of Israel in November 1988. Its charter, published in August 1988, opposed any bid by the PLO to compromise or to establish an interim government in part of the Occupied Territories. 'The only solution to the Palestinian problem is *jihad*,' it pronounced; 'all peace conferences and proposals are no more than a waste of time.'[27] Hamas took the ideological line that all Palestine was a Muslim endowment (*waqf*) 'placed in trust with Muslims till the end of time', a mirror image of the Eretz Yisrael view of the Jewish patrimony.

Initially Israel had been pleased to see dissent within Palestinian ranks. Successive Israeli administrations back in the 1970s had nurtured and even, it was widely believed, funded the Islamic movement in the Territories as an instrument with which to undermine the secular nationalist constituents of the PLO. While these revivalists remained committed to social and religious activities, Israel's policy seemed yet another weapon in its armoury of divide and rule. During the following years Israel began to reap what it had sown, as Hamas started to prove itself more ruthless and more efficient in its attacks on government troops than the PLO had ever been.

# 9

# THE 1990s:
# PALESTINE LOST OR REGAINED?

## The Gulf crisis

The 1990s began with a cruel exposure of Arab disunity. In August 1990 Iraq suddenly invaded Kuwait and threw the entire Arab world into disarray. After the initial paralysis of shock, each Arab community found itself forced to take sides. Few contradicted the flagrant illegality of the invasion, nor its wide and damaging impact. But the immediate and forceful decision of the United States to threaten war on Iraq if it did not withdraw completely and unconditionally provoked dismay and anger. Many Arabs, including Jordanians and Palestinians, had looked to Iraq as the vanguard of Arab military power after Egypt had capitulated as Arab world leader in 1979. Jordanians (and Palestinians in Jordan) immediately began to feel the acute economic impact of the US-led Coalition blockade on Aqaba. At another level, the almost collective acquiescence to US policy left Iraq looking like the one Arab state willing to defy the West and all that it stood for – its hypocrisy, its support for Israel, its imperial history and its exploitation of the Arab world since 1945. All over the Arab world it was noted that the USA was, on the one hand, meticulous in demanding Iraq's respect for international law and, on the other, flagrantly indulgent of Israel's violations.

This feeling was reinforced by widespread ambivalent feelings regarding Kuwait and its professed loyalty to the Arab world. It was easy to view Kuwait's heavy investment in the West, rather than in infrastructural development of poorer Arab countries, as poor evidence of pan-Arab solidarity. In reality it did more than any other Gulf state for Arab development.[1] Envy no doubt played a major part. As Kuwait's oldest expatriate Arab workforce, it was understandable that Palestinians felt these ambiguities more acutely than most.

By 1992 there were an estimated 400,000 Palestinians in Kuwait, many of whom had been there since 1970 or earlier. They spanned the social classes, from wealthy businessmen to skilled or semi-skilled workers. Their remitted savings made life bearable back in Jordan, the West Bank and Gaza, and Lebanon. In the Occupied Territories some villages were almost entirely economically dependent on Gulf remittances.[2]

Yet the relations between Palestinians and Kuwaitis were uneasy. Kuwait had supported Palestinian rights in Palestine more assiduously than other Gulf states, but it had also denied Palestinians any civil rights in Kuwait. Palestinians felt looked down upon. Their presence, in some cases for more than two decades, remained subject to the whim of their employer. Once retired or redundant they had to leave the country immediately. Palestinian businessmen could start their own business only if Kuwaitis held a 51 per cent share, and the company was registered in a Kuwaiti's name. There was no question of Palestinians being allowed to participate in national life, no matter how long they had worked in the country, nor even if they had been born and grown up there. Only a small fraction of Palestinian children were allowed into Kuwaiti government schools; the vast majority had to be educated in schools the Palestinians funded and ran themselves.[3] Many Palestinians, too, were painfully familiar with the heavy hand of the bureaucracy and the police.

In such circumstances, in response to the Iraqi invasion, over half the Palestinians in Kuwait fled the country. Some (mainly, it seems, those brought down from Iraq) openly sided with their Iraqi masters, while others merely stood by to await the outcome. Those in the Occupied Territories demonstrated their approval for Saddam Hussein and their hostility towards Israel's ally, the USA. To many intellectuals such a reaction was short-sighted and irresponsible. The PLO initially sat on the fence, seeking to settle the crisis by conciliation. But Egypt and the Gulf states demanded absolute support for the US-led Coalition, something the PLO could not easily give in view of popular Palestinian reaction to the US move. The PLO leadership had learnt throught the trials of the 1980s that it could afford to lose everything save the support of the mass of Palestinians. So, while privately dismayed at the turn of events, it began to identify more clearly with the position of its constituents, the source of its legitimacy, and thus with Iraq. Financially this proved devastating.

It is hardly surprising that Kuwait reacted bitterly towards its Palestinians, for it recalled its support for the Palestinian cause over many years, and its employment of hundreds of thousands of refugees. It forgot the daily humiliations inflicted on Palestinian workers, the complete absence of civil or worker rights for its foreign labour force, and its failure to use the greater part of its huge wealth to help Arab development.

When Iraq was successfully evicted, the Kuwaitis were swift to revenge themselves on the Palestinians, who became subject to revenge attacks, arrest, torture and extra-judicial killings.[4] Those who had not left Kuwait as a result of Iraq's invasion now did so as a consequence of its liberation. Kuwait announced that it would not offer work to more than 40,000 Palestinians. By September 1991 only 60,000 were still in the country, and a year later this had dwindled to about 30,000.[5] At least half of these were would-be returnees to Gaza, who found that Egypt would not allow them transit permits and were thus stranded in a country where they were now detested.[6]

The economic effect of this migration was considerable. Widespread hardship was experienced in the remittance areas. In the West Bank and Gaza, Gulf remittances probably dropped by over 80 per cent.[7] Of those who returned to Jordan and the Territories, fewer than 20 per cent were able to find employment. Those Palestians hitherto shielded from the real economic cost of the *intifada* now began to feel its true effect. Refugees in Lebanon, too, experienced the loss of jobs and remittances.

Moreover, a completely new set of circumstances now prevailed in the region. A collective Arab bargaining position had ceased to exist. Instead, the Arab world was now bitterly divided. Relations even among Arab members of the Coalition were fraught.[8] Egypt could now boast its 1979 treaty with Israel as the model for others to follow, rather than an abject desertion of the Arab position. The consequences were naturally more severe for those who had opposed the Coalition. Iraq lay in ruins. Jordan found itself struggling on the edge of bankruptcy, its port of Aqaba under embargo, its vital transit trade now at a halt, and Gulf remittances down to a mere trickle. Gulf states made their anger with Jordan clear.[9] But it was the PLO that suffered most. For years the PLO coffers had been filled by Gulf contributions – both governmental and popular. Now this practically all ceased, and the PLO's resources soon proved insufficient to maintain the former level of services and subsidies to institutions and to the families of those killed in action.

### Peace process or fig-leaf?

The end of the Cold War in 1989 and the manifest collapse of the Eastern bloc had given the United States a relatively free hand. It certainly could not have gone to war against Iraq with the same confidence had the Soviet Union still been in a position to oppose it. Now, as undisputed master of the political terrain, the United States announced its intention of settling the Arab–Israeli dispute under its own aegis. It applied considerable pressure to get the Likud government to agree to peace discussions, a considerable feat since Likud was ideologically committed to retaining the whole of Eretz Yisrael. Israeli-American relations deteriorated sharply as the United States delayed (and then witheld) approval for a $10 billion loan guarantee because Likud refused to give an undertaking not to settle current Russian immigrants in the Occupied Territories. It was a measure of the meagre level of its constraints on Israel that the United States did not insist on a freeze on settlement construction, let alone initial measures to reduce illegal Jewish settlement. Nor did the United States threaten to suspend its enormous annual aid package to Israel, running in most years to at least $1,000 per Israeli citizen and in 1991 amounting to $5.6 billion. In order to obtain Likud's agreement, however, the United States sidelined the United Nations, agreed to Likud's conditions restricting Palestinian representation (see below), and made it clear that the PLO could not be a formal participant in this peace process. It still did not require a halt to Israel's settlements programme.

The PLO now found itself under intense pressure. The situation in the Occupied Territories had deteriorated not only because of the loss of remittances but also because Israel made conditions unprecedentedly harsh for the Palestinian population, while stepping up its encroachment on, and seizure of, Arab property, especially around Jerusalem. In October 1990 this reached a bloody crescendo when Israeli police opened fire on a demonstration in the Haram al-Sharif (Temple Mount) in Jerusalem, killing seventeen and wounding another 150. It was the worst day of the *intifada* and of all twenty-three years of Israel's occupation. Although it had supported the UN resolution regarding the applicability of the Fourth Geneva Convention,[10] the United States resisted the idea of UN observers or protectors for the Palestinian people, and the UN Secretary-General's proposal that Israel should be 'persuaded' to accept the *de jure* applicability of the Fourth Geneva Convention fell into abeyance. All this hardly suggested that the United States desired implementation of international law.[11] It was clear that, faced only with verbal censure, Israel's policies and practices would remain unconstrained. A handful of Palestinians reacted to the Haram massacre with random stabbings of Jews, inciting Israel to yet harsher methods.

The PLO also had to contend with dangers implicit in the profound disunity of the Arab world. It was under pressure from Egypt to negotiate with Israel. It was rebuffed by the Gulf states, which wished to punish it for siding with Iraq. It no longer could call on Iraq for support, and Jordan was largely in the same boat as itself, helpless and threatened. Above all, the PLO was in grave danger of being outflanked by Syria, which had already indicated its willingness to consider peace negotiations and now enjoyed improved standing with the Western peace brokers in consequence of its assistance in the Gulf War. Had relations between Syria and the PLO been better, there could have been co-operation. But Syria had always suspected the PLO as a 'loose cannon' in the Arab–Israeli conflict,[12] while the PLO feared that Syria really wished to make the PLO a Syrian satellite like Lebanon.

Under such circumstances, arguably the worst it had ever faced, the PLO reluctantly authorized Palestinian involvement in the US-sponsored peace talks. The decision was highly controversial, above all in the Occupied Territories and in Lebanon, where it was feared that the PLO was taking part in little more than a process of unconditional surrender behind a fig-leaf named 'peace process'. Indeed, it said much about the United States' vaunted role as impartial mediator that it accepted Israeli demands: that Palestinians must be vetted by Israel and must be part of a joint Jordanian–Palestinian delegation; that Palestinians from East Jerusalem and from outside Palestine were disqualified from the delegation; and that neither the status of East Jerusalem nor the issue of Palestinian self-determination was an acceptable item for the agenda. Thus, while Israel was free to choose its own representatives, Palestinians were not; while Israel required, and indeed obtained, Palestinian recognition of its right to exist, the PLO was unable to obtain from either the United States or Israel recognition of any Palestinian rights at all. This was hardly an advertisement for the United States' professed commitment to the principles of equality, democracy or self-determination.[13]

There was a widespread feeling that the Palestinians at the opening meeting of these negotiations in Madrid in October 1991 were sacrifical lambs likely to be dealt with as *ingénues* by Israel's sophisticated diplomatic machine. In fact the dignity, moderation and candour of Palestine's leading representatives, Drs Haidar Abd al-Shafi from Gaza and Hanan Ashrawi of Bir Zeit University, stole the show. By contrast, Likud's negotiators appeared strident and extreme. Madrid represented two important achievements for Palestinians; Palestinian interlocutors demonstrated to the world the reasonableness of Palestinian demands, and the more significant achievement was that for the first time Israel had negotiated with Palestinians, something it had strenuously avoided doing since 1947.[14]

However, Palestinian euphoria soon proved misplaced. By the tenth round of negotiations in Washington in June 1993 no progress had been made. On the contrary, Palestinians began to feel that the peace process served merely to disguise the reality of deteriorating prospects in Palestine and the intention of the

United States to massage the Palestinian case out of existence.

There was good reason for Palestinian scepticism, besides the obvious fact of PLO political impotence. In December 1991 the United States refused PLO officials access to Washington to advise their formal delegates from 'behind the scenes', something that had been possible in Madrid. This may have been symptomatic of President Bush's rapidly declining standing in domestic opinion polls, and his need to placate the Zionist lobby. That month, too, under US pressure the UN General Assembly repealed UNGA Resolution 3379 of 10 November 1975, which had described Zionism as a form of racism, despite the twin facts that Zionism's objective had always been to transfer Palestine from Arab to Jewish control, and that Zionist policy as executed by Israel had been systematically discriminatory against the Arab population of Palestine, whether Israeli citizens or under military occupation.

Meanwhile in the Occupied Territories, Israel was busy establishing new facts to restrict Palestinian hopes further. A new master plan was published by the Ministry of Housing for the construction of 4,000 dwellings in twenty-two Arab neighbourhoods – for new Jewish settlers – and this news was quickly followed by the eviction of Arab inhabitants of five houses in Silwan, a long-standing Arab village on the edge of Jerusalem.

The human rights situation seemed to deteriorate, too, with allegations of electric shock torture being applied to children and young men, and with fresh cases of detainees dying in custody.[15] The fact of routine torture practised on Palestinian detainees since the occupation began was well attested, not least by the Israeli government Landau Commission in 1987.[16] Meanwhile, in January, Israel had announced its intention to deport another twelve Palestinians in addition to the sixty-six already deported since the beginning of the *intifada*.

In June 1992 Israel's electorate returned Yitzhak Rabin to office. Rabin promised a peace agreement within six months, and announced a freeze on settlements. This announcement reflected the domestic priority of absorbing and settling Russian immigrants, and the need to secure US financial support. In August, Rabin visited Washington to repair the damage done during the Likud period. Not only did he secure the $10 billion loan guarantee but he was able to exclude the 'thickening' of existing settlements with another 50,000 settlers and the establishment of fresh settlements in East Jerusalem from the general restrictions on use.

This implied that the USA was now willing to disregard East Jerusalem as occupied territory in order to make progress towards a settlement.[17] By spring 1993 this so called 'thickening', in fact the construction of 11,000 dwellings, constituted 'the biggest building boom in the history of the settlement',[18] with the prospect of the number of Jewish settlers in East Jerusalem rising from 125,000 to 170,000 during the 1990s. The United States seemed unconcerned.

In fact the US election in November 1992 had ushered in a Democrat administration under Bill Clinton, whose electoral vote-seeking utterances warned of his strong pro-Israeli stance:

*'America and Israel share a specific bond. Our relationship is unique among all nations. Like America, Israel is a strong democracy, a symbol of freedom, an oasis of liberty, a home to the oppressed and persecuted... If I ever let Israel down, God would never forgive me.'*[19]

The Clinton administration soon demonstrated its desire to protect Israel from international constraint. The fifth anniversary of the *intifada* was marked by the killing of three IDF reservists by members of Hamas. In response, Rabin authorized the arrest and expulsion of 415 alleged Hamas supporters, who were summarily dumped on the Lebanese border. Lebanon refused to accept people illegally expelled from Palestine, and their predicament at Marj al-Zuhur rapidly became a *cause célèbre*. A substantial proportion of those expelled were professionals, doctors, engineers or academics. On 18 December 1992 UN Security Council Resolution 799 reaffirmed the applicability of the Fourth Geneva Convention and required Israel to take back all the expellees immediately and unconditionally. Although the United States had supported this resolution, it soon accepted Israel's compromise offer of allowing 100 back, as a 'sufficient' conformity with UNSCR 799, as if the remaining

315 expulsions no longer constituted a violation of international law. Falling in now with the US desire to banish this problem, the President of the European Community described Israel's offer as 'helpful'. Once again, the international community was demonstrating its feebleness and cowardice in the face of Israeli law-breaking, and its facile willingness to set aside international law in favour of the 'peace process'. But this put immense pressure on the PLO, now acutely short of funds and desperate for tangible progress in the negotiations.[20] It was widely believed that the PLO, while embarrassed by Israel's action, was secretly glad to see Hamas cut down to size. If that was so, it was a misplaced sentiment. The expellees became national symbols and as such drew more, not less, support for Hamas. Indeed, only the expellees acted with dignity and honour in the affair. They insisted that UNSCR 799 should be upheld, and that either all or none would return to Palestine. Instead of pursuing the enforcement of UNSCR 799, the PLO sought an assurance that there would be no more deportations, but it was unable to obtain even this face-saving commitment.

Perhaps inevitably, conflict in the Occupied Territories intensified during this period, with more Palestinian attacks on Jewish settlers, and more killings by the security forces. It was a striking indication that, while expulsions removed community leaders, they did nothing to reduce the level of violence. Israeli pacification measures intensified. During the first quarter of 1993, fifty-eight Palestinians were killed and another 2,300 injured. Over a hundred homes were also shelled, as Israel resorted to new methods of house demolition, abandoning bulldozers in favour of hitting the homes of suspects with anti-tank missiles and high explosives.[21] Hundreds of homes were searched, many were vandalized, machine gun fire being used to destroy furniture and other movable property. In May alone thirty-four people were killed, bringing the total of Palestinian deaths at the hands of soldiers and settlers since the beginning of the *intifada* to more than 1,200.

Rabin had pledged to achieve a deal with the Palestinians and he now used pacification to achieve his aim.[22] Soldiers and snipers shot men, women and children where no disorders were taking place.[23] Undercover squads roamed the camps carrying out extra-judicial killings. Fear became widespread. At the beginning of March 1993 Rabin declared the closure of the Gaza Strip and West Bank, thereby cutting them off both from Israel and from occupied East Jerusalem. This closure had devastating economic consequences, since it prevented day labourers crossing into Israel and led to an estimated loss of $725,000 for Gaza families daily.[24] The average Gaza income per head of population now fell to $12 monthly, a decrease of 13 per cent, and a drop of 66 per cent from pre-*intifada* days.[25] It also cut off the West Bank from its economic capital, East Jerusalem, with serious consequences for the hundreds who normally commuted to the city to work or to market produce. Besides, this breached Israel's undertaking to allow free access to the holy places of the city.

In July 1993 Israel launched a reprisal raid into Lebanon in retribution for the killing of five Israeli soldiers in its occupied zone of south Lebanon. The vast majority of the 130 killed were civilians. Once again, despite UNSCR 425 (requiring Israel's immediate and unconditional withdrawal), the international community did nothing except express concern.

## The Declaration of Principles: a Palestinian state in sight?

By now the PLO's increasingly parlous financial and ideological situation made it desperate to strike whatever deal it could. It also believed, with reason, that the people suffering Rabin's pacification policy were now desperate for a solution. Yet as so often in the past, those suffering the real hardships, both in the Territories and outside, were less willing than the PLO leadership to sell their birthright for a mess of pottage. Indeed, there was increasing frustration at the PLO's apparently endless political concessions, its alleged corruption and mismanagement, and growing public dissonance between leading Palestinians in the Territories and the PLO leadership in Tunis.[26]

Why was Rabin driving the Palestinians so hard? The Occupied Territories had become, if not ungovernable, at least very costly in lives and cash to keep under direct control. So it made sense to delegate government of the West Bank and Gaza (or the Arab population) to the PLO, if it could be persuaded to act under

Israeli tutelage. Rabin knew that the PLO was already under huge financial and political pressure. The pressure he now applied in the Territories may have been to force the PLO to an agreement.

There was another important Israeli motive, an economic one.[27] The Occupied Territories had once been profitable to Israel, but the *intifada* changed that. Subsequently, the influx of Russian immigrants from 1989 to 1992 produced a severe economic and ideological crisis for Israel. The ideological dilemma concerned whether Zionism's mission concerned redemption of the whole of biblical Israel or something short of it. The 1992 election indicated that a slight but apparently decisive majority favoured the latter. The most crucial issue was economic. The burden of sudden *aliya* (incoming) brought to a head the debate between traditionalists, who upheld principles of state ownership and intervention in the national economy, and those who favoured economic liberalization.

Israel, it seems, has opted for the latter course, but in order to play a full part in the global economy Israel must have unfettered access to Arab, eastern European and non-aligned states, most of which observe the Arab boycott. Striking a deal with the Palestinians is the essential precondition to ending the Arab boycott. Given its enormous skills resources, Israel may now become a vibrant and economically dominating player in the Middle East. It remains to be seen whether Palestinians can capitalize on that or not (see Chapter 10).

While the eleventh fruitless round of talks was taking place in Washington in late August 1993, it was suddenly announced that secret direct negotiations had been taking place under the aegis of the Norwegian government, and had led to a decision for formal mutual recognition between the PLO and Israel as a prelude to an open-ended autonomy arrangement commencing with limited self-government for Jericho and Gaza. Rabin and Arafat travelled to Washington and formally shook hands on the White House lawn on 13 September.[28]

That act marked the most important watershed in Israeli–Palestinian relations since 1948. The PLO, it will be recalled, had recognized Israel in November 1988, but had been scantily rewarded at the time. Israel's formal recognition of the PLO as the representative organization of the Palestinian people reflected a remarkable and almost unprecedented change in Israeli popular attitudes. In 1977 only 2 per cent of the Israeli electorate wanted direct talks with the PLO. By September 1993 that figure had risen to 57 per cent,[29] and with this slender majority the 'doves' of the Labour Party, led by Yossi Beilin and Shimon Peres,[30] were able to prevail over Rabin's instinctive reluctance.

The immediate impact throughout Israel/Palestine was a brief moment of euphoria. At the time an opinion poll indicated that 63 per cent of the Gaza Strip population favoured the accord. The prevailing mood, however, was a mixture of relief, anger and regret. One man expelled from Majdal (Ashkelon) in 1950 spoke for thousands when he said:

*'I feel like a man who has lost a million dollars and been given ten. But you see, I lost the million dollars a long time ago. So I will keep the ten. We cannot go on the way we are. I accept, I accept, I accept. After so many rejections, I accept. But please, don't ask me how I feel.'[31]*

The terms of the Declaration of Principles (DoP) were sufficiently vague to allow a variety of interpretations. Over the next few weeks the implications were hotly debated. The Declaration proposed an agreement to recognize mutual and legitimate rights, and to 'achieve a just, lasting and comprehensive peace settlement and historic reconciliation'.

To this end it was agreed (Art. 1) to establish an interim Palestinian National Authority (PNA), pending an elected Council for Palestinians in the West Bank and the Gaza Strip for a transitional period not exceeeding five years, leading to a permanent settlement based on UNSCR 242; to hold free and general political elections (Art. 3) for the Council with international observers, constituting a 'significant interim preparatory step towards the realisation of the legitimate rights of the Palestinian people and their just requirements'. The Council's jurisdiction was to cover the West Bank and Gaza Strip which would be viewed as a single entity (Art. 4). A five-year transitional period would begin upon Israeli withdrawal from the Gaza Strip and Jericho area (Art. 5). Permanent status negotiations would cover Jerusalem, refugees, settlements, security arrangements, borders, relations and co-operation with other neighbours. On the withdrawal of Israeli forces from the Gaza Strip and Jericho area, authority would be transferred to the Palestinians for education and culture, health, social welfare, direct taxation and tourism (Art. 6). An interim agreement was to be negotiated to specify the structure of the Council and the transfer of powers and responsibilities. This Council would establish relevant authorities for economic growth (Art. 7). A Palestinian police force would be established for public order and internal security, but Israel retained respon-sibility for defending against external threats and also for the 'overall security of Israelis [e.g. settlers] for the purpose of safe-guarding their internal security and public order' (Art. 8). Both parties would review jointly laws and military orders presently in force in remaining spheres (Art. 9). Israeli military forces would be withdrawn from populated areas before Council elections (Art. 13). A withdrawal agreement regarding Jericho and the Gaza Strip was to be reached by 13 December 1993 (in fact not concluded until 4 May 1994), and implemented within four months of that agreement. Israel was anxious to be rid of polic-ing Gaza, while Jericho offered the PLO a symbolic foothold in the West Bank.

Those who wholeheartedly welcomed the accord argued that the drift of such an agreement led unmistakably towards state-hood, particularly in view of the reference to UNSCR 242. For how could Israel, at the end of a five-year transitional period, pre-vent Palestinians from declaring independence? And if thwarted, would not Palestinians revert to revolt again? Experienced diplo-mats recalled that other liberation struggles tended to end with erstwhile masters forced by unfolding circumstances into progres-sive concessions until full independence was granted.

At the other end of the spectrum were opponents of the accord, members of Hamas and the Rejection Front (primarily the PFLP and DFLP), who accused Arafat of abject surrender of every principle on which their national struggle was predicated. Outside Palestine many refugees, particularly in Lebanon, were profoundly embittered by an accord that apparently consigned them to oblivion.

These two clear-cut positions, of outright acceptance or rejection, were mirrored by Israeli reactions. Some who welcomed the agreement as leading to an end to an occupation that had progressively impaired the moral quality of the state, while for others, still committed to 'Greater Israel', as for Hamas, control over the whole of Eretz Yisrael/Palestine remained axiomatic.[32]

Yet even among many Palestinians who had striven for peace, notably those who had actually negotiated in Madrid and Washington, there was now dismay at Arafat's reckless acceptance of such unpromising conditions. They were appalled by the undemocratic secrecy of the negotiations, the way in which the PLO seemed to 'rubber-stamp' Arafat's deal, and the danger of ending not with an independent state but with a series of cantons or bantustans under an authoritarian Palestinian administration (see Map 5). They were quick to remind Arafat that their lack of progress in Washington had centred on principles now so casually thrown away: a total freeze on Jewish settlement activity; the subordination of settlers to the jurisdiction of the self-governing authority; explicit Israeli recognition of the West Bank and Gaza Strip as occupied, not merely 'disputed';[33] and the inclusion of Arab Jerusalem within the territorial jurisdiction of self-rule. Now, in their view, Arafat had waived internationally recognized rights of the Palestinians and yielded implicit recognition of Israeli jurisdiction over the Territories.[34] Furthermore, Arafat had failed to obtain an assurance that the principle of self-determination would ultimately be recognized, and accepted deferment of crucial issues such as the status of East Jerusalem, the fate of the refugees and the Jewish settlements. To those living in the Territories it was crystal clear that Israel was moving fast to consolidate its hold on East Jerusalem and other West Bank settlements.

Al-Haq, the internationally respected West Bank law centre, expressed various concerns that (1) ambiguity in the text could impair the Palestinian right to self-determination; (2) the failure to agree expressly to the amendment of Israeli military regulations raised serious questions about human rights; (3) the failure to define respective Israeli and Palestinian jurisdiction could lead to a problem of accountability; (4) economic proposals could perpetuate current Palestinian dependency. Finally, it made the

MAP 5

## One example of the West Bank cantonization that Palestinians fear

Based on Dr Clinton Bailey's map, *Ha'aretz*, 7 May 1993, and *Jerusalem Post*, 18 June 1993

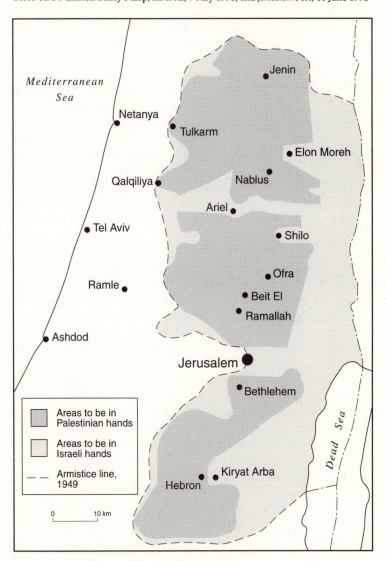

point that all territory, even that from which Israel withdrew in the transitional phase, remained 'occupied' under international law.[35] As Raja Shehadeh, al-Haq's founder, pointed out: 'Despite Israel's well known legalistic and Talmudic approach to negotiations, the Palestinian team negotiating in Oslo did not consult with any legal adviser. No Palestinian jurist was ever present or consulted throughout the process.'[36]

The failure of Israel and the PLO to reach agreement on the details for Gaza–Jericho by 13 December greatly increased Palestinian scepticism, and strengthened the position of opponents of the deal.[37] Major sticking points were the physical extent of Jericho, the question of border controls especially at the river Jordan bridge, prisoners and legal powers.[38] Israel did little to sweeten the atmosphere. It did not fulfil its promise to release some or all of the 11,000 political prisoners it held. As the weeks slipped by, Arafat's reputation plummeted, and killings became more frequent. Hamas activists ambushed and killed IDF reservists and settlers, while troops, settlers and undercover squads killed Palestinians with a new intensity.

## Mayhem in Hebron, while Hamas changes tack

In the West Bank it was perhaps inevitable that Hebron became the epicentre of conflict, given its religious importance to both Muslims and Jews. At the heart of the city stands the Ibrahimi mosque on the traditional site of Abraham's burial place. After 1967 the victorious Israelis allowed the mosque to be used also as a synagogue. IDF troops were permanently stationed at the mosque, supposedly to ensure the safety of all worshippers.

Given the clear intention of Jewish and Muslim ideologues to wreck the Oslo Accord, one might have expected these to have been particularly vigilant during this difficult period. In practice the 100,000 Palestinians were subjected to intensified harassment from the 400 armed Jewish settlers in the centre of the city, and their associates in the nearby settlement of Qiryat Arba. In January 1994 al-Haq publicly warned that it was 'deeply concerned about the escalation of attacks by Israeli settlers in the Hebron district'.[39]

Yet on 24 February a Jewish religious zealot, Dr Baruch Gold-stein, entered the mosque and opened fire on the Muslim wor-shippers marking the end of Ramadan. Twenty-nine died before he was overpowered and killed by surviving worshippers. Israeli troops failed to intervene, except to shoot another six Palestini-ans dead. It subsequently emerged that they were under standing orders never to fire on Jews even if these were killing Palestinians, stark evidence that the inherent racism of the occupation is not confined to ideological settlers but to the whole system of con-trol. Far from being a single demented individual, as Rabin argued, Goldstein represented the views of many of his fellow set-tlers. At his funeral oration the words of Rabbi Perrin – 'one mil-lion Arabs are not worth a Jewish fingernail'[40] – testified to a state of mind more readily identifiable with the Third Reich than with 'an oasis of liberty' as so recently praised by President Clinton.

There could have hardly been clearer evidence of the error in postponing discussion of the illegal settlements. With one bloody deed, Goldstein demonstrated the threat that these settle-ments posed to peace in the Occupied Territories. Now it was the turn of Hamas to take revenge. On 6 April Hamas operatives blew up a bus in 'Afula, killing seven Israelis, including school children. One week later a bomb in Hadera claimed another five lives. These murderous acts inside Israel naturally outraged Jew-ish opinion, but they also suggested that a peaceful disengage-ment required not only the dismantling of the settlements but also a reimposition of the armistice line. Israel responded to these attacks, as it had done to the Hebron massacre, with the imposition of almost the tightest restrictions the Territories had ever known. In both cases it was Palestinians rather than settlers who were put under curfew.

With the apparently inexorable, if delayed, transition to autonomy, however, Hamas began to trim its sails. It did not wish to exclude itself from the political arena; nor did Israel (in spite of its pronouncements) wish it to. It now indicated that it might be willing to abandon its attacks on Israeli civilians, if Israel was willing to withdraw completely from the Occupied Territories, and might even abandon its claim to all Palestine.[41] It also began to negotiate co-operation with the PLO, skilfully positioning itself always to drive a slightly harder bargain than Arafat, and thus appeal to the overwhelming majority of Palestinians. Arafat was well aware that Hamas commanded a solid constituency of approximately 20 per cent, too many simply to be driven off the streets, a proportion that could easily double to reflect disenchantment with the official Fatah line.[42]

On 4 May 1994 Rabin and Arafat finally signed the Jericho–Gaza withdrawal agreement in Cairo. During the five months' delay the confidence of their respective constituents in the peace process had largely evaporated. Israelis felt outraged by Hamas attacks and by Arafat's slippery political style. Palestinians felt left in ignorance as to the precise terms to which they now had to humble themselves. In negotiation Arafat began to discover his previous failure to examine the 'small print'. He then discredited the PLO by attempting to negotiate new conditions consistent with Palestinian rights but in violation of the DoP.

Most of the leadership under occupation which had participated in official peace negotiations – for example, Faysal al-Husayni, Haidar Abd al-Shafi, Hanan Ashrawi and the lawyer Raja Shehadeh – now expressed their dismay. Twenty-three leading figures issued a statement declaring the non-binding nature of the interim agreement since it legitimized Israel's violations of international law.[43] Of the fifty leading Palestinians invited to the Cairo ceremony, forty-nine declined to attend. Most Palestinians responded to so highly circumscribed a self-rule with cynicism.

In Gaza and Jericho there was deep relief that Israeli forces would no longer apply curfews, nor storm into homes, beating up people, taking others away and vandalizing property. But it hardly constituted a withdrawal, more a redeployment of Israeli forces. In Gaza, Israel remained in control of approximately 35 per cent of the land area, including settlements and access roads. It only required thirty minutes to reoccupy the rest of the Strip, should the need arise. Access in and out of both areas remained tightly controlled, and Israel demonstrated their prison-like quality by closing the Strip after Hamas had ambushed and killed two soldiers. This was all a far cry from what Palestinians conceived to be their rights. It remained to be seen what could be built upon such unsure foundations.

# 10

## A NATION IN THE MAKING:
## THE PALESTINIANS TODAY

The greater part of this book has attempted to show how and why the Palestinian people were dispossessed, and to give an account of their struggle to regain a foothold in Palestine. Little has been said so far concerning the Palestinian population and its characteristics. This chapter explores some of the issues which are now of vital concern to Palestinians.

The Palestinian population, both inside and outside geographical Palestine, is extremely young, like the population of most non-industrialized countries. Approximately 50 per cent of the population is 15 years old and under. This implies continued major growth in human numbers for the foreseeable future. Population growth is likely to slow down only with substantial overall economic improvements, economic opportunities for women and the ability of women to determine for themselves how many children they wish to bear. Population growth is particularly high in the Gaza Strip, which is one reason why Israel wishes to slough it off. Growth of the Palestinian population in Israel is now slowing down but remains substantially higher than for the Jewish population. As Table 2 (p. 126) shows, Palestinians overall outnumber Jewish Israelis and within fifteen years will almost certainly outnumber Jews worldwide.[3]

However, except for those concerned merely with a crude demographic competition with the Jewish population, the prospect of unremitting population growth, with numbers doubling every twenty years or so, poses major problems in each political zone, for the Palestinian National Authority and for its

TABLE 2

**Estimated current and projected Palestinian population[1]**

| Country | 1986 | 1993 | 1995 | 2000 |
|---|---|---|---|---|
| INSIDE PALESTINE | | | | |
| W. Bank/ | | | | |
| E. Jerusalem | 951,520 | 1,150,000[a] | 1,250,000 | 1,500,000 |
| Gaza Strip | 650,000 | 795,000 | 880,000 | 1,050,000 |
| Israel | 608,200 | 785,000 | 810,000 | 920,000 |
| OUTSIDE PALESTINE | | | | |
| Jordan | 1,398,050 | 1,850,000 | 2,170,000 | 2,597,000 |
| Lebanon | 275,000 | 360,000 | 395,000 | 465,000 |
| Syria | 242,474 | 325,000 | 360,000 | 410,000 |
| Other Arab | | | | |
| states | 583,000 | 450,000 | 517,000 | 600,000 |
| Rest of world | 400,000 | 450,000 | 500,000 | 550,000 |
| **Total** | 5,108,344 | 6,165,000 | 6,882,000 | 8,092,000 |

[a] An independent study suggests the true figure is already of the order of 1,550,000.[2]

economic body the Palestine Economic Council for Development and Rehabilitation (PECDAR), for Israel and for the governments of neighbouring states. These problems range from potential political challenges through questions of employment and wealth generation to the ability to provide adequate basic facilities in terms of food, shelter, health and education.

These problems lie largely outside the scope of this short book, although some of the challenges facing the PNA and Israel are discussed below. The long-term implications of Palestinian population growth, however, demand serious and urgent study if timely steps are to be taken to provide for these future challenges.

## Christian Palestinians

An estimated 400,000,[4] or 6.7 per cent of all Palestinians, are Christian. Only 50,000 of these live in the Occupied Territories, 2.9 per cent of the population there. Half these Christians belong to the Greek Orthodox Church. About 114,000 Christians live in Israel, forming 13 per cent of the Israeli Palestinian community. The disparity of proportion between the Territories and Israel is immediately striking. It is partly explained by the fact that the Palestinian remnant left in Israel had a disproportionately large Christian component. But it is also explained by the rapid shrinkage of the West Bank Christian population through emigration. An estimated 40 per cent have left since 1967. The Christian exodus has been blamed on the Islamic revival. Although many Christians view this revival with unease, there is no evidence that it has affected their decision to emigrate, which has been determined almost exclusively by the economic and political repression of Israeli rule, and by their better mastery of European languages. Unemployment among Christian graduates is approximately 50 per cent. Most emigrants are young and male, exacerbating the problem of community viability since insufficient men are left available for marriage. Once they begin a family and become enmeshed in children's education abroad, very few are likely to return. Since Christians are well represented among the most educated and skilled cadres in society their emigration represents a disproportionately damaging loss to the whole Palestinian community.

## Islam, Hamas and the PLO

Islam, as discussed in the previous chapter, has played an increasingly important part in Palestinian society over the past two decades. Regardless of the current but possibly cyclical emphasis on Islamic revival, the Palestinian nation is becoming progressively more Muslim in numerical terms, even in Israel where there is a proportionately stronger Christian presence. In 1950 Muslims constituted only two-thirds of Israeli Palestinians; today they are three-quarters.[5]

127

There has been a rediscovery of Islam as a powerful taproot of Palestinian identity. Palestinian society has recently been moving away from secular liberal values so fashionable in the 1960s and 1970s, back to greater social conservatism. Both the PLO and Hamas have tried to exploit this trend. The PLO has made increasing use of appeals to Islamic sentiment,[6] though Hamas has inevitably had the edge. Yet it would be simplistic to suppose that the revival represents solely a conscious return to Islam. The skill with which al-Mujamma' and Hamas sought to serve community needs and political aspiration has left Fatah looking crudely incompetent. The comparison ranges from kindergartens to the conduct of guerrilla war against Israel. Qualitatively the Islamic movement has greater efficiency, commitment and integrity. Even among Christian Palestinians who feel apprehensive about the progress of a militant Islam, there is respect for Hamas's skill and adherence to fundamental objectives. Unlike Fatah, it dislikes vainglorious posturing. Even before the Declaration of Principles, Hamas demonstrated that it enjoyed multi-confessional support by its victory in the Ramallah Chamber of Commerce election in 1992.[7]

The future challenge for Hamas is to retain and strengthen its position as leading opponent of the Arafat concessions. While the official PLO has made one concession after another to Israel, it has not been difficult for Hamas to reflect and garner the popular voice of protest. It has skilfully shifted its stance from wholesale rejectionism (in favour of the recovery of all Palestine) to a strategy of stages, being willing to live with a progression of piecemeal agreements. It has also displaced the PFLP as the leading Palestinian party of opposition to Fatah. Such is its strength that the PLO has been compelled to seek a public *rapprochement* with Hamas. Israel too, while publicly denouncing it, has covertly negotiated with Hamas leaders, most notably the imprisoned and crippled Shaykh Ahmad Yasin.

So far it has been easy for Hamas always to outflank Arafat, taking a harder line that appeals to the mass. This has cost it nothing and enhanced its prestige. It is less certain that Hamas would be able to sustain this position if it found itself sharing power. Its strength lies in opposition. While Fatah remains a coherent force, it is unlikely Hamas will overtake it.[8] Indeed, given economic progress, Hamas is likely to decline in influence. Yet the possibility remains that Fatah (and the PLO) will fragment under the political and economic stress implicit in the limited self-rule arrangements. Hamas has greater flexibility. While the PLO cannot declare its objectives no longer attainable without risking disintegration, Hamas technically can revert to the Mujamma' position of liberation deferred. Yet it, too, must satisfy popular expectation. Besides, large segments of Palestinian society are uneasy with the movement's social outlook. These segments include secular (or *privately* observant) Muslims, Christians and many women. Such people believe that a secular democratic movement will be essential to containing the threat of obscurantism. Through its close links with the Ikhwan in Jordan (where the Ikhwan has accepted the electoral system), Hamas has indicated its commitment to the democratic process but possibly only as a stepping stone to power and the introduction of an Islamic state. It is unlikely that Hamas will achieve the necessary electoral power. For Israel, however, which nurtured the Islamic movement to undermine the PLO, Hamas represents a wider danger than that of Palestinians or Arabs. In the words of a noted leader of the Ikhwan in Egypt, an Islamic solution to the Palestinian problem requires 'the mobilization of the Islamic nation'.[9]

## Women: full participants in society?

Women remain the invisible part of Palestinian history, even though peasant women were among the first casualties of the conflict with Zionism at the end of the nineteenth century. A brief account of the development of the women's movement, up to the *intifada*, has already been given (Chapter 9).

As elsewhere, and particularly in non-industrialized countries, women have found it difficult to exercise choice, over marriage or occupation. They are more subordinate to family pressure and the requirements of tradition than men. Indeed many women find themselves confined by both social custom and the formal requirements of Islamic culture, particularly with regard to personal status.[10] A Muslim man may marry a Christian, but a Muslim woman may not do so. A wife promises obedience, and may not work outside the home without her husband's permission. Muslim women are discriminated against in matters of inheritance from both the father and the husband.[11]

Many women find themselves subject to authoritarian male rule,[12] probably the product of very ancient custom but often dubiously justified in terms of Islam.[13] Those who have sought work outside the home have tended to be confined to 'women's work', mainly as kindergarten or primary school teachers or in health-care services. Like women almost everywhere, they have been denied open access to power. Those who rise to prominence, like Hanan Ashrawi, tend to be the exception rather than the rule. However, there are women in all parts of society who have asserted an independence of mind and spirit, some with encouragement from their husbands.

Once the *intifada* had started, women had the opportunity to co-operate openly to a far greater extent,[14] even though Hamas was able to enforce head-scarves for women in Gaza. It has remained unclear whether women will be able to retain the social relaxations brought about by the *intifada*. Moreover, it has remained a moot point whether greater female participation in the economy reflects dire economic distress or a determination for economic development and a willingness, therefore, to abandon prohibitions against female emancipation. This may not be clear until the Israeli occupation ends.

During the *intifada* the women's committees supported and reinforced women's mass participation in the struggle. They also participated in the creation of neighbourhood and popular committees. With Israel's suppression of the neighbourhood and popular committees, the women's committees began to plan for embryo state structures.

In 1988 a Higher Women's Committee was established to co-ordinate the efforts of the networks associated with the four major political groupings.[15] It was hoped that joint action would make progress possible on two crucial issues, education and legal status. But it has also been a vehicle for a more important process among the campaigners themselves. As the *intifada* has given way to diplomacy, so women have lost much of their participatory role. This has led many in the women's movement to recognize how easily men persuaded them to subordinate women's issues to party loyalty during the *intifada*. In retrospect, a basic dilemma of the women's movement has been the conflict of interest between the national and women's movements. Logically, women would argue, the two should be complementary. But that is only possible if male-dominated structures of the national movement take women's rights and aspirations seriously. There is little evidence that the national movement thinks of women's committees as anything more than appendages to its own organizations. Women must admit their failure to renounce the partisan ideologies thrust upon them by men.

Sceptics can fairly question how far the women's committees have affected the broad sweep of social attitudes among women, let alone among men. One disturbing piece of evidence is the fall in enrolment of female university entrants. Before the *intifada*, for example, women formed 40 per cent of the student body at Bir Zeit University, but this had fallen to 31 per cent by 1994.[16] Faced with economic hardship, higher education for daughters is an early casualty. Growing social conservatism may reduce numbers in the longer term. Yet a growing body of educated, articulate and self-confident women is essential not only to women's achievement of full and equal participation in national life, but also to the realization of the whole of society's potential.

Consequently, leaders of the various women's groups now work much more closely together to advance women's concerns, aware that their parent political parties have never given their gender rhetoric any substance. This has not been made any easier by the basic political divide between those prepared to support the current peace process and those who reject it as unprincipled surrender.

Many Palestinian women recall the fate of Algerian women after their participation in the liberation struggle of 1958–64. Anxiety is increased by the rise of Hamas, and fears that Muslim conservatism would deny women the social advances they seek.[17] This fear is based upon the clear aim of Hamas to preserve the role of the *shari'a* (Islamic law) in personal status law, governing

marriage, divorce, inheritance, child custody and marital relations, all of which weigh against women.[18] Women are cautious
of exaggerating the Islamic challenge to a secular order, but perceive the threat to be focused on the status of women and possibly education. Their opportunity to work may nevertheless
depend more on economic imperatives than on conceded freedom. Only 15 per cent of the workforce in the West Bank and
only 5 per cent in Gaza are women, in both cases mainly in government or UNRWA work. While 80 per cent of women think
they should be entitled to work outside the home, only 50 per
cent of men apparently agree.[19] Women remain a good deal more
restricted in the public domain than men.[20]

If young Palestinian women in their pre-marriage years were
more aware it might be possible to advance the gender issue substantially. Men would find prospective spouses negotiating a
greater measure of functional equality in marriage. Currently,
however, marriage is perceived as an overriding goal by most
young women, and it is only once they are caught in the marital
web of domesticity and child rearing that they face the full force
of gender inequality.

It is feared that the PLO may have already decided to surrender to Hamas on the personal status issue. Unlike the Declaration of Independence of 1988, which put forward principles of
non-discrimination in race, religion and gender, the draft constitution for Palestine avoids mentioning gender entirely, apparently because Palestine has a 'conservative society'.[21] This is
manifestly unacceptable to both women and men who desire
genuine democracy (see p. 145), since it diminishes the political,
economic and social power of half the population.

How can the women's movement respond to such difficulties?
The temptation is to crusade for a secular personal status law, but
this risks a backlash, particularly since many feminists are Christian (and must therefore act with great tact). Tactically there is a
need to advance the gender issue step by step, avoiding direct
confrontation and gradually winning over increasing numbers of
women (and men) to seek progressive expansion of their political,
social and cultural domain.[22] One intention is to present a newly
formed Palestinian government with a unified and articulate pro-

posal for women's legislation, regarding family, employment and other issues, possibly to seek a civil personal status law alongside current *shari'a*-based law, thereby providing people with choice. Yet it is recognized that enlightened legislation without consensus support will simply be ignored.[23] In other words women, ideally well supported by men who recognize that they too need release from traditional stereotyped expectations, must labour hard and long within the engine room of society if traditionalists are to be persuaded that the demand for social progress can no longer be withstood. The women's movement is about liberating the potential and creativity of an entire society.

## Children: Palestine's future

Like women, children tend to be ignored in the Palestine conflict, although under-15-year-olds form half the population. For a brief period, the youth of Palestine stole centre stage during the *intifada*. But as with women, the diplomatic process has swept them aside, frequently into deep disillusionment. Few political pundits make much of the fact that, since today's children will be tomorrow's adults, childhood experience will prove crucial to the future of Palestine. Cast in those terms, the situation for children should be a cause for grave concern.

A substantial proportion of West Bank children grow up in villages in a lifestyle similar to other Third World villages.[24] They have physically freer lifestyles than their urban or refugee camp counterparts. Until the age of 9 or 10 they tend to play together without regard for age or sex, but thereafter begin to assume expected gender roles, household tasks for girls, wage labour, stone-throwing and tyre-burning for boys.

Children face severe shortcomings in the health and educational fields. Throughout the Occupied Territories severe domestic overcrowding exposes children to diarrhoeal diseases and acute respiratory infections, accounting for over half the infant mortality rate, which probably stands at about 50 per thousand.[25] Since the occupation has been so prolonged, this redounds greatly to the discredit of the occupation authority.

There has been growing concern regarding the inadequacy of

educational facilities. Only 25 per cent of children have access to pre-school facilities, which are more necessary in deprived conditions than elsewhere. The quality ranges from the excellent to the abysmal, and refugee camps, probably the most needy areas, have proportionately fewest.[26] Formal education was disastrously interrupted during the *intifada* (see the discussion below).

Even before the *intifada*, virtually all West Bank and Gaza children were exposed to the brutalities of occupation, particularly in the camps and other foci of resistance. Throughout the 1970s and 1980s small children were eyewitnesses to land confiscation, settler violence, night raids and house searches, the arrest of close relatives, beatings, shootings, compulsory family separation or deportation and general harassment. As one might imagine, there have been both physical and psychiatric responses.

Long before the *intifada*, children acquired stone-throwing skills during their secondary school years and used them when they could on passing soldiers or settlers. It was their own form of resistance.[27]

It was perhaps inevitable that the direct combat of the *intifada* should have been dominated by young people; 23 per cent of the resulting fatalities have been among those aged 16 or under.[28] It is estimated that 40 per cent of those injured in the *intifada* sustained permanent injury requiring rehabilation, for example, spinal-cord injuries, loss of sight and amputations.

Military occupation, particularly during the *intifada*, has resulted in severe trauma also, with symptoms such as hyperactivity, withdrawal, anxiety, nightmares, depression and bedwetting. Both the *intifada* and the presence of Israeli soldiers and settlers have become the primary preoccupation of children, most clearly demonstrated in their artwork. Alongside these negative and profoundly damaging characteristics, the *intifada* has also generated a deep degree of group identity.[29]

In the diaspora there must also be grave concern for refugee children in Lebanon who are exposed to violence and hostility on the part of elements within the host country. Elsewhere, in Jordan and Syria, Palestinian children grow up learning of their identity but also aware that the expression of national identity must be made with care, to avoid trouble.

Everywhere there is an urgent need to engage Palestinian youth with a vibrant vision for the future. This must include providing realistic opportunities for them – girls as well as boys – to acquire the necessary skills to play a significant role in the building of tomorrow's Palestine. At present they remain largely ignored.

## Education

Palestinians are thought of as among the most highly educated people in the Arab world. Partly thanks to UNRWA, Palestinians have a reputation for high educational standards and high female enrolment. Yet in 1991 and 1992, when a series of school tests were carried out in twenty countries worldwide, Jordan came second to last, and the West Bank (which follows the Jordanian curriculum) performed significantly worse than Jordan.[30]

Given the circumstances this result is unsurprising. Since 1967 the West Bank and the Gaza Strip have been saddled with the progressively irrelevant curricula of Jordan and Egypt respectively. Israel has banned or censored many textbooks, in some cases violating international copyright to produced sanitized or bowdlerized versions. Above all, repeated closures and curfews culminated in two crucial years of schooling being lost during the *intifada*.

Three educational systems operate. The vast majority of children, certainly for the secondary cycle, attend government schools operating under the civil administration (until August 1994 this was Israeli). Refugee children obtain their elementary education at UNRWA schools but in the West Bank go on to government secondary schools. Almost half the children of East Jerusalem attend private schools, but this is exceptional. Most schools suffer severe inadequacies in facilities and crumbling, overcrowded classrooms which, in many cases, must cope with two separate shifts each day. Laboratories and libraries, essential prerequisites for sound education, are either absent or very poorly equipped. Government education is also characterized by rigidity, low morale and a poorly trained teaching cadre. A number of vocational training centres exist, of which the best are probably run by UNRWA. There are seven universities, all established as such during the 1970s, all offering a four-year degree programme.[31]

It was inevitable that educational establishments should become flashpoints of conflict between Israel and its subject population. Students felt passionately about their subjugation to Israeli rule. Israeli troops frequently chose to enter campuses rather than leaving student demonstrations to burn themselves out.[32] The government also used the compulsory closure of educational establishments as a form of collective punishment. In December 1987 it responded to the *intifada* by closing down the entire education system. Kindergarten children are not usually classed as agents of sedition, but that is how Israel treated them. Schools remained closed for two consecutive years, universities for four or more years. Neighbourhood committees sought to continue education provision in homes, mosques and churches, but in August 1988 such activities were banned with threats of ten years' imprisonment. UNRWA and private schools sought to distribute homepacks for students to continue their studies. This, it could be argued, might have kept some students off the streets, something in Israel's interest. But Israel was bent upon collective punishment and banned these efforts. Thus the children of the *intifada* lost not only two vital years of school but also the skill of prolonged concentration which children learn in study. When schools reopened in 1990, there was a substantial drop-out rate.[33]

Even if they had inherited a healthy system, Palestinians educators would now face a severe test. The economic challenge for any Palestinian entity will be Herculean (see p. 141). To meet that challenge, educators must strive to produce young men and women with appropriate intellectual and manual skills. But in fact they must meet that challenge through an archaic, underfunded and under-equipped system. An entirely new Palestinian curriculum must be designed to replace the Jordanian and Egyptian curricula curently in use; buildings and plant must be renewed, and teachers helped to improve their skills; and a more efficient administrative structure must be installed. This is not merely a question of finance but also a qualitative shift that will produce an intellectually critical younger generation. Whether that can happen will depend in great measure on those chosen to guide and inspire the Palestinian educational sector. To achieve national consensus in that area, it is important for all factions to be involved. Educationalists are dismayed by the refusal of Hamas to participate and fear that either Hamas will lack commitment to the end product or alternatively will seek to influence the PLO leadership arbitrarily to amend the proposed curriculum.

By mid-1994 the question of educational leadership was still confused. In theory there were three distinct institutions involved: the PLO leadership in Tunis, the PLO's Amman-based Department of Education, and the key local player, the Council for Higher Education (CHE). The latter was established in 1977 with a remit limited to tertiary education. With the problems of the *intifada*, the CHE widened its remit to include primary and secondary education. It is the front-runner regarding curriculum reform and may well prove to be so in other spheres, because it has the 'hands-on' experience that Tunis and Amman lack. People tend to look to the CHE to deliver, but it labours under severe constraints – understaffed, underfunded, without specialist experts and operating on an entirely voluntary basis. This is no way to create a new system of education. What is needed is a properly funded exercise involving local experience and outside expertise to formulate Palestinian education. The PLO, in the form of the PNA, must give a lead but there is a widespread fear that as in other fields it simply is not up to the task.

**Health provision and disability**

For many years the population of the Occupied Territories was largely dependent on an urban-based health provision. This care was delivered by four different channels: the civil administration, UNRWA, voluntary agencies and private (commercial) clinics and hospitals. In 1967 virtually all primary health care was provided either by the government (75 per cent) or by UNRWA (17 per cent). Progressively, however, Palestinian services have overtaken this provision, which has now declined to 28 per cent and 4 per cent respectively. Indigenous clinics now account for

68 per cent of the whole provision.[34] The rise in indigenous provision was the result of inadequate government services in both quantity and quality, worse than the provision either in Israel or in Jordan. Annual governmental expenditure on health services in the Territories amounted to a mere $30 per person compared with $350 per person in Israel.[35] UNRWA services remained heavily overstretched and underfunded. The hospital bed provision had fallen from 2.2 to 1.6 per thousand in 1985. Malnutrition, parasite infestation, gastro-enteric disorders and respiratory infections were commonplace.

The infant mortality rate in the West Bank is about 40 per 1,000 live births, though in certain poor villages the level is more than twice that.[36] While 75 per cent of the population of the West Bank live in rural localities or refugee camps, less than one third had basic mother-and-child facilities until the 1980s. Research showed that the infant mortality rate among girls was higher than among boys, a fact that reflected adversely not on the occupation but on traditional social values.

Such factors prompted health professionals to begin to build the indigenous primary health care service already described (see Chapter 8). During the *intifada* these networks greatly extended their services to assist the injured. The stress induced by the *intifada* has also led to the creation of a limited mental health service in the Territories, a service which will almost certainly require major expansion as the long-term effects, particularly on today's children, become more apparent.

The Union of Palestinian Medical Relief Committees now provides an astonishingly extensive health service, but it remains a voluntary agency.[37] With progressive self-rule, there is an urgent need to create an overall policy framework to harmonize and streamline the services available. Currently 12 per cent of the Territories' GDP goes on health care.[38] There is no doubt that, with four different kinds of service operating across the curative, high-tech and primary health fields, there are major areas of duplication, sectorally and geographically. Voluntary agencies account for one-fifth of total health spending. These networks more than doubled the primary health care facilities over the first six years of the *intifada*, but they competed fiercely with each other for foreign funds and for clients.

There is an urgent need to move forward now, to harmonize the various networks and dovetail them with curative facilities, and also to expand and equip hospitals and clinics. A fundamental question concerns who will conceive and oversee the harmonization and development of health services. Some fear that Fatah will control the health system, despite the fact that many view Fatah's health provision as significantly weaker and less participatory than the others. There is a self-evidently strong argument in favour of a national health system into which the different networks should be brought. However, the success of such an operation lies in the maximum participation in planning and implementation of those currently providing the greater part of the health care services. By mid-1994, however, there was a widespread impression that the PLO and its health arm, the Palestine Red Crescent Society, wished to control everything, despite their absence from the Occupied Territories, and therefore lack of local experience.

Before the *intifada*, the provision for disabled people reflected outdated concepts dominated by professionals, a 'charity' approach and the removal of the disabled from their own environments. Because those injured in the *intifada* were regarded as heroes, millions of dollars were poured into large, well-equipped but inappropriate rehabilitation centres, but with no thought for community-based rehabilitation. The Swedish government, for example, funded a centre in Ramallah with money that 'would have been enough to fund dozens of neighbourhood rehabilitation centres for years'.[39] The real needs start once a paraplegic or disabled person gets home, not when they are receiving treatment, and that calls for strategies to help them, their family and their community discover in themselves how to rebuild worthwhile lives.

UNRWA has taken a lead in community-based solutions to disability. Following a highly successful community-based project in Suf camp, Jordan, it encouraged the establishment of disabilty committees in the Occupied Territories.[40] Where such initiatives exist the disabled and those who work with them are discovering inner resources they never previously suspected.

## Infrastructural development and public services

After over a quarter of a century of neglect the development of infrastructure is now an urgent prerequisite for economic development. Israel's control and seizure of West Bank groundwater are a fundamental issue. Theoretically the average urban water supply in the Occupied Territories is 60 litres per day compared with 137 litres in Jordan, but in practice it is about half this because of water loss from the distribution system. Even with increased access to groundwater reserves, there is an urgent need to explore the means for controlling water consumption and reducing waste.[41]

A proper waste disposal system is also a priority. Services are as primitive as in 1967 but have inevitably deteriorated because the population has more than doubled since then. Burning off waste pollutes and creates a health hazard, with the consequences of added morbidity and health expenditure. In a situation of comparatively cheap labour, the recycling of materials and composting should offer substantial benefits.

During its occupation Israel has developed a road system specifically designed to benefit settlers and to bypass Palestinian population areas. These roads are intended to integrate Jewish settlements with Israel, and to make any return to the 1949 armistice line virtually impossible. Apart from its territorial claims up to this line, the Palestinian National Authority will have to construct a road system to meet its own requirements. It will also have to transform the telecommunications system. Currently the telephone availability is 1:46 for Palestinians in the Territories, compared with 1:15 in Jordan. No serious economic growth is likely without a proliferation of telephone and facsimile facilities.

How should the national authority fund its health, education infrastructural and municipal services? Economic prosperity is the strongest argument in favour of streamlined and co-ordinated systems answerable to government. A cleaner environment, an efficient communications system and effective primary health and education services are all essential to optimal economic and social development. There can be no question, therefore, of treating these issues in the way they have been in the past, as areas in which local and foreign voluntary agencies simply do what they can. The involvement of these agencies will doubtless remain essential for many years, but their co-ordination and conformity with a national plan are essential.

Such services should be funded by pump-priming infrastructural grants made by the international community and, far more importantly, by taxation. Psychologically this may prove a real challenge for the Palestinian population. Taxation is closely associated in the popular mind with Israeli oppression. The national authority will have to levy income tax and enforce national and health insurance contributions at similar or even higher levels to create the services necessary for a developing economy. Many people are so used to the free services of UNRWA or of voluntary agencies operating on foreign donations that there is likely to be dismay at facing the real costs involved. This is psychological dependency, and it is essential that the national authority helps people break free from it. That means a phased programme of withdrawal of foreign donations over the forthcoming decade in order for the community to learn to live within its means. This is likely to be an acutely hard test. It will probably necessitate introducing user fees for public services in addition to taxation (particularly since it will be difficult to introduce an efficient income tax net). Israel's prohibition on the application of VAT (tax on purchases) removes the easiest system of revenue-raising and leaves the national authority with a major challenge. In order to raise taxes with popular consent, it is essential for the PLO to demonstrate accountability and transparency in its financial dealings.

Perhaps most seriously, the PLO lacks the experience and the administrative abilities relevant to the operation of state institutions. There are two fundamental requirements: skills and integrity. By the summer of 1994 suspicions of the PLO's shortcomings in these areas were already being borne out.

## The economy

Few countries can have looked forward to independence with such unpromising economic circumstances. The West Bank and Gaza Strip have suffered economic stagnation ever since 1948. Jordanian neglect was followed in 1967 by a deliberate policy on the part of Israel to stifle economic growth through the use of prohibitions and obstructive regulations in the areas of production and marketing. These restrictions include capping Palestinian access to agricultural water at the 1967 level, setting limits on agricultural production and, since 1984, requiring a permit to replace or plant any fruit tree. These were deliberate measures to stifle competition with Israeli agriculture. Restrictions on the issue of factory licences told potential capital providers to invest their money elsewhere. Trade and the free movement of goods have also been restricted. Only in the late 1980s did Israel begin to allow the Territories to export to Europe, but since these products had to pass through the hands of Israeli export agents, Palestinian trade remained controlled and in practice discouraged.

Those concerned with the Palestinians' economic development[42] face huge obstacles: an almost total absence of industrialization, widespread remittance dependency, high unemployment, subservience to and almost total dependence on the Israeli economy. Furthermore the geographical configuration of the Palestinian territories militates against development, with Gaza and the West Bank cut off from each other. The West Bank economy faces a major threat from the apparent Israeli intention to flout international law by retaining Arab East Jerusalem. This would leave the northern and southern parts of the West Bank without their natural economic head and effectively cut off one from the other.

In April 1994 Israel and the PLO concluded an economic agreement in Paris which allowed the PNA in Gaza and Jericho to open banks, collect taxes, trade oil and other goods with Arab states and have free access to Israeli markets for the export of certain agricultural produce. Palestinians will continue to be allowed to work in Israel, and 75 per cent of the tax on their income will be remitted to the PNA. However, the PNA may not mint its own currency.

There can be little doubt that the Palestinian economy will remain subservient to Israel, probably on a permanent basis. In that sense Palestinian independence, if ever granted, will be robbed of much of its meaning. Palestinians will find relatively full employment only by providing cheap labour to carry out tasks that richer Jewish Israelis are unwilling to perform inside Israel. Palestinian trade will remain dependent on the goodwill of Jordan and Israel in order to export. Both countries will apply formal or informal restrictions in order to protect their own interests.

In May 1994 the World Bank finalized an emergency assistance programme for Jericho and Gaza, with a three-year budget of $1.2 billion, a sum woefully inadequate for the tasks involved. This aims to provide employment on infrastructural improvement, and to stimulate investment in housing, agriculture and industry. By September 1994 this money had still not been transferred. It was significant that PECDAR, the PNA's economic organization, would administer these funds in association not only with the World Bank and other donors but also with Israel, an indication that Israel had no intention of allowing any kind of development that did not suit its own purpose.

It will not be difficult for Israel to concede apparent sovereignty while retaining effective economic control. In practice, a federation of two economies based upon separate development may emerge – in other words a form of apartheid without the need for legislation – since the Palestinians will have been granted their own homelands in which to live. That is the negative prognosis, one of economic masters and helots.

The alternative is that Israel recognizes that its own stability will remain contingent on Palestinian prosperity and relative freedom, and that it therefore is willing to encourage Palestinian economic growth independently of the Israeli economy. Palestinian marketing independent of Israeli intermediaries is important, because most of the value added goes to the marketer not the producer. The more that Israel ties the Palestinian economy in a relationship subservient to itself, the more likely it is that frustrated Palestinian nationalism will bleed into Israel, undermining and sapping its internal security. Palestinian and other investors must be attracted by the likelihood both of Israel supporting Palestinian prosperity and of the Palestinian governing authority being able to offer a stable and corruption-free environment in which development can take place.

## Social cohesion and democracy

In the summer of 1993 an important article appeared entitled 'Gaza: new dynamics of civic disintegration',[43] which warned of impending social implosion. Such a forecast might have been dismissed as alarmist had it not been written by a leading authority on Gazan affairs, Sara Roy. Economic collapse and military repression since the *intifada* have brought about rapid social transition in which the old structures of social authority have been under intense challenge. The economic output of the Strip fell by up to 50 per cent between 1987 and 1993. The *intifada* and loss of work opportunities for about 70,000 people (supporting approximately 350,000) were followed by the greater economic crisis of the Gulf War and a massive loss in foreign remittances in 1990–1.[44] The rapid impoverishment of an already poor society may be measured in the steep increase in food aid provided by UNRWA: from only 9,838 needy refugee families in June 1990, recipients increased to 120,000 families (including non-refugees) by 1993.[45] In both parts of the Territories, cases of malnutrition became more common. Roy spoke of 'psychological exhaustion' and 'collective self-withdrawal', symptomatic of the failure of the *intifada* to resolve the Palestinian predicament.

A crucial problem lies with the way Israeli violence has traumatized and damaged a whole generation. By 1994, 70 per cent of Gaza's population had known nothing except Israeli rule. Five years of *intifada* had left a profound mark. There are barely any children who are not familiar with night-time troop raids during which homes are ransacked, old people and women humiliated and young men dragged away. Such actions – arguably a form of state terrorism – have grievously damaged social authority, whether exercised by parents, teachers or community leaders. Children can conceive of authority only as a form of hostile repression: 'Authority is now the enemy and is inherently evil. Law and order do not exist in Gaza, in concept or in practice, and therefore chidren have no boundaries and no markers for distinguishing good behaviour from bad.'[46]

During the period of the *intifada*, Gaza society moved through an initial phase of impressive collective effort by the community before descending into factional rivalries as Israel imprisoned thousands of community leaders and the resistance fragmented along factional lines. It was not long before factions clashed either physically or in their efforts to assert territorial control.

Roy concludes: 'The creation of *structures*, once a prominent feature of the uprising, is steadily giving way to the creation of constituencies in institutional guise.'[47] External Palestinian donors, most notably Fatah, supported their favoured factions. Even foreign non-governmental organizations found it increasingly difficult, as in Lebanon during its civil war, to provide 'impartial' aid. Thus the foreign assistance intended to help make life bearable has also strengthened factionalism and thereby weakened the social fabric. Of all the factions, Hamas is undeniably the most impressive social network, operating effective and impartial institutions unlike some secular nationalist ones that are considered venal and corrupt.

Gaza is a more extreme case than the West Bank, but the problem exists in both areas. Furthermore, the psychological distance, a long-standing tension, between Gaza and the West Bank has grown. Gaza bitterly resents being the poor relation of the West Bank.

Gaza now stands on the threshold of a new beginning, and one by one West Bank towns and villages may follow suit. Any new Palestinian authority must provide the inspirational leadership whereby social cohesion, solidarity and discipline may be rebuilt. There is little evidence, so far, that the leadership has the qualities necessary for what amounts to moral and social regeneration, to restore society from the baleful effects of Israeli manipulation and repression and of Palestinian factionalism, authoritarianism and communalism. As Dr Haidar Abd al-Shafi remarked in July 1993: 'I tell you plainly that the negotiations are not worth fighting about. The critical issue is transforming our society. Only once we achieve this will we be in a position of strength.'[48]

Nothing in the field of self-rule has worried Palestinians intellectuals, voluntary agencies and, above all, women more than the question of establishing democracy. Many express the fear that the PLO will usher in an authoritarian, corrupt and incompetent regime, having absorbed in exile the authoritarian culture which pervades the whole Arab world outside Palestine and Lebanon.[49] They are particularly concerned by the apparent intention to incorporate or subordinate the myriad voluntary agencies in the territories within the PNA, and PECDAR. They have also watched unhappily what they perceive to be a one-man show in which loyalty and acquiescence are bought, and political principles casually abandoned. Some even unflatteringly describe Arafat as an agent of Israel's political will.

The fear is that the autonomy agreement will prove incompatible with democracy. Al-Haq was quick to point out the danger of delaying free elections, originally scheduled to take place within ten months of the DoP, of the need for mandatory international supervision of elections, and that all decisions by PNA in the interim should be subject to ratification by its elected successor.[50]

However, concern is much wider than this. With good reason, Palestinian voluntary agencies see themselves as guardians of democratic freedoms. They see the work and advocacy of voluntary agencies as crucial to democracy. Palestinian intellectuals and voluntary agencies are determined to avoid the authoritarianism prevalent elsewhere in the Arab world. Ironically, in view of its consistent denial of their own freedoms, they acknowledge the example of the democracy in Jewish Israel. In spring 1994, thirty-three voluntary associations issued a declaration affirming the essential and complementary role of voluntary bodies within a democracy, and that these bodies form the bedrock of civil society:

> 'The freedom to associate, organize and operate within the framework of non-governmental organizations and societies is a basic human right that must not be prejudiced. This freedom forms the principal foundation for the participation of individuals in serving their society. Democratic society cannot exist without a clear recognition of this right, and without safeguarding it in law.'[51]

By June 1994 over eighty voluntary agencies were involved in the democracy movement, and a number of these resolved to monitor the development of democratic institutions and practices.[52]

Only time will tell how successful such institutions will be. It must remain open to question whether intellectuals and voluntary agencies (regardless of their excellence) are able to prevail against authoritarian tendencies and the absence of a democratic tradition.

# 11

## PALESTINE AND ISRAEL:
### IN SEARCH OF PEACE WITH JUSTICE

The fate of the peace process hangs, above all, on the intentions of the two contestants. The Palestinian intention is clear: self-determination in a Palestinian state. The Israeli intent is less clear. Indeed, it is unlikely the government fully knows its own mind yet. Optimistic doves believe the process will lead inexorably to a complete withdrawal, excluding East Jerusalem, and to a productive economic relationship, because the logic of the situation demands it.

Many Palestinians doubt this outcome because they are well aware of strong Israeli arguments in favour of allowing them to govern themselves in specified cantons, with Israel still firmly in charge of political and economic sovereignty. Within the Israeli establishment there is a tension between doves and hawks; and having 'lost' the first round, the indications are that the hawks of Labour and Likud will work in coalition to limit the progress of the peace process.[1]

It is with such uncertainties that the protagonists must look at the outstanding problems. Article V (3) of the Declaration of Principles provides for discussion of certain critical issues to commence by May 1996. These issues include the refugees, Jerusalem, boundaries and security, Jewish settlements, and water, but not those Palestinians living in Israel today.

### Refugees

Israel has always been reluctant to discuss the Palestinian refugees. It views them as the responsibility of the countries in which they find themselves, and has argued that they constitute a population exchange with those Jews who left the Arab world for Israel in 1948–51. It has refused responsiblity for them itself. Since the Madrid conference, Israel has reluctantly agreed to discuss the refugee question, provided the 'right of return' is not raised. Shortly after the Declaration of Principles was issued, Israel agreed to discuss certain categories of Palestinians outside Palestine. It announced willingness to process 2,000 applicants for family reunion yearly, having dragged its feet on this issue for years.[2] The number of those awaiting family reunion – spouses and children unable to live with their husbands in the West Bank and Gaza – may be as many as 120,000.[3] By mid-1994 there was a French-sponsored attempt to persuade Israel to process 6,000 cases yearly and to raise the age of child qualification from 16 to 18.

Then there are another 100,000 who have been denied re-entry having stayed abroad longer than the Israelis permitted. No progress has been made yet on allowing these back. Finally, before discussing the question of the 1948 refugees, there is the question of the 350,000 or so displaced by the 1967 war, and their descendants. Consideration of their case and the modalities of their return is allowed for in Article 12 of the DoP. No progress, however, had been made on this question by summer 1994.

In such unpromising circumstances it is difficult to see how or when the question of the 1948 refugees might be tackled. Inevitably there is enormous apprehension among the refugees concerning the final outcome of the peace process. There is a wide belief that, in spite of the repeated public commitment of the United States and the European Union to Resolution 194 (calling for the right of return) and Resolution 242 (calling for a just settlement of the refugee problem), they will be left languishing in their present predicament, that there is no chance of returning to what is now Israel, and only a token number out of almost 3 million registered refugees will return to any part of Palestine.

Refugee claims tend to be cast in terms of rights rather than negotiable conditions. In the end, however, clearly those 'rights' must be cast in terms that the refugee population accepts. If the Israel/Palestine conflict is to be fundamentally resolved, the refugees must accept a negotiated solution, whatever that may be. If that solution does not satisfy the refugees, a new movement of the dispossessed is likely to reawaken tension and conflict between Israel and Palestinians with whom it thinks it has made peace. This is a crucial issue not only for Israel and the United States, but also for those Palestinians who have not experienced the hardships of life in the diaspora. There is no evidence, so far, that either Israel or the United States has begun to understand what the refugee experience has been like, or its potential to give rise to more conflict.

Zionism was born out of growing fear and insecurity long before the rise of the Third Reich, out of memory kept alive over two thousand years, and out of huge energy generated during the first half of this century. It would be rash to suppose that the Palestinian refugees, all of whom are condemned to live under conditions of semi-permanent insecurity and surveillance, will neither keep their own memory alive, nor continue to generate energy for 'the return'. *Aliya* (Hebrew for 'the return') cuts both ways. Most Palestinians are in exile, and their numbers alone makes the continued growth of a diaspora Palestinian national identity virtually inevitable unless the problem is satisfactorily resolved.

By and large, refugees remain on the periphery of the communities among whom they live, except in Jordan. Nowhere are they able to organize themselves as they wish. Everywhere they are subject to the political pressures of the host government, and this is bound to continue. In Jordan they must subordinate their sense of Palestinian identity in order to be loyal Jordanian citizens and the ambiguity of their position leaves them under observation by the security services.[4] In Lebanon the refugees will be increasingly confined, physically, economically and psychologically, as the government reasserts its authority. In early 1994 the government decided not to allow reconstruction of four camps destroyed by war, nor any expansion of existing camps (despite the growing population and the predicament of the displaced), nor the construction of new camps. The degree of displacement is exemplified in the predicament of the 930 refugee families squatting in Sikki, a locality of Sidon, after their expulsion from their previous places of abode in Lebanon.[5] In

April Lebanon's Foreign Minister stated that 'Under no circumstances will Lebanon agree to give Palestinians citizenship.'[6] In fact Lebanon wants to 'redistribute' the refugees, an infelicitous euphemism for transfer. What will happen to the people of Sikki, and many others like them? They fear yet another expulsion, in addition to those they have already experienced. Chaim Weizmann's plea for Europe's Jews, 'They cannot stay where they are, yet have nowhere to go', has now become a leitmotif of the Palestinian diaspora, the wandering Jew replaced by the wandering Palestinian.

In April 1994 the Multilateral Refugee Working Group visited refugee camps in Lebanon and Jordan. Delegates were shocked by what they found, and came to the staggeringly understated conclusion that 'the refugee problem has gone on for too long'.[7]

Perhaps the most remarkable conclusion of this international delegation was that 'there is a just and feasible solution to this issue. There are numerous options which can contribute to a solution, but they are complicated.'[8] One must hope that it will succeed where the international community has remained flummoxed ever since Israel stonewalled at Lausanne in 1949.

Of 3.5 million Palestinians currently living outside Palestine, it is unlikely that most will wish to return, at any rate until a Palestinian entity has demonstrated its political and economic viability. One might therefore suppose that those most anxious to return are those living in the Lebanon, and a smaller number from elsewhere, probably not more than 750,000 in all.

There is little chance of Israel allowing more than a nominal number into the area of Israeli sovereignty, and possibly not even that. It is conceivable that Israel might accept 50,000 returnees and that the refugee community might accept this as token amends for its dispossession.

Israel will probably try to prevent a return of large numbers to the West Bank. It will not want a numerically superior Palestinian community alongside Israel. Yet to prevent such a return not only violates UNGAR 194 and every legal instrument concerning refugee rights, but invites irredentism. Israel must weigh up how badly it wants a complete and final settlement that will stick.

This is where the international community is under a serious misapprehension in referring to the 'right of return' as a political issue.[9] UNGAR 194 says nothing of a political settlement. On the contrary, only one condition is placed on the refugees, a condition which is manifestly non-political: 'those refugees wishing to return to their homes *to live at peace with their neighbours* [my emphasis] should be permitted to do so at the earliest practicable date'. This is the position, hardly a political one, to which the international community, with the exception of Israel, is formally committed.

So far there has been great reluctance to revisit the circumstances whereby the refugee problem arose. It is only when the governments concerned with reaching a settlement openly face *how* so many people became refugees that they are likely to recognize that the principle of the right of return remains fundamentally a moral and humanitarian rather than political imperative for the international community. The distinction therefore between current relief and 'a just solution' is that between a temporary and a permanent settlement, not between the humanitarian and the political.

This is not casuistry but a fundamental principle regarding refugee rights that the international community would be mistaken to depart from. It is also the reason why any political agreement negotiated bilaterally between Israel and the PLO that fails to meet the requirements of UNGAR 194 may be legitimately disregarded both by the refugees themselves and internationally. In view of the growing evidence of widespread 'ethnic cleansing' during and after the 1948 war, a mean-spirited accommodation now may threaten Israel's long-term hopes for peace.

## Jerusalem

Technically, Jerusalem's status internationally is still defined by UN Resolution 181 of 1947, as an international zone. In practice it falls under Israeli *de facto* sovereignty. Since it was annexed in 1967 (and more formally in 1980) the Arab sector has been ringed with apartment blocks. As a proportion of the population of Jerusalem municipality, the Palestinian Arabs fell to and then stabilized at about 28 per cent. Jewish 'Greater Israel' ideologues, both *yeshiva* students and also secular nationalists like Ariel Sharon, have sought to make inroads into the Arab quarters of the Old City. The intention seems to be to gradually 'redeem' all Jerusalem to Jewish tenure (see Map 6).

Since 1992, when Arab Jerusalem was excluded from the settlement freeze Israel conceded to the USA, a major new housing programme has been adopted.[10] The intention is to establish a Jewish majority in the Arab sector of Jerusalem. Two major road plans to serve Jewish interests are to be pushed across Arab Jerusalem. Arab housing located within 10 metres of the planned highways is liable to demolition; it is most unlikely that the residents will find alternative housing within Arab Jerusalem and indeed the drift of Palestinians to beyond the municipal boundary seems to be part of a deliberate policy. Meanwhile Jewish settlements in the Arab sector qualify for priority housing benefits.[11] This is demographic planning along racist lines, akin, for example, to Iraq's replacement of Kurds and Turkomans with Arabs in the oil city of Kirkuk.

Israel's intention is clear. It wishes to pre-empt any chance of Palestinian sovereignty over any part of Jerusalem. In 1993 Prime Minister Rabin gave an assurance that 'Palestinian autonomy will not include Jerusalem.'[12] It is possible that Israel, while retaining total control of the city, will offer West Bank Palestinians the free access they are currently denied. The portents, however, are ominous. In March 1993 Jerusalem was 'closed' to residents of the rest of the West Bank and Gaza Strip. The seriously damaging effect of this has been outlined in Chapter 9. The argument that the closure is still for security reasons hardly bears scrutiny. Its apparent permanence points to the physical detachment of West Bank Palestinians from East Jerusalem so as to render it no longer seriously negotiable in 1998.[13]

Palestinians will never accept either the *de facto* or *de jure* loss of Jerusalem. They, and the wider Arab and Muslim worlds, will alway lay claim to it, as the third holiest city of Islam, as the historic capital of Palestine and, most compellingly of all, because the heart of the city is largely Muslim or Arab in construction. However successfully Israel has created a sanitized version of what happened to Arab properties inside Israel now inhabited by

MAP 6

## Israel's expansion of Jerusalem's municipal boundary in 1967 and intended vast enlargement of 'Greater Jerusalem'

Based on United Nations map no. 3640, rev. 1, September 1991; *al-Quds* (Jerusalem), 4 January 1993

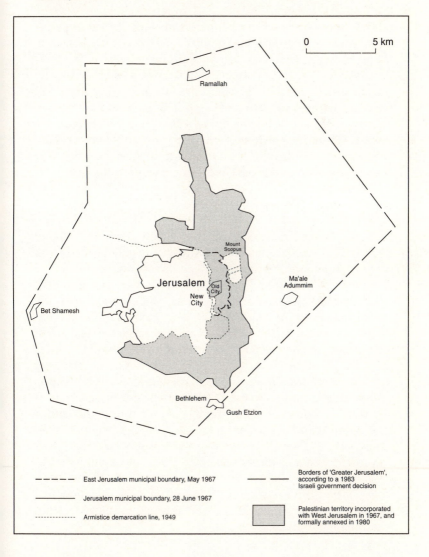

| | | |
|---|---|---|
| – – – – East Jerusalem municipal boundary, May 1967 | ——— | Borders of 'Greater Jerusalem', according to a 1983 Israeli government decision |
| ——— Jerusalem municipal boundary, 28 June 1967 | | |
| ·············· Armistice demarcation line, 1949 | ▨ | Palestinian territory incorporated with West Jerusalem in 1967, and formally annexed in 1980 |

Jews, it has little chance of achieving the same illusion with Arab Jerusalem.

The struggle to recapture Jerusalem from the Crusaders changed the Muslim perception of the city.[14] History is most unlikely to repeat itself in similar terms, but the Jewish state, like the Crusader kingdom, will be able to retain Jerusalem only by military superiority, which will have to be maintained in perpetuity. There is a considerable difference between the foreseeable future, in which Israel has little to fear, and perpetuity. The Muslim claim will always be there, in abeyance possibly but easily reawakened. It remains an open question how long Israel will maintain its hold on Jerusalem, but it is likely to find that an insistence on exclusive sovereignty will impede the regional reconciliation upon which its long-term prospects may depend. Israeli policy makers will have to decide whether retaining sole sovereignty is worth the risks and permanent costs implied.

## Boundaries and security

UNGAR 181 set out clear boundaries for the partition of Palestine. Israel's armistice agreements with its neighbours defined a new line which in due course came to be accepted as the new *de facto* boundary of Israel. UNSCR 242 made two vital principles clear regarding the territories that Israel had captured: first, the inadmissibility of the acquisition of territory by war; second, the requirement that Israel withdraw from territories it had occupied. Israel has argued that the wording of the second requirement did not necessarily mean *all* the territories it occupied, but the first principle (admurbrated in the resolution's preamble) precludes such casuistry. If the Palestinian authority agreed to a boundary amendment – for example, to hand over the Latrun salient (the West Bank salient pointing towards Lod and Ramle), lands in the Tel Aviv commuter area or possibly land that Israel considered essential for its security – this could presumably be offset against the allocation of compensating land to the Palestinian entity, perhaps specifically designated as a reception area for some returning refugees, if Israel was serious about tackling Palestinian grievances.

What Palestinians fear is that, far from having a territorial exchange in mind, Israel actually intends to retain not only the Latrun salient but large slices of the West Bank (and possibly the Gaza Strip). In this the plans of Labour and Likud have not been significantly different.[15] The significant difference has lain in Labour's willingness to consider Palestinian areas forming a confederation with Jordan, while Likud has preferred them to remain under Israeli control. Either way they will remain under Israeli control economically, and probably also geographically and physically. If Israel retains control of the arterial road system, and thus of Palestinian entities, this will leave the Palestinian authority in control of little more than its population areas. It is conceivable that the Palestinian authority might act in a manner similar to the homelands governments in South Africa, but this would be liable to open the way for a new liberation movement. Arbitrary retention of parts of the West Bank is unlikely to create the conditions of peace necessary for Israel's future.

Israel's requirement – strategic and tactical security – will remain a major consideration of any settlement; but the question of how this can be achieved falls outside this study. In practice, Palestinians have been greater victims of Israeli armed action than vice versa. It seems sensible, therefore, to review the security of both parties and to build into any border settlement mutual security arrangements which will contribute to confidence building. Joint patrols in the Occupied Territories seem likely to persist for a long time. The principle of reciprocity would suggest joint patrols in areas of Israel, but there can be no prospect of Israel agreeing to that.[16] This is a pity, since the sight of joint patrols on both sides of the border could have an important psychological effect on popular perception, that old antagonisms are being replaced by mutual co-operation.

## Settlements and settlers

The question of retention of territory leads naturally to that of Israel's settlers and settlements. Critics of the DoP were swift to pinpoint the deferment of this question as a serious error. Electorally, however, the government of Israel may be unable to declare the withdrawal of the settlements without risking alienation of the electorate and possibly civil conflict with the settlers. No government is likely to risk either. Indeed, in order to demonstrate its commitment to the settlers (surely an expensive cosmetic exercise rather than a sincere expression of its position), the government laid roads and provided armed guards for the 3,500 settlers in the Gaza Strip, in the case of one settlement at the rumoured cost of $1 million per family. But it is difficult to imagine that Israel seriously intends to protect the settlements permanently at such enormous expense. More probably it will allow economic attrition to wear down the inhabitants of most settlements, possibly inviting settlers to share the costs of their protection. This is likely to be true in Gaza and possibly in the West Bank settlements outside the commuter areas for the coastal plain and Jerusalem. Here Israel will face a problem, since these are also large Palestinian population areas, and it will not wish to incorporate Palestinians into the Israeli state. One obvious solution is for settlers to be evacuated from settlements and for Palestinian refugees to inhabit them.

## Water

Israel's thirst for water is well known. It has drawn off water from the Sea of Galilee, leading to dangerously low levels that could permanently change the ecology of the lake. It almost certainly draws water illegally from the Lebanon's Litani River (acquired during its occupation of south Lebanon since 1982), and it takes a greater share of the river Jordan than either Syria or Jordan. It also draws heavily from the groundwater reserves of geographical Palestine. In May 1990 senior Israeli hydrologists warned that water consumption exceeded replenishment of groundwater resources at a current annual rate of 15 per cent, and that the country faced a 'catastrophe' within five years.[17] Forty per cent of Israel's consumption comes from the West Bank. Israel therefore will be most unwilling to surrender control of the water resources of the Occupied Territories, even though it is depleting these groundwater reserves also. So far it has insisted that it must retain full control of the water found in the West Bank and Gaza Strip.

Yet Israel must forge an equitable agreement on the use of water resources with Palestinians and its other neighbours. In the case of its riparian neighbours there are formulas to achieve this,[18] and one must hope that the protagonists will agree where they failed over the Johnston Plan in the early 1950s. Palestine will understandably require a share of the Jordan waters.

Leaving aside the question of the Jordan waters, the current situation in the West Bank is wholly inequitable. Apart from the loss of 40 per cent of their groundwater to Israel, Palestinians are hardly likely to accept that their consumption should be limited to an average of 35 cubic metres yearly per capita compared with a settler consumption (as in Israel) of 170 cubic metres.[19]

In principle, a Palestinian state should have sovereignty over its own groundwater. A reasonable alternative would be to share the groundwater resources of the whole of geographical Palestine on an equal per capita basis under a joint Israeli/Palestinian authority. This would encourage co-operation on water use, control, conservation and recycling.[20] If Israel retains control and the greater part of the region's water resources for itself, this will remain a potential source for conflict.

## The Palestinians in Israel

The more repugnant of South Africa's apartheid laws referred to the mixing of black and white people, and the prohibition of sexual relations. These, however, were only the uglier features of a system which intended to exclude blacks from any political or economic power by consigning them to zones of impoverishment, geographically, economically and socially as well as politically. With the same intention, Israel has implemented an informal separate development system which allows Jews and Arabs to mingle for work, but with one group firmly subordinated to the other, and which makes it difficult for Arabs to escape their 'native reservations', hidden away from the main roads of the country.

Although off the international agenda, the question of Israel's handling of its own Palestinian citizens is possibly the most crucial issue in resolving the Palestine/Israel dilemma. The formidable problems of the Occupied Territories, and perhaps even the refugees, pale compared to those implicit for Israel in its own growing Palestinian constituency. This is because Israeli Palestinians impinge upon Israel's Jewish identity and psychology, and are destined to do so increasingly in future.

So far it has been possible for Israel to ignore its Palestinians. But it may be unable for much longer to ignore rising Palestinian protest against discrimination. As the population balance begins to change, it is almost inevitable that Palestinians will begin to recognize their latent electoral power. In 1992 Palestinians still constituted just over 18 per cent of the Israeli population, a proportion that has remained static since 1987 on account of the immigration of Russian Jews. By 2005, however, their proportion will probably be 21 per cent. Bearing in mind that 24 per cent of Israelis aged 20 and under are Palestinian, one may anticipate that by 2020 or so the Palestinian minority as a whole will be at least a quarter of the population. Unless the Palestinian birth rate flattens out, Israel faces the longer term prospect of a Palestinian population reaching 35 or 40 per cent by the middle of the twenty-first century.

What will Israel do? It faces serious choices. Some will be tempted to head off the ethnic growth by offering Palestianans autonomous areas, or finding some other means of avoiding the political effects of demographic change.[21] This suggests a formalizing of the notion of separate development, but this is likely to work only in the short term. Some Israeli Palestinians still express the fear that, in the end, trucks will come to transfer them out of their homeland.

The real crunch is whether Israel can abandon its status as the state of the Jewish people in favour of becoming the bi-national state of its Jewish and Arab citizens. That requires Israel's abandonment of ethnic nationalism, with all its sinister racial implications, in favour of civic nationalism in which citizenship is the basis of national identity: the nurturing of community values regardless of religious or ethnic difference. If it is able to accept such an outcome, the logical progression in due course would be the reintegration of all geographical Palestine, hopefully embodying the full reconciliation of Arab and Jew in Palestine and the genuine integration of the Jewish community into the region. That, whatever the means, is the kind of miracle to which one must hope the inhabitants of the land will aspire during the course of the twenty-first century.

# 12

## PALESTINIAN RIGHTS: THE INTERNATIONAL AGENDA

The story of Palestine is a major international scandal. In retrospect, the progressive dispossession of the indigenous people of Palestine and the consequent destructive conflict, with its waste of human life and resources, seem a terrible folly both in conception and execution. It was both foreseeable and foreseen at any early date. Palestinians were made scapegoats for Zionist ambition, for British imperial strategy, for the Jewish Holocaust in Europe and finally for the United States' Cold War regional conflict with the Soviet Union.

The performance of the international community, and of the United States and Britain in particular, has been morally abject. Because of its competition with the Soviet Union, and its reliance on Israel as its regional ally, the United States undermined virtually every attempt to bring Israel into line with international law. It has largely averted its gaze as Israel has increased its living space and stripped the indigenous population of its basic rights.

Britain also has nothing to be proud of. Responsible for the Balfour Declaration, it fled its obligations in 1947 when unable to handle what it had unleashed. To its credit it took a leading role in drafting UNSCR 242 in 1967. But that apart, it has been reluctant to take a stand of principle where this would be unpopular with the United States.[1] More than any other outsider, it had the responsibility and authority to stand up for the victims of its own disastrous policies. Instead it pursued a path of pusillanimous obedience to US objectives, as Israel settled the Occupied Territories, stole their water and subjected their people to a whole generation of brutal military rule.

Governments pursue 'state interests', and no permanent member of the UN Security Council, certainly neither the USA nor UK, has any vital interests which necessitate safeguarding the basic rights of the Palestinian people. So one may expect that they will now allow Israel to dictate the terms it wishes to a weak and essentially defenceless people, as seems to be happening.

This may seem sound like realpolitik, but in reality it is profoundly short-sighted, and hardly a commendation of the moral quality of the world's leading states, or of their commitment to the rule of law internationally. For it reveals that they appeal to international law only when it is either in their own interest to do so (as with Lockerbie and Kuwait) or when it can be done at little cost.

If they had had any serious concern for the people of Palestine, the USA and its allies would have warned Israel in 1967 that serious breaches of the Fourth Geneva Convention would not be tolerated, and that those individuals of whatever rank or status involved in committing grave breaches (i.e. war crimes) would be 'sought out and prosecuted', as all contracting parties are obliged to ensure.[2] The settlement programme, the annexation of Arab Jerusalem and widespread individual human rights abuses would have been thwarted by warnings, followed if necessary by appropriate action to ensure respect for the law. In reality the Western alliance has quietly accepted such violations, because it rates those of its strategic interests linked to Israel more highly than the fate of the Palestinian people.

Until the election of President Clinton the USA still formally accepted the applicability of the Fourth Geneva Convention and UNSCR 242 (in its generally accepted meaning). Since then there have been growing fears that it is quietly distancing itself from such norms, referring to the Territories as 'disputed' rather than occupied, and indicating that it no longer necessarily views Israel's permanent possession of East Jerusalem as unacceptable. It has still not recognized that the Palestinian people have the right to self-determination, an eccentric position for the world's 'greatest democracy'.

In such dismal circumstances it may be naive to propose what steps the international community could usefully take in order to uphold the political, civil and human rights of the Palestinian people. However, at that risk, the following proposals may be made:

## 1 Refugees

The international community must reaffirm its commitment to Resolution 194, and lay down the principles whereby the original intent of this resolution can now best be implemented. That must include facilities for the return of those who desire it to geographical Palestine, and adequate compensation for those who do not. It should reaffirm that the refugee question is a humanitarian matter, not a political one, and should therefore be negotiated on practical considerations (e.g. timescale, absorption capacity and location) and not political ones.

## 2 The Palestinians in Israel

The West has averted its gaze from the system of separate development evolved for the Arabs inside Israel. With a peace process now under way in the Occupied Territories, the international community must express its disquiet and encourage Israel to take the steps necessary to avoid communal conflict in the twenty-first century. These steps include:

(a) allocation of national resources on the basis of equality, regardless of ethnic identity, in all fields of state funding;
(b) cancellation of the Jewish National Fund's and Jewish Agency's role as agents for government land management and development, and of all other means whereby the government allows its agents to operate on a discriminatory basis between communities;
(c) recognition of the Palestinian Arab community as a national minority;
(d) the participation of Palestinian Arabs in all sectors of national life, including senior government posts, military (or equivalent national) service, employment possibilities (with legislation to prevent covert discrimination) and

qualification for state benefits;

(e) a review of land expropriations since 1948 with a view to making restitutions where practicable, possibly on a phased basis;

(f) encouragement to redefine the State of Israel as the state of all its citizens, with a new law of return which offers equal opportunity for both Jews and Arabs of their respective diaspora who yearn to 'return'.

## 3 Law

The international community, led by the United States, should remind Israel that the requirements of the Fourth Geneva Convention must be met, particularly:

(a) that all Jewish settlements in the Occupied Territories are illegal, and must be dismantled in due course unless those who inhabit them are able to negotiate an agreement to enter the jurisdiction of an administration representing the inhabitants of the Occupied Territories;

(b) that all forms of collective punishment must cease;

(c) that the basic rights of the people under occupation must be respected, as framed by the Convention;

(d) that Israel must abandon its use of the defunct and draconian British Defence (Emergency) Regulations of 1945, its practice of detaining people without trial, demolishing homes on suspicion and other practices that violate international law and norms of behaviour;

(e) that regardless of agreements reached between Israel and the PLO the territories occupied by Israel in 1967 will retain 'occupied' status until Israel has completed a physical and legal withdrawal;

(f) that Clause 14 of the Cairo Agreement binds Israel and the PLO to comply with human rights norms (i.e. international human rights law). The international community must ensure that both parties honour this undertaking.

## 4 Jerusalem

The international community should lay down principles whereby the city can be shared as functional capital of both an Israeli and a Palestinian entity, with the security of both communities safeguarded.

## 5 Land

The international community must uphold the principle of the inadmissibility of the acquisition of territory by war and insist that Israel may retain areas that it considers vital to its interests only subject to compensation, territorial or otherwise, acceptable to an elected Palestinian administration.

## 6 Water

The international community should advance principles of joint planning, management and distribution of the river and groundwater resources of geographical Palestine on the basis of equality of consumption (presumably on a per capita basis for domestic use, and acreage for agricultural use).

## 7 Aid

As the Palestinian people enter a critical phase of self-administration, they need financial and skills support in order to transform a situation that has stagnated since 1967. A prosperous and well-ordered Palestinian community is vital to the well-being of Israel as well as to Palestinians. So far there is little indication that this has been understood in the West. Substantial, but properly accountable and monitored, funds need to be made available, alongside expert consultancy and skills transfer where this seems necessary in order to assist the new Palestine to create the health, education, economic (production and marketing), civil service and local government structures which will equip it for the challenges ahead.

## 8 Human rights protection and Palestinian voluntary agencies

Until an electoral system and sound government services are firmly established, donors like the European Union should continue to support local voluntary agencies as a vital component of democratic growth and local services.

## 9 Accountability

The international community should hold the Palestine National Authority accountable to the standards of human rights expected internationally on the basis of customary law. To that end, it should support the creation of a legal and constitutional order that will ensure an independent judiciary, a rights-based legal system and fair elections.

Only an *ingénue* would believe Western governments will take even a fraction of these proposals seriously unless a significant proportion of ordinary people, voluntary agencies and media remind their governments of the consequences of not doing so. In the end, as the case of South Africa demonstrated, democratic governments can be persuaded to abandon so-called 'state interests', in favour of pressure on offending governments to observe basic human rights. Popular action is a long-term task with no guarantee of success, but that is no argument for doing nothing.

# NOTES AND REFERENCES

*Chapter 1*
**The Palestinians and early Zionism**

1 The lands stretching between the Mediterranean Sea in the west, the Syrian desert in the east, and between the Taurus in the north and Sinai and the Arabian peninsula in the south.
2 The Prophet Muhammad first designated Jerusalem as the *qibla* (prayer direction), before changing it to Mecca. Al-Aqsa mosque in Jerusalem is the third holiest shrine of Islam.
3 See Scholch, Alexander, *Palestine in Transformation, 1856-1982: Studies in Social, Economic and Political Development* (Washington, 1993), and Scholch, 'The emergence of modern Palestine (1856-1882)', in Nashabe, Hisham (ed.), *Studia Palaestina* (Beirut, 1988).
4 Bedouin encroachment into these areas had largely occurred during the eighteenth century because of the decline in government authority.
5 I do not propose to go into the complex question of Ottoman landholding. Suffice it to say there were at least six different categories of landholdings, only a small proportion of which conceded outright title to land to a private individual.
6 Graham-Brown, Sarah, *Palestinians and their Society, 1880-1946* (London, 1980), p. 73.
7 The Vilayet Law provided for local administrative assemblies in which local magnates were usually represented.
8 Smith, Pamela Ann, *Palestine and the Palestinians, 1876-1983* (Beckenham, 1984), p. 11.
9 Stein, Kenneth W., *The Land Question in Palestine, 1917-1939* (Chapel Hill, NC, and London, 1984), p. 21.
10 Max Nordau, who had proposed the term *heimstatte* ('homeland') later wrote 'we all understood what it meant...to us it signified "Judenstaat" (Jewish state) and it signifies the same now...' in Sykes, Christopher, *Two Studies in Virtue* (London, 1953), p. 160, quoted in Hirst, David, *The Gun and the Olive Branch* (London, 1977), p. 20.
11 Herzl wrote in 1898 'Were I to sum up the Basle Congress in a word – which I shall guard against pronouncing publicly – it would be this: at Basle I founded the Jewish State', in Herzl, Theodor, *The Complete Diaries of Theodor Herzl* (New York, 1960), vol. ii, p. 581, quoted in Hirst, *The Gun and the Olive Branch*, p. 20.
12 Quoted in the introduction to Dinur, Ben-Tzion, and Ben-Tzvi, Yitzhak

(eds), *The Book of the History of the Haganah* (Ma'arakhot/Armed Forces Edition, 1959).

13  Hirst, *The Gun and the Olive Branch*, p. 16.

14  Khalidi, Rashid, 'Palestinian peasant resistance to Zionism before World War I', in Said, E.W. and Hitchens, C. (eds), *Blaming the Victims: Spurious Scholarship and the Palestinian Question* (London and New York, 1988), p. 213.

15  Reelef, Rabbi Yitzhak, *Healing Of My People* (in German), published 1883, quoted in the introduction to Dinur and Ben-Tzvi, *The Book of the History of the Haganah*. Reelef was inspired to join the Zionist movement following the publication of Leo Pinsker's *Autoemancipation* in 1882 (see Avineri, Shlomo, *The Making of Modern Zionism: The Intellectual Origins of the Jewish State* (New York, 1981), Chapter 7.

16  Bohm, Adolf, *Die Zionistische Bewegung* (Berlin and Jerusalem, 1935), vol. i, p. 706.

17  *The Complete Diaries of Theodor Herzl* (New York, 1960), vol. i, p. 343, quoted in Hirst, *The Gun and the Olive Branch*, p. 18.

18  See Masalha, Nur, *Expulsion of the Palestinians: The Concept of 'Transfer' in Zionist Political Thought, 1882-1948* (Washington, 1992), for a scholarly but compelling analysis of this concept. A shorter treatment may be found in McDowall, David, *Palestine and Israel: The Uprising and Beyond* (London, 1989), Chapter 8.

19  Masalha, *Expulsion of the Palestinians*, p. 6.

20  Zangwill, Israel, *The Voice of Jerusalem* (London, 1920), p. 104.

21  See Teveth, Shabtai, *Ben-Gurion and the Palestinian Arabs: From Peace to War* (Oxford, 1985), p. 94; Flapan, Simha, *Zionism and the Palestinians, 1917-1947* (London, 1979), p. 135; Eban Abba, *The Voice of Israel* (London, 1958), p. 11.

22  Lehn, Walter, with Davis, Uri, *The Jewish National Fund* (London, 1988), p. 2, which discusses the issue in detail.

23  See Mandel, Neville J., *The Arabs and Zionism before World War I* (Berkeley, Los Angeles and London, 1976), p. 103f; Khalidi, 'Palestinian peasant resistance', p. 222; Hirst, *The Gun and the Olive Branch*, p. 29.

24  Even taking into account the economic pressures of the 1920s and 1930s, over 60 per cent of the land sold to the Yishuv was sold by absentee landlords, Khalidi, 'Palestinian peasant resistance', p. 225.

25  See Lehn, with Davis, *The Jewish National Fund*, Chapter 2.

26  Khalidi, 'Palestinian peasant resistance', p. 213; Mandel, *The Arabs and Zionism*, pp. 34-7.

27  Khalidi, 'Palestinian peasant resistance', p. 222.

28  Mandel, *The Arabs and Zionism*, p. 39.

29  Mandel, *The Arabs and Zionism*, pp. 7-31.

30  Mandel, *The Arabs and Zionism*, p. 46.

31  Mandel, *The Arabs and Zionism*, p. 128.

32  Mandel, *The Arabs and Zionism*, p. 220.

Notes and references

Chapter 2
British rule: 1917–48

1 The classic work on the emergence of Arab nationalism is Antonius, George, *The Arab Awakening* (London, 1938); see also Haim, Sylvia, *Arab Nationalism: An Anthology* (Los Angeles, 1962), and Hourani, Albert, *The Emergence of the Modern Middle East* (London, 1981).
2 In 1915 Britain had given vague undertakings to the Hashemite leaders of the Hijaz that, if successful in their 'Arab Revolt' against Ottoman rule, they would gain independence subject to a number of modifications, one of which was that 'the two districts of Mersina and Alexandretta and portions of Syria lying to the west of the districts of Damascus, Homs, Hama and Aleppo cannot be said to be purely Arab and should be excluded from the limits demanded'. Palestine lay indisputably south of the district (*sanjak*) of Damascus, and it was stretching a point to suggest the *province* (*vilayet*) of Syria (which stretched further south) was intended. If it had been it would have said so, and not bothered to refer to Homs, Hama and Aleppo. In November 1917 the Bolsheviks revealed details of a secret Anglo-French plan (the Sykes-Picot Agreement of 1916) to carve up the Arab region and Anatolia into spheres of direct rule and of influence. Palestine was marked to come under 'international control'.
3 Verite, Mayir, 'The Balfour Declaration and its Makers', in Kedourie, Elie and Haim, Sylvia, *Palestine and Israel in the 19th and 20th Centuries* (London, 1982).
4 The full text may be found in Antonius, *The Arab Awakening*, Appendix E.
5 For the whole text, see Ingrams, Doreen, *Palestine Papers, 1917-1922: The Seeds of Conflict* (London, 1972), p. 73.
6 Zangwill, Israel, *Speeches, Articles and Letters* (London, 1937), p. 342.
7 Curzon memorandum of 26 January 1919, Ingrams, *Palestine Papers*, p. 58.
8 Khalidi, Walid, *From Haven to Conquest* (Beirut, 1971), pp. 189-90.
9 The full text of the July 1919 Memorandum of the General Syrian Congress to the King-Crane Commission may be found in Antonius, *The Arab Awakening*, Appendix H. In fact they soon parted company with Damascus Syrians because the latter seemed willing to compromise with the Zionists if they united in the cause of independence from Britain and France.
10 *League of Nations Covenant*, Article XXII (4), reads: *'Certain communities formerly belonging to the Turkish Empire have reached a stage of development where their existence as independent nations can be provisionally recognized subject to the rendering of administrative advice and assistance by a Mandatory until such time as they are able to stand alone. The wishes of the inhabitants must be a principal consideration [author's emphasis] in the selection of the Mandatory.'* Britain took the Mandate since it was already in physical and political control. The League, essentially a club of 'winners' in the war, confirmed possession of the spoils.
11 The relevant articles are 4 and 11, and the whole text may be found in Ingrams, *Palestine Papers*, pp. 177-83.
12 For statistical evidence of growing Jewish economic control see Zureik, Elia, *The Palestinians in Israel: A Study in Internal Colonialism* (London, 1979), pp. 54-9. There had been rapid Arab industrialization, 1,373 new enterprises between 1918-28. These represented 60 per cent of all enterprises started in this period , but they tended to be significantly smaller scale than Jewish

enterprises which enjoyed foreign capital backing and previous large enterprise experience. By 1928 Jewish enterprises employed 75 per cent of the workforce, see Gottheil, Fred, 'Arab immigration into pre-state Israel 1922-1931', in Kedourie and Haim, *Palestine and Israel*, p. 147. See also Himadeh, Said, *The Economic Organization of Palestine* (Beirut, 1938), and Stein, Kenneth, *The Land Question in Palestine, 1917-1939*.

13   The best account of him is Mattar, Philip, *The Mufti of Jerusalem: al-Hajj Amin al-Husayni and the Palestinian National Movement* (New York, 1988). He was widely condemned for befriending the Third Reich in the hope it would help Palestinians get rid of both their British rulers and the Jewish settlers; see Nicosia, Francis, *The Third Reich and Palestine* (London, 1985).

14   In fact the Council was to be composed of ten government appointees, plus twelve elected members: eight Muslims, two Christians and two Jews, and one can see the Palestinian suspicion that this might also leave the two Jews with the deciding vote.

15   On the Arab response to British rule, see Porath, Yehoshua, *The Emergence of the Palestinian-Arab National Movement, 1918-1929* (London, 1974), and *The Palestinian-Arab National Movement, 1929-1939* (London 1977). On this particular point, see *The Emergence*, pp. 150-8. See also Kayyali, A.W., *Palestine: A Modern History* (London, 1978).

16   Resolution of the 12th Zionist Congress, 1921, quoted in Porath, *The Emergence of the Palestinian-Arab National Movement*, p. 146.

17   Quoted by Ziff, William, *The Rape of Palestine* (New York, 1938), p. 171, and Hadawi, Sami, *Palestinian Rights and Losses in 1948 – A Comprehensive Study* (London, 1988), p. 17

18   Certain Hebron Arabs sheltered and saved Jews. According to Rabbi Meir Franko of Hebron 200 Jews were sheltered and 420 rescued from probable death, Jabara, Taysir, *et al.*, *Madina Khalil al-Rahman* (Hebron, 1987), p. 136.

19   Muslims were very sensitive concerning Jewish attempts from 1918 onwards to acquire practical and legal control of the Wall. By 1929 tensions had reached the point of explosion, Storrs, Ronald, *Orientations* (London, 1937), pp. 407-8.

20   The best account is probably in Porath, *The Emergence of the Palestinian-Arab National Movement*, pp. 150-8.

21   Hope-Simpson Report of 1930, quoted in Erskine, Beatrice Stewart, *Palestine of the Arabs* (London, 1935), p. 103.

22   It might be assumed that the number of evicted peasants had reached cataclysmic proportions, but this was clearly not so. The impact of those evicted, however, was heightened by the general economic transformation from subsistence to a market economy now taking place. Jewish economic activity may have been the main stimulus for this transformation but it was not the only one. Moreover, this economic activity acted as a magnet, attracting an increasing number of Palestinians down to the coastal plain: see Zureik, *The Palestinians in Israel*, p. 46.

23   Zionist and British discussion of transfer during the 1920s and 1930s is best covered in Masalha, *The Expulsion of the Palestinians*, pp. 14-92; but see also Flapan, *Zionism and the Palestinians*; Teveth, *Ben-Gurion and the Palestinian Arabs*; Gorny, Yoset, *Zionism and the Arabs, 1882-1948*, (Oxford, 1987).

24   Ben-Gurion, David, *Memoirs* (Hebrew, Tel Aviv, 1974), vol. ii, pp. 330-1, quoted in Flapan, *Zionism and the Palestinians*, p. 246.

25 Porath, *The Palestinian Arab-National Movement*, pp. 283-4. In late 1935, before the outbreak of revolt, Hajj Amin al Husseini tried to strike a compromise deal with Ben-Gurion of allowing the Jewish proportion to become 44 per cent of the total population (it was only 25 per cent at the time of the offer), provided the Arab majority was guaranteed. Ben-Gurion would have none of it, for that would have defeated the purpose of Zionism: Teveth, *Ben-Gurion and the Palestinian Arabs*, p. 157.

26 A useful explanation of not only British but also US vacillation between the options of partition and trusteeship right up to April 1948 is provided in Louis, Roger, and Stookey, Robert (eds), *The End of the Palestine Mandate* (London, 1986); Cohen, Michael, *Palestine and the Great Powers, 1945-1948* (Princeton, 1983). What remains clear is that the issue hinged more on British strategic interests, the US desire to reduce these, and the Zionist lobby in the US, than the perceived interests of either Arabs or Jews in Palestine.

## Chapter 3
## Partition and dispossession: 1947–9

1 Perhaps the best account of this whole dismal episode, out of which no state emerged with much credit, is Pappé, Ilan, *The Making of the Arab-Israeli Conflict, 1947-1951* (London 1992).

2 Space does not permit a résumé of the various strands of the Jewish struggle to gain control of Palestine. The following may be usefully consulted: Hurewitz, J.C., *The Struggle for Palestine* (New York, 1950, 1976); Sykes, Christopher, *Crossroads to Israel* (London, 1965); Cohen, *Palestine and the Great Powers, 1945-48*. Regarding Jewish terrorist groups, see Begin, Menachem, *The Revolt* (London, 1951); Ben-Ami, Yitshaq, *Years of Wrath, Days of Glory: Memoirs from the Irgun* (1982); Wilson, R.D., *Cordon and Search: With 6th Airborne Division in Palestine* (Aldershot, 1949). Furthermore, the extermination of European Jews had driven its survivors in desperate search of refuge to Palestine. Hitler's genocide of the Jews wracked Europe and the US with guilt and with a desire to provide a safe haven for the survivors. That guilt was turned to popular disgust by British government attempts to limit Jewish immigration by turning back illegal immigrant ships.

3 In particular Transjordan hoped to acquire the Arab part of Palestine, while Egypt and Syria fearing Hashemite regional ambitions, were particularly anxious to thwart it. None of the Arab states were disposed to fight the putative Jewish state except for Transjordan. It wished to in order to gain Arab Palestine. If it chose to fight alone, the other Arab states would be seen as betraying the Arab cause.

4 'Binationalism not partition', UN Ad Hoc Subcommittee 2 Report, 11 November 1947 (A/AC 14/32 and Add I), reprinted in Khalidi, *From Haven to Conquest*, p. 687.

5 Porath, *The Emergence of the Palestinian-Arab National Movement*, pp. 253-4, and *The Palestinian-Arab National Movement*, pp. 283-91.

6 Their first blunder was with the Anglo-American committee of Enquiry, 1946. Committee members came from visiting the Displaced Persons camps of Europe, deeply moved by the Jewish plight and receptive to the

possibilities the Yishuv could offer them. The Committee consequently strongly embraced the link between the European Holocaust and the creation of a Jewish state. Instead of presenting a cogent argument for protecting the rights of the indigenous population, the Arab Higher Committee boycotted the Committee.

7   UNSCOP was composed of Australia, Canada, Czechoslovakia, Guatemala, India, Iran, Netherlands, Peru, Sweden, Uruguay and Yugoslavia. The US had opposed a committee made up of Security Council members since this would have allowed the USSR (and Britain) a say in the outcome. The US preferred to exercise its influence through lesser UN members.

8   It was symptomatic of that lack of understanding (regardless of their expectation of massive Jewish immigration) that they favoured the establishment of a Jewish state that would contain 498,000 Jews and 407,000 Arabs at its foundation, see note 13.

9   'Haiti, Liberia, the Philippines, China, Ethiopia and Greece – all of which opposed partition – were given concentrated doses of political and economic pressure', Gilmour, David, *Dispossessed – The Ordeal of the Palestinians* (London, 1980), p. 59, based on Roosevelt, Kermit, 'The partition of Palestine: a lesson in pressure politics', *Middle East Journal*, vol. ii, no. 1, 1948, pp. 1-16.

10  Ben-Gurion to the Histadrut Executive, 3 December 1947, in Flapan, Simha, *The Birth of Israel: Myths and Reality* (London and Sydney, 1987), pp. 32-3. Flapan believed 'acceptance of the UN Partition Resolution was an example of Zionist pragmatism par excellence. It was a tactical step in the right direction – a springboard for expansion when circumstances proved more judicious (*sic*)'.

11  Ben-Gurion, *Memoirs*, vol. iv, p. 278, quoted in Flapan, *The Birth of Israel*, p. 22. See also Teveth, *Ben-Gurion and the Palestinian Arabs*, pp. 102, 136, 185, and Flapan, *Zionism and the Palestinians*, p. 265.

12  Segev, Tom, *1949 – The First Israelis* (New York, 1986), p. xviii.

13  In fact, based on the 31 December 1946 official census figures (used by UNSCOP) the Jewish state would be 50.5 per cent Arab, for UNSCOP left out of its demographic calculations 92,000 Negev bedouin, leaving their existence as a mere footnote: see United Nations, *United Nations Special Committee on Palestine*, Document A/364 of 3 September 1947, p. 11, note 1, and p. 54, compared with the census figures set out in United Nations, *Ad Hoc Committee on the Palestine Question*, Document A/AC 14/32, 11 November 1947, Appendix I, Annex I, pp. 304-7.

14  The only shrewd move they made was to seek a UN vote on referring to the International Court of Justice in the Hague the question of the partition's legitimacy, since it violated the right of self-determination adumbrated in Article 1 of the UN charter. They failed by one vote to carry the resolution. Had they succeeded, and had the Hague ruled that partition against the will of the majority violated the UN charter, the history of Palestine might have been significantly different: Pappé, *The Making of the Arab-Israeli Conflict*, p. 37.

15  Weitz Diary A246/7, 20 December 1940, quoted in Masalha, *Expulsion of the Palestinians*, p. 131. See also p. 159.

16  Minutes of the Jewish Agency Executive's meeting of 2 November 1947, quoted in Morris, Benny, *The Birth of the Palestinian Refugee Problem, 1947-1949* (Cambridge, 1987), p. 28.

17 Ben-Gurion, David, *War Diary* (Hebrew, Tel Aviv, 1982), vol. i, p. 22.
18 Ben Gurion, *War Diary*, 19 December 1947, p. 58, quoted in Flapan, *The Birth of Israel*, p. 90.
19 Ezra Danin, in Rivlin, Gershon, and Orren, Elhanan (eds), *Yoman Hamil-hama-Tashah 1948-1949*, 3 vols (David Ben-Gurion's War Diary) (Tel Aviv, 1982), 11 December 1947, p. 37, quoted by Pappé, *The Making of the Arab-Israeli Conflict*, p. 82.
20 Gad Machnes, in Rivlin and Orren, *Yoman*, 11 January 1948, p. 97, quoted in Pappé, *The Making of the Arab-Israeli Conflict*, p. 82.
21 Pappé, *The Making of the Arab-Israeli Conflict*, pp. 52, 65.
22 Furthermore, the commander of the ALA, Fawzi Qawuqji, made secret overtures to all the other contestants in Palestine, including the Jewish leadership. It seems he wanted to establish his own area of control in northern Palestine: Pappé, *The Making of the Arab-Israeli Conflict*, p. 84.
23 Bar Zohar, *Ben-Gurion*, vol. ii, p. 703, quoted in Masalha, *Expulsion of the Palestinians*, p. 178. See also Lorch, N., *The Edge of the Sword: Israel's War of Independence, 1947-49* (London, 1961), pp. 87-9.
24 Pappé, *The Making of the Arab-Israeli Conflict*, p. 55.
25 The indispensable work on this subject is Shlaim, Avi, *Collusion Across the Jordan* (Oxford, 1988).
26 Armies fighting against interior lines of defence are always seriously disadvantaged, since exterior lines make the problems of co-ordination, movement and concentration of forces immensely difficult even among co-operating forces. A defender can always move forces more rapidly from one sector to another. Without a numerically or qualitatively superior force, it is virtually impossible to win a war fought on exterior lines.
27 This was only 4,500 strong: see Glubb, John Bagot, *A Soldier with the Arabs* (London, 1957), for an account of the Arab Legion's war.
28 Shlaim, *Collusion Across the Jordan*, pp. 337, 368, 442, 515, 533.
29 Estimates of villages emptied range from 360-472. Morris in *The Birth of the Palestinian Refugee Problem* estimates 369, while Khalidi, Walid, in *All that Remains: The Palestinian Villages Occupied and Depopulated by Israel in 1948* (Washington, 1989), lists 418 villages.
30 Quoted by Ben-Gurion, *Medinat Yisrael Hamehudeshet*, pp. 164-5, in Morris, *The Birth of the Palestinian Refugee Problem*, p. 141.
31 Segev, *1949 – The First Israelis*, p. 29.
32 United Nations General Assembly Resolution No. 194 (III) of 11 December 1948, Article 11.
33 The disparity between 369 villages abandoned and 386 destroyed is explained by the forcible removal of inhabitants who had not left during hostilities. Some of these were expelled from the Jewish state, others were forcibly transferred to Nazareth, or nearby villages between 1948 and 1953: see Morris, *The Birth of the Palestine Refugee Problem*, and *1948 and After: Israel and the Palestinians* (Oxford, 1990); Khalidi, *All that Remains*; Zayyad, Tawfig, 'The Arabs in Israel', in Zogby, J. (ed.), *Perspectives on Palestinian Arabs and Israeli Jews* (Wilmett, IL, 1977), p. 50; Kanaana, Sharif, *Still on Vacation! The Eviction of the Palestinians in 1948* (Jerusalem, 1992), p. 26.
34 Pappé, *The Making of the Arab-Israeli Conflict*, p. 88.
35 Weizmann himself was convinced transfer was crucial to the Zionist programme: Flapan, *Zionism and the Palestinians*, pp. 70, 82. On the whole question of transfer in Zionist thinking see Masalha, *Expulsion of the Pales-*

*tinians;* Morris, *The Birth of the Palestinian Refugee Problem;* and Morris, Benny, 'Josef Weitz and the Transfer Committee, 1948-1949', *Middle Eastern Studies,* vol. xi, no. 1, Winter 1986, republished in Morris, *1948 and After.*

36  Ben-Gurion, David, *Behilahem Yisrael* (Tel Aviv, 1952), pp. 86-7, in Masalha, *Expulsion of the Palestinians,* p. 181.

37  Aharon Cohen, Director of Mapam's Arab Committee, 10 May 1948, in Morris, 'Josef Weitz and the Transfer Committee', p. 522, and in Masalha, *Expulsion of the Palestinians,* p. 181.

38  Their first request to the United Nations was to arrange their return. For the evidence of the refugees themselves, see Sayigh, Rosemary, *Palestinians: From Peasants to Revolutionaries* (London, 1979), Chapter 2.

39  A number of accounts are available but easily the most important must be that of an early eyewitness, J. de Reynier, head of the Red Cross delegation, reprinted in Khalidi, *From Haven to Conquest,* pp. 761-6. See also the horrific account of a survivor who witnessed the slaughter of most of her family: Kanaana, *Still on Vacation!,* pp. 69-71, and the version given by Menachem Begin the Irgun leader and subsequent Prime Minister denying a massacre took place in *The Revolt,* pp. 162-5. Also worth consulting are Sykes, Christopher, *Crossroads to Israel,* pp. 416-18, and Gilmour, David, 'The 1948 Arab exodus', *Middle East International,* no. 288, 21 November 1986, which cites a Haganah intelligence officer who claimed he was forbidden to warn the inhabitants to leave the village before the Irgun attacked.

40  Quoted in Morris, Benny, 'The causes and character of the Arab exodus from Palestine: the Israel Defence Forces Intelligence Service Analysis of June 1948', *Middle Eastern Studies,* vol. xxii, no. 1, January 1986, p. 9.

41  Begin, *The Revolt,* p. 164.

42  *Middle East International,* no. 288, 21 November 1986, and Pappé, *The Making of the Arab-Israeli Conflict,* p. 85.

43  Morris, Benny, 'The harvest of 1948 and the creation of the Palestinian refugee problem', *The Middle East Journal,* vol. xi, no. 4, Autumn 1986, p. 684.

44  Morris, *The Birth of the Palestinian Refugee Problem,* p. 204.

45  Morris, Benny, 'Operation Dani and the Palestinian exodus from Lydda and Ramle in 1948', *The Middle East Journal,* vol. xi, no. 1, Winter 1986, p. 94.

46  Morris, *The Birth of the Palestinian Refugee Problem,* p. 207.

47  Morris, *The Birth of the Palestinian Refugee Problem,* p. 210.

48  The most serious of these was at Duwayma, southern Palestine, on 29-30 October 1948 when about 100 villagers perished, but there were at least six serious atrocities in the Galilee; Nazzal, Nafiz, *The Palestinian Exodus from Galilee, 1948* (Beirut, 1978), describes six such atrocities; see also Chacour, Elias, *Blood Brothers* (Eastbourne, 1985), pp. 36-53, and on Duwayma, *Davar,* 6 September 1979, *al Fajr* (English edition), 31 August 1984, and Morris, *The Birth of the Palestinian Refugee Problem,* pp. 222-3. Regarding the massacre of the al-Azazma bedouin tribe, see Maddrell, Penny, *The Bedouin of the Negev* (London, 1990), p. 6. One alleged massacre, in which 70 men were reportedly killed in a mosque, occurred at Hula just inside Lebanon in 1949: Sayigh, *Palestinians: From Peasants to Revolutionaries,* p. 156. It was not as if Arab irregulars did not also commit atrocities, but they were far fewer and smaller in scale. Three days after Deir Yassin, Arab forces took revenge, ambushing and killing a convoy of 77 Jewish medical and acade-

mic personnel. Four weeks later at the fall of Kfar Etzion, 15 Jews were shot after their surrender, although the majority were saved by the Arab Legion.

49  Umm Ibrahim Shawabkeh, refugee from Bayt Jibrain, a village midway between Hebron and Majdal (Ashkelon), sacked by Israeli troops in October 1948: in Najjar, Orayb Aref, *Portraits of Palestinian Women* (Salt Lake City, 1992), p. 30, quoted by Holt, Maria, *Half the People: Women, History and the Palestinian Intifada* (Jerusalem, 1992), p. 26.

50  Minutes of cabinet meeting, 17 November 1948, Kibbutz Meuhad Archive, sec. 9, container 9, file 1, cited by Segev, *1949 – The First Israelis*, p. 26.

51  Morris, 'The causes and character of the Arab exodus', pp. 5-19.

52  Morris, 'Operation Dani and the Palestinian Exodus from Lydda and Ramle in 1948', *Middle East Journal*, vol. xi, no. 1, Winter 1986, p. 104.

53  Morris, 'Josef Weitz', p. 550.

54  Morris, 'Josef Weitz', p. 556; on alleged radio broadcasts, see *The Spectator*, 12 May 1961.

55  Morris, *The Birth of the Palestinian Refugee Problem*, pp. 243, 246-52.

56  Maddrell, *The Bedouin of the Negev*, p. 6.

57  The first was that between Hindus and Muslims on the eve of India's partition.

58  Conditional, that is, on their willingness 'to live at peace with their neighbours'.

59  Morris, *The Birth of the Palestinian Refugee Population*, p. 269 and footnotes.

60  'Israel's reactions to Za'im's offer ranged from indifference to distrust to contempt': Flapan, *The Birth of Israel*, p. 210. Ben-Gurion was unwilling to make any concession to Syria until it withdrew its troops unconditionally from the ceasefire line inside Palestine. Control of the river Jordan's tributaries was a key issue.

61  Morris, *The Birth of the Palestinian Refugee Problem*, pp. 263-4, and footnote.

62  Flapan, *The Birth of Israel*, 205-7.

63  Morris, *The Birth of the Palestinian Refugee Problem*, p. 277.

64  Al-Hawwari, Nimr, *The Secret of the Catastrophe* (Nazareth, 1955), pp. 376-87, quoted in Flapan, *The Birth of Israel*, p. 222. See also Pappé, *The Making of the Arab-Israeli Conflict*, pp. 209-23 passim.

*Chapter 4*
**Deepening conflict: 1948–67**

1  See Shlaim, *Collusion across the Jordan*.

2  Flapan, *The Birth of Israel*, p. 150.

3  Smith, *Palestine and the Palestinians, 1876-1983*, p. 95.

4  By 1967, after 19 years of Hashemite rule the industrial sector of the West Bank had not only shrunk from 12 per cent to 9 per cent of the gross domestic product but was now smaller than in any neighbouring Arab area, and particularly in comparison with the East Bank; see Owen, Roger, 'Economic history of Palestine under the mandate, 1914-48', paper given at the Welfare Association International Symposium, Oxford, January 1986.

5  It should be remembered that, as hereditary custodians of the holy cities of Mecca and Medina, the Hashemites hailed from the Hijaz, now part of Saudi Arabia. Their strength in Transjordan rested on tribal support, and

was rooted in a social culture different from that of peasant or urban Palestine.

6 Morris, Benny, *Israel's Border Wars, 1949-1956* (Oxford, 1993), provides essential reading on this period, and explains how the situation on the borders and Israel's policy of reprisal led inexorably towards war. Jordan, Syria and Egypt all at first made sincere efforts to prevent border violations, see pp. 67, 91 and 88.

7 Morris, *Israel's Border Wars*, p. 27.

8 Morris, *Israel's Border Wars*, p. 98, gives annual figures.

9 Public Record Office, FO 371/104778, General Glubb, 'Note on refugee vagrancy', quoted in Morris, *Israel's Border Wars*, p. 37.

10 For example, see orders issued by Israel's Southern Command, Morris, *Israel's Border Wars*, pp. 125, 129, 132, 414.

11 Morris, *Israel's Border Wars*, p. 135.

12 Morris, *Israel's Border Wars*, p. 157.

13 MM to *al Hamishmar*, *al Hamishmar* to Mapam Knesset faction, 20 June 1950, quoted in Morris, *Israel's Border Wars*, p. 148. See also pp. 157, 160.

14 Morris, *Israel's Border Wars*, p. 166.

15 In Jordan's case, Israel rejected the suggestion of joint patrols.

16 As late as July 1954 a senior US diplomat reported 'On the Arab side, small-scale infiltration persists on the part of individual and small groups acting on their own responsibility. There is no evidence of organised military activity by the Arab states acting in concert or by any individual Arab state': Executive Secretary James Lay, memorandum, 6 July 1954, appended to National Security Document 155/1, quoted in Green, Stephen, *Taking Sides: America's Secret Relations with a Militant Israel, 1948-1967* (London, 1984), pp. 117-19, and for the early 1960s, p. 192.

17 Morris, *Israel's Border Wars*, Chapter 11. In fact Moshe Sharett (briefly Prime Minister of Israel) had initiated secret diplomacy with Nasser who, faced with overwhelming economic problems, was amenable to a settlement. Secret meetings in 1954, however, were deliberately undermined by Pinhas Lavon (Minister of Defence) and Moshe Dayan (Chief of Staff) at the instigation of Ben-Gurion. In 1954 Israeli agents attempted to bomb British and French installations in Egypt in an attempt to damage their relations with Cairo. The agents were caught, and Nasser suspended talks. The Gaza raid some months later convinced Nasser of Israel's bellicose intent. It took place only four days after Nasser had taken a formal stand against the Baghdad Pact, and only 11 days after Ben-Gurion had resumed office as Prime Minister.

18 Morris, *Israel's Border Wars*, p. 408; Locke, Richard, and Stewart, Anthony, *Bantustan Gaza* (London, 1985), p. 6.

19 Apart from Morris, *Israel's Border Wars*, see also Green, Stephen, *Taking Sides*, pp. 104-92 passim.

20 Israel had acquired passage through these Straits by an act of war, namely its Sinai campaign of November 1956.

21 Davis, John, *The Evasive Peace* (London, 1970), p. 69.

22 *The Independent*, 11 April 1994.

23 See Hirst, *The Gun and the Olive Branch*, pp. 227-9; 'West Bank Story' published in *Private Eye*, 10 November 1967; and the statement of a 5th Division reservist, Tel Aviv, 10 September 1967, issued by *Haolam Hazeh*, and republished in the Institute for Palestine Studies, *Israel and the Geneva Con-*

*ventions* (Beirut, 1968).

24 These were Menachem Begin and Yigal Allon and Pinhas Sapir and Abba Eban respectively, private diaries of Ya'acov Herzog, cabinet secretary, cited in Melman, Yossi, and Raviv, Dan, 'A final solution of the Palestinian problem', *Guardian Weekly*, 21 February 1988.

25 The scheme lasted for only three years and was made public in 1987 by Ariel Sharon when advocating Arab emigration, *Guardian Weekly*, 21 February 1988; see also Reinhard Wiemar, 'Zionism and the Arabs after the establishment of the State of Israel', in Scholch, Alexander, *Palestinians over the Green Line* (London, 1983), p. 47.

26 *Christian Science Monitor*, 3 June 1974, quoted in Chomsky, Noam, *The Fateful Triangle* (London, 1983), p. 116.

*Chapter 5*
## The Palestinian Arabs inside Israel

1 Many Palestinians congregated in Nazareth who either fled in 1948 and were not allowed to return to their villages or were expelled from their homes after the cessation of hostilities.

2 Many internal refugees and inhabitants of the area ceded by Jordan were not given citizenship. For a discussion of the question of citizenship, see Halabi, Usama, 'The impact of the Jewishness of the State of Israel on the status and rights of the Arab citizens, in Israel' in Masalha, *Is Israel the State of All its Citizens and 'Absentees'?*.

3 Jiryis, Sabri, 'Recent Knesset legislation and the Arabs in Israel', *Journal of Palestine Studies*, vol. i, no. 1, 1971, p. 54; Zureik, *The Palestinians in Israel*, p. 121. See also McDowall, *Palestine and Israel*, p. 130.

4 Gavison, Ruth, 'Minority rights in Israel: the case of army veteran provisions', in International Centre for Peace in the Middle East, *Relations between Ethnic Majority and Minority* (Tel Aviv, 1987), p. 21. *Yeshiva* (religious seminary) students benefit from from this law even though they are exempt from military service.

5 Smooha, Sammy, 'Political intolerance: threatening Israel's democracy', *New Outlook*, July 1986; see also Sims, Emily, and Kana'aneh, Hatim, 'The problems faced by the Palestinian community in Israel' (unpublished paper, Shafa Amr, 1994), and Davis, Uri, and Richardson, John, 'Zionism and democracy: a contradiction in terms', in Masalha, *Is Israel the State of All its Citizens?*.

6 At the same meeting Dayan urged Mapai to consider these Arabs 'as if their fate is not yet determined. I hope that there will perhaps be another opportunity to transfer these Arabs from the Land of Israel': minutes of Mapai Knesset faction and party secretariat meeting, 18 June 1950, in Morris, *Israel's Border Wars*, p. 162.

7 Masalha, Nur, 'Operation Hafarfaret and the massacre of Kafr Qassim, October 1956', *The Arab Review*, vol. 3, no. 1, Summer 1994.

8 On 18 June 1950: Litani, Yehuda, *Hadashot*, 7 December 1990, quoted in Masalha, 'Operation Hafarfaret'.

9 Rosenthal, R., 'Mitzva Hafarfaret', *Hadashot*, 25 October 1991, in Morris, *Israel's Border Wars*, p. 417.

10 From the two villages of Krad al Baqqara and Krad al Ghannama, on 30

October 1956: Masalha, 'Operation Hafarfaret'.

11  See Jiryis, Sabri, *The Arabs in Israel, 1948-66* (Beirut, 1968), Chapter 2, and Lustick, Ian, *Arabs in the Jewish State: Israel's Control of a National Minority* (Austin, 1980).

12  Israel, *Report of the State Controller on the Ministry of Defence for the Financial Year 1957-58*, no. 9, February 1959, p. 56, in Jiryis, *The Arabs in Israel*, p. 20.

13  This was the assessment of the Palestine Conciliation Commission in 1951: Hadawi, *Palestinian Rights and Losses*, p. 94. See also Jiryis, *The Arabs in Israel*, pp. 58ff.

14  Lustick, *Arabs in the Jewish State*, p. 60.

15  In both cases villagers won court orders entitling them to return. In order to thwart the court's will, the IDF demolished the dwellings before the inhabitants could return. As Maronite Christians, the villagers were the least likely to be a security risk. By 1994 the villagers had still not obtained implementation of the court ruling: see Jiryis, *The Arabs in Israel*, pp. 65-71.

16  The title is an illuminating one since, if acts needed validating retrospectively, they were presumably either unlawful or of dubious legality when done.

17  The main legal instrument was the 'Emergency Articles for the Exploitation of Uncultivated Lands', *Official Gazette*, no. 27, 15 October 1948, (b) p. 3, cited in Jiryis, *The Arabs in Israel*, pp. 72-3.

18  Israel created the Israel Land Administration, which is jointly administered by the JNF and the Ministry of Agriculture, and the Land Development Authority (the JNF having exclusive responsibility for land development). Even where the JNF does not exercise direct control, the Zionist-JNF principle of inalienability has been applied to state holdings: Lustick, *Arabs in the Jewish State*, pp. 99, 107-8. In certain limited contexts Arabs receive short leases (nine months) on ILA/JNF land.

19  Most of the rest is in Arab hands, and only about 4 per cent is in private Jewish hands.

20  Sims and Kana'aneh, 'Problems faced by the Palestinian community in Israel'. Five settlements were 'recognized' in 1992 but none have so far received any basic services extended to all other recognized settlements.

21  Lustick, *Arabs in the Jewish State*, pp. 59, 189-90. On the whole question of the *waqf* both in Israel and in the Occupied Territories in detail, see Dumper, Michael, *Islam and Israel: Muslim Religious Endowments and the Jewish State* (Washington, 1994), especially Chapters 2 and 3.

22  Defence Laws (State of Emergency) 1945, Article 125, empowered the government to declare areas closed. A permit was required to move in or out of a closed area. Beersheba was outside the closed area of the Negev. A member of one tribe was also forbidden to cross into the territory of another: Jiryis, *The Arabs in Israel*, pp. 17-19; al-Atawna, Shaykh Musa, 'What the bedouin want', *New Outlook*, vol. 3, no. 9, September 1960, p. 16 in Lustick, *Arabs in the Jewish State*, p. 134.

23  For a general briefing see Maddrell, *The Bedouin of the Negev*.

24  For details of how Arab inhabitants were denied permission to repair their homes, and the plan to make the centre exclusively Jewish, see McDowall, David, *Palestine and Israel: The Uprising and Beyond*, pp. 128-9 and endnotes. By 1994 this policy had apparently been abandoned, partly because of the difficulty of achieving this figure but also because it was decided that old Acre, after all, would remain more attractive as a tourist site with its Arab

population still in residence.

25 One Palestinian is currently legally contesting his disqualification from subsidized housing in the Wadi Ara settlement of Katzair on racial grounds. The outcome should be interesting.

26 For a more detailed description, see Masalha, 'Operation Hafarfaret'; Jiryis, *The Arabs in Israel*, Chapter 3; Morris, *Israel's Border Wars*, p. 417; or McDowall, David, *The Palestinians* (London, 1987), p. 14.

27 In fact these regulations were revoked by the British on the eve of their departure from Palestine in May 1948, but it suited Israel to consider them still in force.

28 Jiryis, *The Arabs in Israel*, p. 4.

29 McDowall, David, 'Are Israel's defence regulations valid?', *Middle East International*, no. 292, 23 January 1987.

30 McDowall, 'Are Israel's defence regulations valid?'. See also Rosenthal, André, 'The 1945 defence regulations: valid law in the West Bank?' (unpublished paper, Jerusalem, 1984); Quigley, John, *Palestine and Israel: A Challenge to Justice* (Durham and London, 1990), pp. 102-4.

31 *Ha'aretz*, 17 January 1986, in *Israeli Mirror*, no. 748. For other examples of discrimination see *Kol Ha'ir*, 15 February 1985, *Jerusalem Post International*, 4, 11, 18 July, *Israeli Mirror*, no. 762, 22 July 1987, with excerpts from *Ha'aretz*, *Yediot Aharanot* and *Hadashot*.

32 While on average, each Arab village in 1948 had 9,136 dunums, by 1974 this had fallen to 2,000 dunums: Zayyad, Tawfiq, 'The Arabs in Israel', in Zogby, *Perspectives on Palestinian Arabs and Israeli Jews*, p. 50; Lustick, *Arabs in the Jewish State*, p. 179, lists a representative number of villages.

33 Between 1977 and 1981, 58 new settlements were established: Scholch, *Palestinians Across the Green Line*, p. 15; see also Yiftachel, Oren, *Planning a Mixed Region in Israel: The Political Geography of Arab-Jewish Relations in the Galilee* (Aldershot, 1992).

34 Carmiel is the classic example: McDowall, *Palestine and Israel*, p. 135.

35 Maddrell, *The Bedouin of the Negev*, p. 8.

36 Maddrell, *The Bedouin of the Negev*, p. 11.

37 Information from the Galilee Society for Health Research and Services, Shafa Amr.

38 McDowall, *Palestine and Israel*, p. 135.

39 Sims and Kanaaneh, 'Problems faced by the Palestinian community in Israel'. See also Falah, Ghazi, 'Pluralism and resource allocation among Arab and Jewish citizens of Israel', in Masalha, *Is Israel the State of All its Citizens and 'Absentees'?*, p. 87, which states that in 1986-7 the smallest allocation made to a Jewish local authority (Yokne'am 'Illit) was still greater than the largest water allocation to an Arab location (Kafr Yasif).

40 By the Ministry of Agriculture and designated marketing boards.

41 For an elaboration, see Khalidi, Raja, *The Arab Economy in Israel: The Dynamics of a Region's Development* (London, 1988), Chapter 5.

42 The American-Israeli owned Phoenicia Glass factory being built near Mashad in the Galilee will produce large quantitites of sulphur dioxide. It is predicted that this toxic matter will create severe ecological and health problems for humans, animals and flora around Mashad and Kufr Kana (biblical Cana). Other factories of toxic output are planned for the same area. Arab localities also suffer pollution from waste disposal from Jewish residential areas.

43  For a discussion with map, see Lustick, *Arabs in the Jewish State*, p. 186; McDowall, *Palestine and Israel*, p. 139; Khalidi, *The Arab Economy*, p. 163.
44  Known as the Ya'cobi Report: McDowall, *Palestine and Israel*, pp. 234-5.
45  Ghanadiri, Samih, *al-Jamahir al-'Arabiya fi Isra'il* (Nazareth, 1987), pp. 34-5.
46  Umm al Fahm was able to construct a partial sewage system in 1990.
47  McDowall, *Palestine and Israel*, pp. 137, 141 and endnotes.
48  McDowall, *Palestine and Israel*, pp. 139-40.
49  McDowall, *Paslestine and Israel*, pp. 137-8 and endnotes.
50  McDowall, *Palestine and Israel*, pp. 234-5.
51  Smooha, Sammy, *The Orientation and Politicization of the Arab Minority in Israel* (Haifa, 1984), p. 81; Government of Israel, *Statistical Abstract for Israel for 1984* (Jerusalem, 1985).
52  *Ha'aretz*, 3 and 7 April 1989, quoted in Halabi, 'The impact of the Jewish-ness of the State of Israel', p. 28.
53  *Al Ittihad*, 16 March 1986, quoted in Laugharn, Peter, and Kana'aneh, 'Development needs and potential of Israel's Arabs' (Galilee, 1987 mimeograph), and in McDowall, *Palestine and Israel*, p. 142.
54  Mari, S.K., *Arab Education in Israel* (New York, 1978), p. 70f, quoted in Minority Rights Group, *Educational Rights and Minorities* (London, 1994), p. 29.
55  The National Religious Party was also popular because it controlled the Ministry of Religious Affairs and could allocate funds.
56  As a Labour supporter, he surprised people by describing the community as part of the Palestinian nation (rather than the preferred Zionist desription of 'Arab'): *al Musawwar*, 20 May 1994.
57  From 1984, for example, Labour preferred a coalition with Likud, to a slender majority in coalition with Rakah and PLP.
58  Lustick, *Arabs in the Jewish State*, p. 249; al Haj, Majid, 'Strategies of mobilization among the Arabs in Israel', in Kyle, Keith, and Peters, Joel (eds), *Whither Israel? The Domestic Challenges* (London, 1993), p. 150.
59  Smooha, Sammy, *The Orientation and Politicization of the Arab Minority in Israel*, p. 37.
60  Miari, Mahmoud, 'They returned to their people', in Masalha, *Is Israel the State of All its Citizens and 'Absentees'?*, pp. 37-9.

*Chapter 6*
**Exile and the rise of the national movement**

1  This figure is disputed. The maximum Arab claim is 900,000 and the minimum (Israeli) claim 520,000: see Morris, *The Birth of the Palestinian Refugee Problem*, p. 297.
2  Sayigh, *Palestinians: From Peasants to Revolutionaries*, pp. 126-7.
3  For personal accounts, see Sayigh, *Palestinians: From Peasants to Revolutionaries*, Chapters 2 and 3.
4  The refugees received citizenship by 1954, but significantly the vast majority of them were only enfranchised by the 1986 Election Law which superseded the previous property ownership requirement: Brand, Laurie A., *Palestinians in the Arab World: Institution Building and the Search for a State* (New York and Oxford, 1988), p. 12.
5  Loescher, Gill, *Beyond Charity: International Co-operation and the Global*

*Refugee Crisis* (Oxford, 1993), p. 61.

6  All descendants of registered refugees are eligible for refugee status, with the exception of females who marry non-refugees: see Cervenak, Christine, 'Promoting inequality: gender-based discrimination in UNRWA's approach to refugee status', *Human Rights Quarterly*, no. 16, 1994, pp. 300-74. See also UNRWA, *UNRWA, Past Present and Future* (Vienna, 1986); Sayigh, Y., *The Implications of UNRWA Operations* (Beirut, 1952); Viorst, Milton, *UNRWA and Peace in the Middle East* (Washington, 1984); Buehrig, Edward H., *The United Nations and the Palestine Refugees* (Bloomington, 1971); Forsythe, David, 'UNRWA, the Palestinian refugees and world politics', *International Organizations*, 25, Winter 1971, and 'The Palestine question: dealing with a long-term refugee situation', *Annals of the American Academy of Political and Social Sciences*, 467, May 1983; and Adelman, Howard, 'Palestine refugees, economic integration and durable solutions', in Bramwell, Anna (ed.), *Refugees in the Age of Total War* (London, 1988).

7  A measure of UNRWA's success its the reduction of infant mortality among refugees in the West Bank from 173 deaths per thousand live births in the early 1950s, to roughly 35 per thousand by the late 1980s.

8  In 1956 girls represented only 26 per cent of UNRWA school enrolment. By the 1980s it had reached 49 per cent: UNRWA, *UNRWA: Past, Present and Future*, p. 9.

9  George McGhee to US Congress, House Committee on Foreign Affairs, 81st congress, 2nd session, *Hearings on Palestine Refugees*, 16 February 1950, p. 9, quoted in Loescher, *Beyond Charity*, p. 61.

10  On the Jordan waters issue, see Stevens, Georgiana Stevens, *The Jordan River Partition* (Stanford, 1965); on the Nile/Sinai schemes see Brand, *Palestinians in the Arab World*, p. 49; also a brief description of the resettlement schemes, UNRWA, *UNRWA: Past Present and Future*. For earlier resettlement plans, see Pappé, *The Making of the Arab-Israeli Conflict*, pp. 250-1.

11  Quoted by Brand, *Palestinians in the Arab World*, p. 8.

12  Brand, *Palestinians in the Arab World*, pp. 28-9, and Cobban, Helena, *The Palestinian Liberation Organisation* (London, 1984), p. 29.

13  For an account of Fatah and the career of Yasir Arafat, see Gowers, Andrew, and Walker, Tony, *Behind the Myth: Yasser Arafat and the Palestinian Revolution* (London, 1990); on the PLO more generally, Gresh, Alain, *The PLO – The Struggle Within* (London, 1985); Cobban, *The Palestinian Liberation Organisation*.

14  *International Documents on Palestine*, 1967, quoted in Cobban, *The Palestinian Liberation Organisation*, p. 52.

15  The DFLP was protected from PFLP punishment by Fatah. Naif Hawatma hails from an East Bank Christian bedouin tribe.

16  Cobban, *The Palestinian Liberation Organisation*, p. 52.

17  For a brief account of the Lebanon's ordeal, and the Palestinian part in it, see McDowall, David, *Lebanon: A Conflict of Minorities*, (London, 1983, 1986).

18  The Palestine National Charter called for an end to the 'Zionist entity' and states (Article 6): 'The Jews who had normally resided in Palestine until the beginning of the Zionist invasion will be considered Palestinians.' The obvious inference was that all other Jews in Palestine could not be considered Palestinians. Arafat's speech, however, implied that the PLO was willing to recognize the legitimacy of all Jews in Palestine *if* Israel would

recognize the same legitimacy for the Palestinian people including those it had made refugees.

19 This was the Saad Haddad militia, established in 1976. Following Saad Haddad's death in 1983 the militia was renamed the South Lebanon Army, under the command of General Antoine Lahad but in practice it was an arm of the IDF.

20 Cobban, *The Palestinian Liberation Organisation*, p. 96.

21 Abu Nidal's Fatah Revolutionary Council was the PLO's mortal foe, already responsible for assassinating PLO diplomats around the world. For more on this organization, see Seale, Patrick, *Abu Nidal: A Gun for Hire* (London, 1993).

22 Kahan Commission Report, *Jerusalem Post*, 9 February 1983, p. 7.

23 Massacres in Nabaa, Maslakh-Qarantina and Tal al-Zaatar camps/slum areas. It was a Phalangist massacre of 27 Palestinian footballers in a bus that had finally triggered the civil war in April 1975.

24 Sayigh, R., *Too Many Enemies: The Palestinian Experience in Lebanon*,(London, 1994), p. 122. There has been a persistent suspicion that some of Saad Haddad's men, too, were involved.

25 Following a popular outcry, the Israeli government agreed to hold a Commission of Enquiry. The (Kahan) Commission Report accepted the justification for entry into West Beirut 'to preserve quiet...otherwise there might have been pogroms'. Yet there was only one group likely to commit pogroms, namely the Phalangists whose leader Bashir Gemayel had just been assassinated, and who were fiercely anti-Muslim and anti-Palestinian. Of all their enemies, the Phalangists hated the Palestinians most. This was well known to Israel's commanders, as the report bears out. Why then did Israeli commanders introduce the Phalange specifically into Palestinian refugee camps? Why, given reports of 2,000 terrorists at large, were only 150 Phalangists sent into Sabra/Shatila? The implication is that they did not expect to encounter serious opposition. The report found Israeli senior officers only 'indirectly' responsible yet, in the words of the Israeli critic Uri Avneri, 'When you put a poisonous snake into a cradle and the baby dies of snake bites, there is no need to prove that the person who let in the snake wanted the baby to die. He who denies the intention bears the burden of proof.'

26 Essential reading on the whole siege, quoting the specific US undertaking (and admission of failure) is Khalidi, Rashid, *Under Siege: PLO Decision-making During the 1982 War* (New York, 1986).

27 The Lebanese police produced figures on a district-by-district basis, totalling just under 19,000.

28 Khalid al-Hassan, quoted in Cobban, *The Palestinian Liberation Organisation*, p. 61.

29 *International Documents on Palestine*, p. 449, quoted in Cobban, *The Palestinian Liberation Organisation*, p. 62.

30 *Life*, 12 June 1970, p. 33, in McDowall, *Palestine and Israel*, p. 201.

31 After the Larnaca killings, Israel bombed the PLO Headquarters in Tunis, killing both Palestinians and Tunisians and demonstrating that it, too, was prepared to flout international norms of behaviour.

32 Rashidiya was subject to fierce seiges, but Burj al-Shamali and Bass, both less easily defensible, surrendered to Amal control virtually without a struggle.

33 For an account of the ordeal of Sabra/Shatila, see Sayigh, *Too Many Enemies*.

## Chapter 7
## Under Israeli occupation, 1967–87

1 See Chapter 4, note 1.
2 For an account, see Grossman, David, *The Yellow Wind* (London 1988), Chapter 13.
3 Israel initially disregarded the Hague Regulations on the grounds that they were not framed to cover such an occupation, which was *sui generis*. Later it accepted a Supreme Court ruling that it was engaged in a military occupation governed by customary international law. In the first flush of victory it had recognized the Fourth Geneva Convention, but soon realized this would inhibit its freedom of action, and withdrew recognition (Military Order No. 3 of 7 June 1967, Article 35). It rejects applicability by the argument that Article 2 of the Convention means that the Convention only has validity where the occupied territory has a legitimate sovereign. It claimed the territories occupied were 'disputed'. No other contracting party accepted this argument.
4 The following articles are relevant: nos 31, 32, 33, 49, 50, 64, 71, 72, 76, 78. Israeli acts also contravene Hague Convention (1907), Articles 23, 43, 46, 48, 49, 50, 55, 56.
5 Easily the best general treatment is Shehadeh, Raja, *Occupier's Law: Israel and the West Bank* (Washington, 1985), but see also the publications of al-Haq (Law in the Service of Man), Ramallah.
6 Shehadeh, *Occupier's Law*, p. 113.
7 Shehadeh, *Occupier's Law*, p. 77.
8 Grossman, *The Yellow Wind*, Chapter 7.
9 This violates the Hague Convention (Art. 55), which specifically charges the occupying power to be only the 'administrator and usufructuary' of state property. See also Lehn, with Davis, *The Jewish National Fund*, Chapter 5.
10 Shehadeh, *Occupier's Law*, pp. 84–90.
11 Shehadeh, *Occupier's Law*, pp. 98–99.
12 Or it may be that the victim is merely a relative of an absent, alleged troublemaker, for example as the author witnessed in al Shati camp, Gaza, December 1989. For a documented case, see Grossman, *The Yellow Wind*, p. 16.
13 Palestine Human Rights Campaign, *Israeli Settler Violence in the Occupied Territories, 1980-1984* (Chicago, 1985); see also *The Karp Report, an Israeli Government Inquiry into Settler Violence Against Palestinians on the West Bank* (Washington, 1984). The Israeli government only published the report after Judge Judith Karp had resigned in protest at the government's failure to respond to her findings.
14 Interrogators exploit the sexual mores and shame/honour codes of Palestinian society, and therefore have subjected Palestinian women to sexual harrassment, or the threat of it, or actual abuse. They know that once a woman's reputation is compromised, it brings shame on her whole family. The threat of rape (in the case of a man, of his wife, sister or daughter) is an efficient way to create a cadre of informers: see Thornhill, Teresa (ed.), *Making Women Talk* (London, 1992).
15 See, for example, Aziz, Fuad, and Shehadeh, Raja, *Israeli Proposed Road Plan for the West Bank, A Question for the International Court of Justice* (Ramallah,

1984), and on the more general issue of land use planning, Rishmawi, Muna, *Planning in Whose Interest? Land Use Planning as a Strategy for Judaization* (Ramallah, 1986).

16 It did this by distorting the definition of state land under Ottoman land laws which require any occupier to be 'usufructuary' of public property, i.e. not to alienate such property from the indigenous population.

17 Goldblum, Amiram, *The Real Map,* Peace Now report no. 5 (Jerusalem, November 1992), pp. 21, 23.

18 Goldblum, *The Real Map,* p. 3.

19 Goldblum, *The Real Map,* p. 6.

20 Goldblum, *The Real Map,* p. 24.

21 In fact, discounting East Jerusalem, the settlers are barely 6 per cent of the West Bank and Gaza populations: Goldblum, *The Real Map,* pp. 5, 29, 36.

22 It is well known that since the *Altalena* affair (between the Haganah and Irgun) in the summer of 1948, government troops have never shot Jews.

23 Military Order no. 158, 1 October 1967. No water installation was allowed without a licence from the military commander. After 1967 there were only five cases of Palestinians being allowed to sink new (and minor) wells.

24 In 1992 Arab per capita domestic consumption was allowed for at an average of 35 cubic metres yearly. The allowed for level of Jewish consumption is over 100 cubic metres. A combined agricultural and domestic consumption for the average Israeli settler is something between 14,000-28,000 cubic metres, while for the average Gazan it is 200 cubic metres: Goldblum, *The Real Map,* p. 5; Roy, Sara, *The Gaza Strip Survey* (Jerusalem, 1986), p. 51.

25 Another reason is the rocky nature of much of the terrain: Goldblum, *The Real Map,* p. 27.

26 There was also the question of high transport costs, fraud in Amman and a high level of spoilage at the Allenby Bridge waiting for Israeli security clearance.

27 Benvenisti, Meron, *The West Bank Data Base Project Report 1986: Demographic, Economic, Legal, Social and Political Developments in the West Bank* (Jerusalem, 1986), p. 10, and Roy, *The Gaza Strip,* p. 58.

28 Benvenisti, Meron, *The West Bank Handbook* (Jerusalem, 1986), p. 96.

29 See, for example, *The Financial Times,* 4 March 1987; *Middle East International,* no. 292, 20 February 1987.

30 Workers from the territories must not be inside Israel between 1 a.m. and 4 a.m. Nevertheless many did so with the connivance of their employers, though running the risk of detection and heavy fines. Harassment during legal hours, however, is frequent and widespread: Benvenisti, *1986 Report,* p. 13.

31 The start of this process, which resulted from global recession and low oil prices, was marked by the Suq al-Manakh crisis in Kuwait, when widespread corruption and highly speculative dealing on the Kuwait stock market became publicly known.

32 Benevenisti, *1986 Report,* p. 19; *1987 Report* (Jerusalem, 1987), p. 11; Roy, *The Gaza Strip Survey,* p. 76.

Notes and references

## Chapter 8
## Resistance and the *intifada*

1 Both had grounds for nervousness, quite apart from PLO activity. The Muslim religious leadership and a group of leftists tried to organize a National Guidance Committee in 1967, but this was quickly smashed by Israel: McDowall, *Palestine and Israel*, p. 285, n. 9.
2 This suppression was achieved by ruthless measures, the bulldozing of refugee shelters to cut wide swathes whereby the camps could be physically controlled, and the smashing of PFLP cells by the torture of captive members of the resistance.
3 Because the Communist Party had been proscribed under Jordanian rule it already had an underground network dating back before 1967. Indeed, it was because it was the only underground network that the PLO used it. The Communists soon found themselves exploited by the PLO, and in the end the PLO tried to replace the Patriotic Front with a right-wing alternative of its own: McDowall, *Palestine and Israel*, p. 99. It is worth noting that the Communist Party was the only Palestinian group that in 1947 had (reluctantly) accepted the partition of Palestine.
4 It also introduced a 'civil administration', implying that the Territories were no longer under military occupation but were integral to Israel.
5 McDowall, *Palestine and Israel*, p. 101.
6 Tamari Salim, 'In league with Zion: Israel's search for a native pillar', *Journal of Palestine Studies*, vol. xii, no. 4, Summer 1983.
7 Essential reading on the popular movement is Hilterman, Joost, *Behind the Intifada: Labor and Women's Movements in the Occupied Territories* (Princeton, 1991).
8 Tamari, Salim, 'The Palestinian demand for independence cannot be postponed indefinitely', *MERIP Reports*, nos 100-1, October-December 1981, pp. 32-3, quoted in Hilterman, *Behind the Intifada*, p. 4.
9 AWA was active hiding escaped prisoners, demonstrating, writing for the nationalist press. From its inception it pressed for equal educational opportunities for girls. AWA showed imaginative flair.
10 Union of Palestinian Medical Relief Committees, *Twenty Years of Occupation: An Overview of Health Conditions and Services in the Israeli-Occupied Territories* (Jerusalem, 1987).
11 These were the Palestinian Women's Action Committees (DFLP); Palestinian Working Women's Committees (CP), Palestinian Women's Committees (PFLP) and the Women's Committee for Social Work (Fatah).
12 Certainly it was the Communist-affiliated women's committee that co-operated with UPMRC to bring health services to villages and camps.
13 The following publications of al-Haq/Law in the Service of Man since 1984 reflect the increasingly adverse conditions in this period: Playfair, Emma, *Administrative Detention* (Ramallah, 1986); Hilterman, Joost, *Israel's Deportation Policy in the Occupied West Bank and Gaza Strip* (Ramallah, 1986); Playfair, Emma, *Demolition and Sealing of Houses as a Punitive Measure in the Israeli-Occupied West Bank* (Ramallah, 1987); Hunt, Paul, *Justice? The Military Court System in the Israeli-Occupied Territories* (Ramallah and Gaza, 1987).
14 In November 1987 an Arab League summit put the Palestine question at the bottom of its agenda from the first time since 1948; the summit host,

King Hussein personally welcomed all heads of state with the notable exception of Arafat. Meanwhile, Syria unsuccessfully presented a conference resolution which omitted the PLO as a participant in any future international peace conference.

15  McDowall, *Palestine and Israel*, p. 2.
16  *The Guardian*, 19 January 1988.
17  *The Observer*, 24 January 1988.
18  Before the facts of the case had been established the army had demolished thirteen homes, and expelled six villagers from the Occupied Territories: McDowall, *Palestine and Israel*, p. 14.
19  *Middle East International*, no. 335, 7 October 1988.
20  *Israel and Palestine* (Paris), no. 144, September 1988, individual cases cited.
21  UNLU communiqués are reproduced in translation in Lockman, Zachary, and Beinin, Joel, *Intifada: The Palestinian Uprising Against Occupation* (Washington, 1989, and London, 1990), and in FACTS Information Committee, *Towards a State of Independence: The Palestinian Uprising, December 1987-August 1988* (Jerusalem, 1988).
22  100,000 dunums of Israeli woodland were burnt that summer, but it is difficult to say how much was caused by arsonists. *Middle East International* no. 328, 25 June 1988, and *al-Hadaf Newsletter*, 7, July 1988, indicated that some of the fires were the result of hot summer winds, a major accident during army training, and the inadvertent spread of fire from burning garbage.
23  *Jerusalem Post International*, 31 March 1990; *The Other Israel*, March-April 1988.
24  Sources on the Islamic revival in Palestine: Jarbawi, Ali, 'Hamas: the Muslim Brotherhood's entry to political legitimacy', and Haydari, Nabil, 'The PLO and the Hamas movement: a struggle for influence', *Mujallat al-Dirasat al-Filastiniya*, Winter 1993; Abu Amr, Ziad, 'Hamas: a historical and political background', *Journal of Palestine Studies*, vol. xxii, no. 4, Summer 1993; Kristianasen-Levitt, Wendy, in *Le Monde Diplomatique*, February 1994.
25  The Muslim Brotherhood was founded by an Egyptian, Hasan al-Banna, in 1928. In 1945 the Ikhwan opened branches in Palestine.
26  One might wonder why a separate organization was established. Al-Mujamma' and the Ikhwan were hedging their bets, in case Hamas or the *intifada* failed, they would be able to continue their social activities hopefully without an odour of failure or Israeli reprisals.
27  Satloff, Robert, 'Islam in the Palestinian uprising', *Orbis*, vol. 33, no. 3, Summer 1989, pp. 403-22, quoted in Haydari, 'The PLO and the Hamas movement'.

*Chapter 9*
**The 1990s: Palestine lost or regained?**

1  Kuwait was the home of two major development funds, the Arab Fund for Economic and Social Development and the Kuwait Fund. Both discharged large sums of money for development, both in the Arab world and further afield. They compared very creditably with the miserly performance of most industrialized countries, but in the light of the enormous oil wealth generated and the rhetoric of pan-Arab solidarity, the aid level was widely

deemed to be derisory.

2  Many also were not. Those villages which were poorly represented in the Gulf tended to derive their income almost entirely from the provision of cheap labour for the Israeli economy.

3  Brand, *Palestinians in the Arab World*, pp. 118-22.

4  These were documented by Amnesty International and Human Rights Watch (Middle East).

5  British Refugee Council, *Gulf Information Project*, September 1991 and January 1994.

6  Egypt feared Israel would deny many re-admittance to the Gaza Strip, and would then be unable to return them to Kuwait.

7  See *Middle East International*, no. 385, 14 September 1990.

8  It had been agreed at the end of the war that Syria and Egypt would provide forces to assist the long-term protection of Kuwait and Saudi's northern borders. Now the Gulf countries made it clear they preferred Western troops, by implication distrusting their fellow Arabs.

9  Memory of the bitter conflict between the Hashemites and the House of Ibn Saud earlier in the century was revived.

10  UNSCR 672, 673.

11  Indeed, it contrasted with the warning Iraq received in September 1990 that those who committed grave breaches (i.e. war crimes) incurred international responsibility under the Geneva Conventions, and the call upon all UN members to pass evidence of such breaches to the UN Secretary General. Never did Israel receive a similar warning.

12  This difficulty existed at two levels. At the institutional level, Syria considered itself, after the Egypt-Israel Peace Treaty of 1979, as Arab leader versus Israel. It demanded but did not receive PLO obedience to this position. Secondly there was a longstanding personal animosity between the shrewd and pragmatic Asad and the mercurial Arafat.

13  As adumbrated, for example, in the US Declaration of Independence, Jefferson's Inaugural Speech and Lincoln's Address at Gettysburg.

14  As the Israeli peace worker Simha Flapan had written in 1987: 'One of Israel's most serious failings was its stubborn refusal to consider the Palestinians themselves as a partner to the negotiations, a position that has been steadfastly maintained to this day and that remains, after Camp David [1979] as well as before, the crux of the problem.' (Flapan, *The Birth of Israel*, p. 215.)

15  Palestine Human Rights Information Centre published a report alleging that several young males aged between 14 and 23 had been subject to such torture, *Middle East International*, no. 415, 20 December 1991. In February 1992 a 35-year-old Palestinian died as a result of torture in custody. Mustafa Akawi was arrested on 21 January 1992 and his family informed of his death on 3 February. The family obtained the services of Dr Michael Baden of the New York State Forensic Science Unit to conduct an autopsy. His report concluded: 'The emotional pressure, physical exertion, the low temperatures he was forced to withstand, and lack of proper medical care caused Akawi's heart attack and death. His body showed evidence of multiple injuries sustained while in custody': *Middle East International*, no. 419, 21 February 1992. Other cases were reported during 1993 of deaths in custody by the Gaza Centre for Rights and Law in its monthly bulletins. Regarding the torture of women, see Thornhill, *Making Women Talk*.

16 In 1987 the Landau Commission had reported that Shabak (the General Security Services) routinely tortured Palestinian detainees. It recommended *against* prosecution of torturers, and accepted the legitimacy of 'a moderate amount of force' and 'non-violent psychological pressure'. It is difficult to avoid the conclusion that while admitting torture went on, the Landau Commission's recommendations constituted a remit for continued torture, since no Shabak operative was likely to be deterred from conducting business as usual.

17 This loophole in the loan conditions contradicted UN Security Council Resolution 726 of 6 January 1992 which reaffirmed the applicability of the Fourth Geneva Convention to the occupied territory, *including* East Jerusalem.

18 *Middle East International*, no. 451, 28 May 1993.

19 *Middle East International*, no. 436, 23 October 1992.

20 It was symptomatic of its desperate straits that at Bir Zeit salaries were being paid two months in arrears, and that funding was withdrawn from the Palestinian daily *al-Sha'b*.

21 Between summer 1992 and April 1993 21 operations were carried out, 17 of them in the Gaza Strip in which a total of 121 buildings were either completely destroyed or seriusly damaged. For example, in a single operation in Khan Yunis (Gaza Strip) involving 18 houses, 98 people were rendered homeless by the total destruction of 12 homes, and an estimated $725,000 worth of damage inflicted. The rationale for such operations is the apprehension of 'wanted' suspects without risk to troops. In fact in only two out of the 21 cases were such arrests made, suggesting such measures are more to do with pacification. In several cases bystanders or those surrendering in the required manner have been shot dead; see Taylor, Tom, *Missiles and Dynamite* (Ramallah, 1993), pp. 4, 7.

22 'Rabin is responsible for the worst year in Gaza human rights conditions so far': Gaza Centre for Rights and Law (GCRL), *Monthly Bulletin for June*, 4 July 1993.

23 The monthly bulletins of the Gaza Centre for Rights and Law make essential but dismaying reading, reporting cases of children under 10 being wantonly, callously and unjustifiably shot. In one disturbing case a 49-year-old woman was knocked down by a jeep which then drove over her body three times. She was sole provider for eight children: GCRL, *Monthly Bulletin for October 1993*, 7 November 1993.

24 *Al-Quds*, 3 March 1993.

25 GCRL, *Monthly Bulletin for June*, 4 July 1993.

26 These leading Palestinians were Hanan Ashrawi, Saeb Erakat, Haidar Abd al-Shafi and Faysal al-Husayni, all of whom were openly critical of the way negotiations were going.

27 For an elaboration of this argument, and the rationale behind it, see Kyle and Peters, *Whither Israel?*, in particular Chapters 1, 4 and 13.

28 The United States now had to swallow its embarrassment. Having so enthusiastically embraced Israel's long-standing refusal to recognize the PLO, it now found itself publicly hosting a man it had branded for many years as a terrorist leader.

29 *Middle East International*, no. 458, 10 September 1993.

30 Peres' desire as Foreign Minister to advance the process of direct negotiation contrasted with his previous position. In the first years of the occupa-

tion he supported the Land of Israel settlement movement in the Territories; in 1984-5 he had initiated the toughest crackdown on the Territories since 1972; in 1986 he had called for Palestinian 'self-expression' but dismissed the idea of free elections in the Territories as an opportunity for terrorists, and he had been unwilling to meet Arafat in 1986; see McDowall, *Palestine and Israel*, pp. 103, 209, 244, and his address at Chatham House, 22 January 1986.

31  *Middle East International*, no. 459, 24 September 1993.
32  The ideological position is set out by Leiter, Yechiel, *Peace to Resist* (Jerusalem, 1993).
33  On 30 June 1993 the Clinton administration had implied its endorsement of the 'disputed' definition.
34  Most laws and military orders introduced since 1967 have no substantive legality under the Fourth Geneva Convention. Article IX of the Declaration implicitly conceded their legitimacy by conceding a joint review of these laws and military orders. It also implied Israel's *de jure* legitimacy throughout the Territories, and thus the implicit legality of its settlements.
35  Al-Haq, *A Human Rights Assessment of the Declaration of Principles on Interim Self-Government Arrangements for Palestinians* (Ramallah, 1993). The argument regarding the Territories remaining occupied centres on Israeli control of boundaries and all external relations, and on its exclusion of certain territory and Jewish settlements from the remit of the Palestinian authority. In other words, withdrawal had only partially taken place.
36  *Middle East International*, no. 467, 21 January 1994.
37  Support for the agreement now fell to 41 per cent, opposition rose to 38 per cent: *Le Monde Diplomatique*, February 1994.
38  The PLO argued that 'the Jericho area' meant the Jordanian adminstrative district of Jericho, Israel insisted it meant only Jericho town.
39  The author of this report was subsequently detained and his colleagues believe that at the time of writing he is being tortured, as he has been before: *Middle East International*, no. 478, 24 June 1994.
40  *Middle East International*, no. 470, 4 March 1994.
41  *Middle East International*, no. 474, 29 April 1994.
42  In the June 1994 elections at al-Najah University, for example, the Hamas-led Rejectionists took 47 per cent of the vote, compared with Fatah's 48 per cent.
43  Undated declaration. Signatories included Haidar Abd al-Shafi, Gabi Baramki, Mustafa Barghouti, Ghassan al-Khatib, Samir Abd Allah, Iyad Sarraj, Raja Shehadeh and Raji Sourani.

*Chapter 10*
**A nation in the making: the Palestinians today**

1  Figures taken from Hallaj, Muhammad, 'Palestinian refugees and the peace process', *Middle East International*, no. 462, 5 November 1993.
2  See Barghouti, Mustafa, and Daibes, Ibrahim, *Infrastructure and Health Services in the West Bank: Guidelines for Health Care Planning* (Ramallah, 1993), pp. 13-24, which makes this estimate after careful study of the existing literature.
3  Jews outside Israel are likely to decline from 9.3 million in 1987 to 8 million by 2000 on account of high assimilation and low birth rates (well

below replenishment level) in diaspora Jewry: McDowall, *Palestine and Israel*, p. 169.

4  Statistics from Prior, Michael, 'Living or dead stones: the future of Christians in the Holy Land' (mimeograph, n.d.).

5  McDowall, *Palestine and Israel*, p. 152.

6  Quranic verses and Islamic phrases were liberally scattered through UNLU communiques.

7  Ramallah still has a large Christian community. Hamas more predictably won the student council elections at Gaza and Hebron universities.

8  In December 1993 Fatah still enjoyed 42.2 per cent of popular support, the largest single faction, compared with 12.6 per cent for Hamas: *Le Monde Diplomatique*, February 1994. Yet it should be noted that it was only a whisker behind Fatah in the al-Najah university election in May 1994.

9  Ma'mur al-Hudaybi, Cairo, 3 May 1992, quoted in Abu Amr, Ziad, 'Hamas: a historical and political background'.

10  The West Bank follows Jordan's Personal Status Law of 1976, which is guided by the Hanafi school of jurisprudence, arguably the most liberal of the four law schools but still one that offers women inferior treatment. For a helpful discussion on the legal status of Palestinian women, see Wing, Adrien Katherine, 'Custom, religion and rights: the future legal status of Palestinian women', *Harvard International Law Journal*, vol. 35, no. 1, Winter 1994. More generally, see Mayer, Ann Elizabeth, *Islam and Human Rights: Tradition and Politics* (Boulder and San Francisco, 1991).

11  Mayer, *Islam and Human Rights*, pp. 123-7; Cervenak, 'Promoting inequality', p. 355.

12  Two good written challenges to patriarchy and its effect on women and society more generally are Saadawi, Nawal, *The Hidden Face of Eve* (London, 1980), and Sharabi, Hisham, *Neopatriarchy: A Theory of Distorted Change in Arab Society* (New York and Oxford, 1988).

13  As in Christianity, it is possible to interpret Holy Writ either in a discriminatory or a liberal manner according to the lights of the reader.

14  For a discussion of women in the *intifada*, see Giacaman, Rita, and Johnson, Penny, 'Palestinian women: building barricades and breaking barriers', in Lockman and Beinin, *Intifada: the Palestinian Uprising Against Israeli Occupation*.

15  Fatah, PFLP, DFLP and the Communist (People's) Party: Holt, Maria, *Half the People: Women, History and the Palestinian Intifada* (East Jerusalem, 1992).

16  Ramsden, Sally and Senker, Cath, *Learning the Hard Way: Palestinian Education in the West Bank, Gaza Strip and Israel* (London, 1993).

17  For a useful discussion of women's legal and human rights status generally under Islam, see Mayer, *Islam and Human Rights*, Chapters 5 and 6.

18  For a statement of Islamic views, see Jarrar, Shaykh Bassam, 'Ruwiya wa mustaqbal 'alaqat al-harakat al-islamiya bi'l sultat al-intiqaliya', in Jerusalem Media and Communications Center (JMCC), *Tahdiyat al-marhallat al-intiqaliya li'l mujtama' al-filastini* (Jerusalem, 1994), pp. 169-73.

19  FAFO, *Survey of Living Conditions* (Oslo, 1992).

20  Though it is noteworthy that with the 1994 Israeli redeployment, women 'repossessed' a stretch of beach in Gaza and the wearing of the *hijab* declined.

21  Women have protested vehemently regarding this draft constitution.

22 Under the auspices of al-Haq there is a programme 'Women, Justice and Law' to stimulate debate at the grassroots level on the following themes: (1) civil and poliical rights, (2) family/personal status law, (3) health, (4) education, (5) labour, (6) protection from violence.

23 This is well argued in Wing, 'Custom, religion and rights: the future status of Palestinian women'.

24 For a good description, see Giacaman, Rita, *Life and Health in Three Palestinian Villages* (London and Atlantic Highlands, 1988), Chapter 7.

25 The government of Israel says the level is half this, 22 per thousand in the West Bank and 26 per thousand in the Gaza Strip, but these figures are based only upon reported deaths: Save the Children Fund (SCF), *Growing Up with Conflict* (London 1992).

26 SCF, *Growing Up with Conflict*, p. 33.

27 For a vivid description, see Giacaman, *Life and Health in Three Palestinian Villages*, p. 121.

28 SCF, *Growing Up with Conflict*, p. ii; see also the reports of the Palestine Human Rights Information Center, Jerusalem.

29 SCF, *Growing Up with Conflict*, pp. 36-7.

30 UNICEF, *Summary of Study of Student Achievement in Jordan and the West Bank: A Comparative Perspective* (Jerusalem, 1993), cited in Ramsden and Senker, *Learning the Hard Way*, p. 11.

31 These are: Bir Zeit, near Ramallah (1972); Bethelehem (1973); Hebron (1972); the Islamic University, Gaza (1978); al-Najah, Nablus (1977); al-Quds, Jerusalem (1978); al-Azhar, Gaza (1978).

32 This was particularly true of Bir Zeit, a small village off the main Ramallah-Nablus road. Nationalist demonstrations there may have been defiant, but in no arguable sense did they cause disorder. It was Israeli troops shooting at students, and sometimes killing them, that caused the real mayhem on campus.

33 UNESCO reckoned at elementary level: 10 per cent, and at intermediate (12-14 years) 35 per cent in Gaza, 53 per cent in the West Bank: Ramsden and Shenker, *Learning the Hard Way*, p. 17.

34 Barghouti and Daibes, *Infrastructure and Health Services in the West Bank*, p. xviii.

35 McDowall, *Palestine and Israel*, p. 113.

36 UNICEF, *The Situation of Palestinian children in the West Bank and Gaza Strip* (Jerusalem, 1992).

37 In 1993 UPMRC treated 400,000 patients, at a cost of $5 per head. UPMRC operates thirty-one centres in the West Bank and Gaza, eleven rehabilitation projects for the disabled covering eighty villages, twenty-seven women's health clinics, eleven laboratories, a large health education programme and health worker training, information from Dr Mustafa Barghouti.

38 UNRWA/WHO figure, in World Bank, *Developing the Occupied Territories*, vol. vi, June 1993, p. 30.

39 For a discussion within the context of disability world-wide, see Coleridge, Peter, *Disability, Liberation and Development* (Oxford, 1993), pp. 170-86.

40 By 1992 eleven in the West Bank and four in the Gaza Strip: Coleridge, *Disability, Liberation and Development*, p. 180.

41 A key means of doing this in urban areas may be by developing 'dry' toilets, already being introduced in other countries. This would reduce a

major area not only of water waste but also of ground water pollution.

42  See PLO's *Programme for the Development of the Palestinian National Economy for the years 1994-2000* (Tunis, 1993).

43  Roy, Sara, 'Gaza, new dynamics of civic disintegration', *Journal for Palestine Studies*, vol. xxii, no. 4, Summer 1993.

44  Roy, 'Gaza: new dynamics', p. 21.

45  Roy, 'Gaza: new dynamics', p. 21. In the West Bank food aid had to be extended to an even greater number, 165,000 families.

46  Roy, 'Gaza: new dynamics', p. 28.

47  Roy, 'Gaza: new dynamics', p. 25.

48  *Middle East International*, no. 459, 24 September 1993.

49  The issue of an authoritarian culture in the Arab world is an extremely serious one. See the work of the Palestinian scholar Sharabi, Hisham, *Neopatriarchy*.

50  Al-Haq, *A Human Rights Assessment*, p. 4.

51  Signatories included al-Haq, the Union of Medical Relief Committees, the Friends School Ramallah, and Muwatin (the Palestinian Institute for the Study of Democracy), a research and educational centre based in Ramallah, producing educational materials for schools and university use.

52  These included al-Haq, the Gaza Centre for Rights and Law, and Muwatin.


*Chapter 11*
**Palestine and Israel: in search of peace with justice**

1  'A new powerful group, "The Third Way" was officially formed on 5 June. This is, arguably, the most important political development in Israel since Menachem Begin won power in May 1977... the beginning of a very profound turn to the right in the Labour party': Haim Baram in *Middle East International*, no. 477, 10 June 1994.

2  This was in 1986, when there were an officially estimated 10,000 applicants for family reunion. Israel was criticized for dragging its feet on this issue when it was so vociferous about the right of family reunion in the case of Soviet Jews: *Jewish Chronicle*, 15 August 1986.
3No one knows the exact figure. Since Israel turned down the majority of applicants, and took a year to reach its decision in each case, many did not even bother to apply. The figure of 120,000 is the estimate of a member of the Multilateral Working Party on Refugees.

4  The conflict of 1970-1 remains an uncomfortable reminder of the political difference between East and West Bankers.

5  Of these, 131 families are from Nabatiya camp, destroyed by Israeli air action in 1974, 119 from Tal al-Za'atar, destroyed by the Phalangists in 1976, 300 from Burj al-Shamali and 120 from Rashidiya, both besieged by Amal in 1985, 75 from the coastal area running north from al-Bass camp, Tyre, and 35 from Jal al-Bahr; in addition there are 43 Lebanese families and another 56 families 'without nationality': memorandum of the Popular Committee for the Displaced People of Sikki, February 1994.

6  *Middle East International*, no. 475, 13 May 1994.

7  International Mission to Palestinian Refugee Camps, *Report* (10-19 April 1994), p. 2.

8  International Mission to Palestinian Refugee Camps, *Report*, p. 3.

9 For example, in International Mission to Palestinian Refugee Camps, *Report*, p. 3.

10 32,200 housing units at Reches Shu'afat west of French Hill, 200 units for Sha ar Mizrah; 2,500 units at Pisgat Ze'ev and 8,000 units at Har Homa, a large new settlement south of Jerusalem. Approximately another 6,000 units are planned in an outer ring around Arab Jerusalem; see *Challenge*, no. 22, September 1993.

11 The government specifies areas meriting development and investment privileges, top priority Zone A, lower priority Zone B. Jewish colonization of East Jerusalem falls within Zone A; see *Ha'aretz*, 3 December 1992, reproduced in Mansour, Awad, *Clever Concealment: Jewish Settlement in the Occupied Territories under the Rabin Government, August 1992-September 1992* (Jerusalem, 1994), p. 12.

12 *Jerusalem Post*, 29 June 1993, quoted in Mansour, *Clever Concealment*, p. 31.

13 In June 1994 Israel also indicated its desire to close longstanding Palestinian institutions in Jerusalem, most notably Orient House, the centre of the local Palestinian leadership. In stormy scenes in the Knesset, Foreign Minister Peres was embarrassed to admit that assurances had been given to the PLO via the United States that Orient House and similar Palestinian institutions in Jerusalem would not be closed down.

14 Porath, Yehoshua 'The awakening of the Palestinian Arabs', in Ma'oz, Moshe (ed.), *Studies on Palestine during the Ottoman Period* (Jerusalem, 1975), p. 354.

15 See for example the two similar regional compromise plans of the Jaffee Centre, Tel Aviv, and the Leonard Davies Institute, Jerusalem, summarized with maps in McDowall, *Palestine and Israel*, pp. 245-8.

16 Israel never even accepted UN observers being stationed on its side of the border.

17 *Jerusalem Post International*, 9 June 1990.

18 The doctrine of Limited Territorial Sovereignty aims at an equitable solution, compared with the notions of Absolute Limited Sovereignty and the Community of Riparian States. See Zarour, H., and Isaac, J., 'A novel approach to the allocation of international water resources', in Isaac and Shuval (eds), *Water and Peace in the Middle East* (Amsterdam, 1994), p. 391.

19 Jaradat, Muhammad, 'The water crisis in the southern West Bank' (Jerusalem, 1993), p. 6.

20 There is an enormous amount of work necessary. Israel has allowed the water systems of the Occupied Territories (as also in the Galilee) to fall into a wasteful state of disrepair, preventing Palestinian municipalities from overhauling local pipe systems (since this would allow the pipes to take greater water pressure and therefore a greater volume). In the case of Gaza, there is a deficit of 50 million cubic metres of water out of yearly consumption of 110 cubic metres. Overpumping has continued since 1967. The situation has been made much worse by Israel's digging of 20 deep wells on the east side of the Strip, and blocking of Wadi Gaza, thus intercepting winter run off and ground water moving into the Gaza Strip. In Gaza average consumption is 50 litres per day compared with 360 litres per settler; source: Gaza Water Resources Action Programme.

21 The two primary Palestinian population areas are the Galilee and the northern Negev. But even elsewhere things are changing. In Haifa, almost wholly evacuated by Arabs in 1948, there was a Palestinian minority of 5.7

per cent in 1980, which had increased to 8.2 per cent in 1986 and 10.6 per cent by 1992, thus doubling in about fifteen years: McDowall, *Palestine and Israel*, p. 227, and Central Bureau of Statistics, *Israel Statistical Abstract* (Jerusalem, 1993), p. 62.

*Chapter 12*
**Palestinian rights: the international agenda**

1  Britain, in its anxiety that membership of the European Community might otherwise strain its alliance with the United States, persuaded other EC members in 1974 that no Arab/Israeli initiative would be taken without first referring it to the United States as leader of the Western alliance.

2  As implicitly required by Article 1 of the Fourth Geneva Convention, and explicitly confirmed by the ICRC Commentary on the Convention: 'the proper working of the system of protection provided by the Convention demands in fact that the Contracting Parties should not be content merely to apply its provisions themselves, but should do everything in their power to ensure that the humanitarian principles underlying the Conventions are applied universally.' See also how Western governments ignored the requests of the UN Human Rights Commission, the Security Council and General Assembly to withhold aid until the Convention was complied with: Quigley, *Palestine and Israel: A Challenge to Justice*, pp. 216-17.

# SELECT BIBLIOGRAPHY

The bibliography of Palestine is immense. I have listed a selection of helpful books in reference to the themes of each chapter of this book, although many of those recommended are relevant to more than one chapter.

*General*
Gerner, D., *One Land, Two Peoples*, London, 1991.
Gilmour, David, *Dispossessed: The Ordeal of the Palestinians*, London, 1980.
Hirst, David, *The Gun and the Olive Branch: The Roots of Violence in the Middle East*, London, 1977.
Khalidi, Walid, *From Haven to Conquest*, Beirut, 1971.
Lacqueur, Walter, *The Israeli-Arab Reader*, London, 1969.
Lukacs, Yehuda, *The Israeli-Palestinian Conflict: A Documentary Record*, Cambridge, 1990.
McDowall, David, *Palestine and Israel: The Uprising and Beyond*, London, 1989.
Quigley, John, *Palestine and Israel: A Challenge to Justice*, Durham and London, 1990.
Said, Edward, *After the Last Sky*, London, 1986.
Said, Edward, *The Question of Palestine*, London, 1980.
Sayigh, Rosemary, *Palestinians: From Peasants to Revolutionaries*, London, 1979.

*Chapter 1*
**The Palestinians and early Zionism**
Antonius, George, *The Arab Awakening*, London, 1938.
Avineri, Shlomo, *The Making of Modern Zionism*, New York, 1981.
Graham-Brown, Sarah, *Palestinians and their Society 1880-1946*, London, 1980.
Gorny, Yosef, *Zionism and the Arabs, 1882-1948*, Oxford, 1987.
Kenyon, Kathleen, *Archaeology in the Holy Land*, London, 1979.
Kushner, D. (ed.), *Palestine in the Late Ottoman Period*, Oxford, 1986.

Le Strange, Guy, *Palestine under the Moslems: A Description of Syria and the Holy Land from* AD *650 to 1500*, London, 1890, Beirut, 1975.

Mandel, Neville, *The Arabs and Zionism Before World War 1*, Berkeley, Los Angeles and London, 1980.

Ma'oz, Moshe (ed.), *Studies on Palestine During the Ottoman Period*, Jerusalem, 1975.

Murphy-O'Connor, Jerome, *The Holy Land: An Archaeological Guide from Earliest Times to 1700*, Oxford, 1986.

Owen, Roger (ed.), *Studies in the Economic and Social History of Palestine in the Nineteenth and Twentieth Centuries*, London, 1982.

Scholch, Alexander, *Palestine in Transformation, 1856-1982*, Washington, 1993.

Smith, George Adam, *The Historical Geography of the Holy Land*, London, 1895.

*Chapter 2*
**British rule: 1917–48**

Flapan, Simha, *Zionism and the Palestinians, 1917-1947*, London, 1979.

Hurewitz, J.C., *The Struggle for Palestine*, New York, 1950.

Ingrams, Doreen, *Palestine Papers, 1917-1922: Seeds of Conflict*, London, 1972.

Kayyali, A.W., *Palestine: A Modern History*, London, 1979.

Lesch, Ann Mosely, *Arab Politics in Palestine, 1917-1939: The Frustration of a Nationalist Movement*, Ithaca, 1979.

Mattar, Philip, *The Mufti of Jerusalem: al-Hajj Amin al-Husayni and the Palestinian National Movement*, New York, 1988.

Porath, Yehoshua, *The Emergence of the Palestinian-Arab National Movement, 1918-1929*, London, 1974.

Porath, Yehoshua, *The Palestinian-Arab National Movement, 1929-1939*, London, 1977.

Stein, Kenneth W., *The Land Question in Palestine*, Chapel Hill, SC, and London, 1984.

Sykes, Christopher, *Crossroads to Israel: Palestine from Balfour to Bevin*, London, 1965.

Teveth, Shabtai, *Ben-Gurion and the Palestinian Arabs*, Oxford, 1985.

*Chapter 3*
**Partition and dispossession: 1947–9**

Abu-Lughod, Ibrahim (ed.), *The Transformation of Palestine*, Evanston, 1970.

Flapan, Simha, *The Birth of Israel: Myths and Realities*, London, 1987.

Hadawi, Sami, *Palestinian Rights and Losses in 1948*, London, 1988.

Khalidi, Walid, *All That Remains: The Palestinian Villages Occupied and Depopulated by Israel in 1948*, Washington, 1989.

Louis, Wm. Roger, and Stookey, Robert W. (eds.), *The End of the Palestine mandate*, London, 1986.

Masalha, Nur, *The Expulsion of the Palestinians: The Concept of 'Transfer' in Zionist Political Thought, 1882-1948*, Washington, 1992.

Morris, Benny, *The Birth of the Palestinian Refugee Problem, 1947-1949*, Cambridge, 1987.

Morris, Benny, *1948 and After: Israel and the Palestinians*, Oxford, 1990.

Nazzal, Nafez, *The Palestinian Exodus from Galilee, 1948*, Beirut, 1978.

Pappé, Ilan, *The Making of the Arab-Israeli Conflict, 1947-1951*, London, 1992.

Segev, Tom, *1949 – The First Israelis*, New York, 1986.

Shlaim, Avi, *Collusion across the Jordan*, Oxford, 1988.

## Chapter 4
### Deepening conflict: 1948–67

Burns, E.L.M., *Between Arab and Israeli*, London, 1962.

Chomsky, Noam, *The Fateful Triangle*, London, 1983.

Davis, John, *The Evasive Peace*, London, 1970.

Green, Stephen, *Taking Sides: America's Secret Relations with a Militant Israel, 1948-1967*, London, 1984.

Morris, Benny, *Israel's Border Wars, 1949-1956*, Oxford, 1993.

Rodinson, Maxime, *Israel and the Arabs*, London, 1968.

## Chapter 5
### The Palestinian Arabs inside Israel

Al-Haj, Majid, and Rosenfeld, Henry, *Local Arab Government in Israel*, Boulder, 1990.

El-Asmar, Fawzi, *To Be an Arab in Israel*, Beirut, 1978.

Firro, Kais, *A History of the Druzes*, Leiden, New York and Cologne, 1992.

Hareven, Alouph, *Every Sixth Israeli*, Jerusalem, 1983.

Jiryis, Sabri, *The Arabs in Israel, 1948-66*, Beirut, 1968.

Khalidi, Raja, *The Arab Economy in Israel: The Dynamics of a Region's Development*, London, 1988.

Kyle, Keith, and Peters, Joel, *Whither Israel? The Domestic Challenges*, London, 1993.

Lustick, Ian, *Arabs in the Jewish State: Israel's Control of a National Minority*, Austin, 1980.

Maddrell, Penny, *The Bedouin of the Negev*, London, 1990.

Minns, A., and Hijab, Nadia, *Citizens Apart: A Portrait of the Palestini-*

*ans in Israel*, London, 1990.

Scholch, Alexander (ed.), *Palestinians Over the Green Line*, London, 1983.

Smooha, Sammy, *Arabs and Jews in Israel: Conflicting and Shared Attitudes in a Divided Society*, Boulder, 1989.

Smooha, Sammy, *The Orientation and Politicization of the Arab Minority in Israel*, Haifa, 1984.

Yiftachel, Oren, *Planning a Mixed Region in Israel: The Political Geography of Arab-Jewish Relations in the Galilee*, Aldershot, 1992.

Zureik, Elia, *The Palestinians in Israel: A Study in Internal Colonialism*, London, 1979.

*Chapter 6*
### Exile and the rise of the national movement

Brand, Laurie A., *Palestinians in the Arab World*, New York and Oxford, 1988.

Buehrig, Edward H., *The United Nations and the Palestinian Refugees: A Study in Non-territorial Administration*, Bloomington, 1971.

Cobban, Helena, *The Palestinian Liberation Organisation*, Cambridge, 1984.

Cutting, P., *Children of the Siege*, London, 1988.

Giannou, C., *Besieged: A Doctor's Story of Life and Death in Beirut*, London, 1991.

Gowers, Andrew, and Walker, Tony, *Behind the Myth: Yasser Arafat and the Palestinian Revolution*, London, 1990.

Jansen, M., *The battle of Beirut: Why Israel Invaded Lebanon*, London, 1982.

Khalidi, Rashid, *Under Siege: PLO Decision Making in the 1982 War*, New York, 1986

Mishal, Shaul, *The PLO under Arafat: Between Gun and Olive Branch*, New Haven and London, 1986.

Sayigh, Rosemary, *Too Many Enemies: The Palestinian Experience in Lebanon*, London, 1994.

Sayigh, Y., *The Implications of UNRWA Operations*, Beirut, 1952.

Schiff, Z., and Ya'ari, E., *Israel's Lebanon War*, London, 1985.

UNRWA, *UNRWA, Past, Present and Future*, Vienna, 1986, mimeograph.

Viorst, Milton, *UNRWA and Peace in the Middle East*, Washington, 1984, revised edition 1989.

*Chapter 7*
### Under Israeli occupation, 1967–87

Abed, George (ed.), *The Palestinian Economy: Studies in Development under Prolonged Occupation*, London, 1988.

Arkadie, Brian van, *Benefits and Burdens: A Report on the West Bank and Gaza Strip Economies since 1967*, Washington, 1977.
Aruri, Naseer (ed.) *Occupation: Israel over Palestine*, London, 1984.
Benvenisti, Meron, *The West Bank Handbook*, Jerusalem, 1986.
Benvenisti, Meron, *The West Bank Data Base Project Report 1986: Demographic, Economic, Legal, Social and Political Developments in the West Bank*, Jerusalem, 1986 [and subsequent reports].
Cossali, Paul, and Robson, Clive, *Stateless in Gaza*, London, 1986.
Grossman, David, *The Yellow Wind*, London, 1988.
Khamsin, *Palestine: Profile of an Occupation*, London, 1989.
Ma'oz, Moshe, *Palestinian Leadership on the West Bank*, London, 1984.
Nakhleh, Khalil, and Zureik, Elia, *The Sociology of Palestinians*, London, 1980.
Palestine Human Rights Campaign, *Israeli Settler Violence in the Occupied Territories, 1980-84*, Chicago, 1985.
Roy, Sara, *The Gaza Strip Survey*, Jerusalem, 1986.
Shehadeh, Raja, *Occupier's Law: Israel and the West Bank*, Washington, 1985.
Shehadeh, Raja, *The Third Way: A Journal of Life in the West Bank*, London, Melbourne, New York, 1982.

*Chapter 8*
### Resistance and the *intifada*
Al-Haq, *Punishing a Nation: Human Rights Violations during the Palestinian Uprising, December 1987-December 1988*, Ramallah, 1989.
Hilterman, Joost, *Behind the Intifada*, Princeton, 1991.
Hunter, Robert, *The Palestinian Uprising: A War by Other Means*, London 1991.
Lockman, Zachary, and Beinin, Joel (eds.), *Intifada: The Palestinian Uprising Against Israeli Occupation*, Washington, 1989; London, 1990.
Peretz, Don, *Intifada: The Palestinian Uprising*, Boulder and San Francisco, London, 1990.
Schiff, Ze'ev, and Ya'ari, Ehud, *Intifada: The Palestinian Uprising – Israel's Third Front*, New York, 1989.

*Chapter 9*
### The 1990s: Palestine lost or regained?
Heller, Mark, and Nusseibeh, Sari, *No Trumpets, No Drums: A Two State Settlement of the Israeli-Palestinian Conflict*, London, 1991.
Khalidi, Walid, *Palestine Reborn*, London, 1993.

King, John, *Handshake in Washington: The Beginning of Peace?*, London, 1994.

Taylor, Tom, *Missiles and Dynamite: The Israeli Military Forces' Destruction of Homes with Anti-Tank Missiles and High-Powered Explosives*, Ramallah, 1993.


*Chapter 10*
**A nation in the making: the Palestinians today**

Augustin, Ebba, *Palestinian Women: Identity and Experience*, London, 1994.

Barghouti, Mustafa, and Daibes, Ibrahim, *Infrastructure and Health Services in the West Bank: Guidelines for Health Care Planning*, Ramallah, 1993.

Giacaman, Rita, *Life and Health in Three Palestinian Villages*, London and Atlantic Highlands, 1988.

Holt, Maria, *Half the People: Women, History and the Palestinian Intifada*, Jerusalem, 1992.

Najjar, Orayb Aref, *Portraits of Palestinian Women*, Salt Lake City, 1992.

Thornhill, Teresa (ed.), *Making Women Talk: The Interrogation of Palestinian Detainees*, London, 1992.

Warnock, Kitty, *Land before Honour: Palestinian Women in the Occupied Territories*, London, 1990.

World University Service, *Learning the Hard Way: Palestinian Education in the West Bank, Gaza Strip and Israel*, London, 1993.


*Chapter 11*
**Palestine and Israel: in search of peace with justice**

Heller, Mark, and Nusseibeh, Sari, *No Trumpets, No Drums: A Two State Settlement of the Israeli-Palestinian Conflict*, London, 1991.

Hurwitz, Deena (ed.), *Walking the Red Line*, Philadelphia, 1992.

Jaffee Center, *The West Bank and Gaza: Israel's Options for Peace*, Tel Aviv, 1989.

Khalidi, Walid, *Palestine Reborn*, London, 1993.

Lowi, Miriam, *Water and Power: The Politics of Scarce Resources in the Jordan River Basin*, Cambridge and New York, 1993.

Peters, Joel, *Building Bridges: The Arab-Israel Multilateral Talks*, London, 1994.

# INDEX

Abdallah, King of Transjordan, 26, 33
  assassination of, 34
Abd al-Shafi, Dr Haidar, 112, 124, 145
Abna al-Balad (Sons of the Land), 59
absentee landlords, 7, 10, 11
Absentee Property Law (1950), 46
Abu Nidal, 74
*Achille Lauro*, 77, 78
Acre, 5, 53
administrative detention, 83
Afula, 10, 123
agriculture, 56
  Palestinian, 88-89, 95, 98, 101
agricultural collectives: *see kibbutzim*
agricultural labour, 52-53, 65
airline hijacking, 76
Algeria, 131
Algiers, 98
Allon, General Yigal, 29
Amal militia, 78, 79
Amman, 34, 81, 82, 93, 99
anti-semitism, 8, 77
anti-Zionism, 12, 15, 17
apartheid laws, 157
Aqaba, 110
Arab Association for Human Rights, 60
Arab Democratic Party, 58
Arab–Israeli conflict, 34, 38, 40
Arab–Jewish relations, 34, 49, 157-58, 159
Arab League, 69, 73
Arab Legion, 26, 29, 34, 35

Arab Liberation Army (ALA), 25, 26
Arab Liberation Front, 71
Arab nationalism, 11, 34, 59, 71, 73
Arab states, 21
  acceptance of Israel, 39, 41, 117
  authoritarian, 146
  conservative, 71, 103
  disunity of, 107-8, 111
  Jews of, 41, 148
  and Palestine, 21-23, 24, 26, 65, 94-95
  and PLO, 70, 74, 94
  poor, 107
  and refugees, 32, 33, 38, 65, 68
Arab Women's Association (AWA), 96
Arab world, 69, 71, 146
Arabic language, 4, 60, 81
Arabs, 10, 152
  conquer Palestine, 3, 4-5
  cultural identity of, 13:
  *see also* Palestinians
Arad, 55-56
Arafat, Yasir, 1, 71, 103, 117
  and peace negotiations, 119, 120, 122, 128
  as PLO chairman, 70, 73-74, 75, 78
arbitrary arrests, 134
Ashkelon, 31, 118
Ashrawi, Hanan, 112, 124, 130
authoritarianism, 120, 146
autonomy plan, 1, 85, 94, 117, 120, 123, 146
Ayyubid dynasty, 5

Baghdad, 5
Balfour, Arthur, 13, 14
Balfour Declaration, 15, 164
Baransi, Salih, 50
bedouin, 5-6, 43, 47, 55, 60
   culture of, 6, 48
   expulsions of, 31, 35, 48, 49,
     50, 52
   resettlement of, 52-53, 55
   tribal rights of, 46-47
Beersheba, 31, 48, 54-55, 61
Begin, Menachem, 29
Beilin, Yossi, 118
Beirut, 5, 7, 10, 11, 63, 69, 72, 78-
   79
Beit Jibrin, 30
Beit Suhur, 102
Ben-Gurion, David, 23-24,
   and Arabs, 10, 19, 25, 26, 28,
     29, 45
Bernadotte, Count, 27
Bethlehem, 102
Bible, the, 6-7, 14
   and Zionism, 8, 10
Bir Zeit University, 112, 131
Black September, 76
British army, 21
British mandate for Palestine, 3, 5,
   13, 19-20
   Arab uprising in, 18-19, 21
   and Jewish settlement, 15-18,
     21
   land deeds issued, 46
   laws of, 50-51, 82, 84
   termination of, 21, 26, 28
British troops, 19
Bronze Age, the, 3
building permits, 56
Burj al-Barajna refugee camp, 78
Burj al-Shamali camp, 78
Bush, President George, 113

Cairo, 11, 38,
   peace agreement, 124, 164
Camp David Accords, 94, 98
Canaan, 3
car bombs, 95
Carmiel, 52, 54
Carter, President Jimmy, 73
central Europe, 21, 24
children, 133-35

Christian Palestinians, 1, 4, 7, 15,
   16, 127
   in Israel, 46, 127
Christianity, 4, 7
civil courts, 83
Clinton, President Bill, 114, 123,
   162
Cold War, the, 110, 161
collaborators, 102
collective punishment, 82, 164
colonization, 9-11, 13-15, 18
Committee on Arab Education, 57
Committee for the Defence of
   Arab Lands, 58
Committee of the Heads of Local
   Councils, 58, 59
Communist Party (Rakah), 58
Communists, 93, 95, 98: *see also*
   Palestine People's Party
construction industries, 53
co-operative action, 98
corruption, 83
Council for Palestinians, 118-19
criminal law, 83
Crusades, 5, 154
cultural societies, 103, 119
curfews, 50, 82, 123, 124
Curzon, Lord, 14
customary law, 82, 166

Damascus, 5
Darawsha, Abd al-Wahhab, 58
David, King of Israel, 3
Dayan, Moshe, 45
Declaration of Principles (DoP),
   60-61, 118, 124, 132, 146,
   156
   provisions of, 148, 155
Deir Yassin, 28-29
Defence (Emergency) Regulations
   (1945), 50-51, 84, 164
defence industry, 54
Democratic Alliance, 78
Democratic Front for the Liberation of Palestine: *see* DFLP
democracy, 15, 18, 23, 34, 44, 51,
   162
   and Arab minority, 59, 162
   establishment of, 143-46, 166
   secular, 129
demolition of dwellings, 56-57,

82, 99, 101, 115, 164
deportations, 83, 113, 115, 134
Deuxième Bureau, 72
detention without trial, 82, 164
development projects, 69
DFLP, 71, 76, 78, 94, 96, 119
    and *intifada*, 101
    women's committee of, 98
Discharged Soldiers Act (1949), 44
DoP (Declaration of Principles),
    60-61, 118, 124, 132, 146,
    156
Druze community, 4, 47
    as border guards, 81
    Israeli treatment of, 47-48, 57,
    60

East Jerusalem, 112, 135, 147
    Israeli annexation of, 41, 116,
    151-54, 162
    Jewish settlers in, 85, 88, 113,
    114, 152, 156
    and Palestinian self-rule, 120-22
eastern Europe, 4
    programs in, 8, 17
Eban, Abba, 10
Eder, Dr, 17
education, 54, 57, 67, 69, 79, 119,
    135-37
    Islamic, 103
    suspension of, 82, 101, 136
    for women, 130, 131
Egypt, 5, 13, 82, 83, 135
    Cairo peace agreement, 124,
    164
    and Camp David Accord, 94
    and Gaza, 33, 82, 93
    and Gulf crisis, 108-9
    and Israel, 38, 39, 41, 110, 111
    and Palestinians, 26, 32, 38, 68,
    109
    Palestinian refugees in, 69
Eitan, Rafael, 75, 88
elections, 148
Eliyahu, Chief Rabbi Mordechai,
    51
Entrance to Israel Law (1952), 44
Europe, 11, 12, 15, 21
European Jews, 8, 11, 17, 150
    extermination of, 21, 161
European Community, 89, 115

European Union, 148, 166
extra-judicial killings, 102, 109,
    116
extended families (*hamula*), 5, 16,
    48-49, 59

Faluja, 31
family, 44, 129
    extended (*hamula*), 5, 16, 48-
    49, 59
    separation of, 134, 148
family reunion, 148
Family Revival Society (Jami'at
    In'ash al-Usra), 96-97
Fatah, 70, 76, 79, 93, 95, 103, 124,
    128-29, 139, 145
    and *intifada*, 101
    rebels against, 78
    women of, 98
Fatah Revolutionary Council, 74
Faysal, Amir, 15
*fidayin* 38, 70
    conflict with Jordan, 71-72
    Lebanese civil war, 73
    pro-Syrian, 71, 75, 78
*Filastin* journal, 12
First World War, 13, 14
Fourth Geneva Convention, 82,
    84, 94, 111, 114, 162, 164
France, 7, 13, 14
    and Suez operation, 38
freedom of expression, 12
Front for Peace and Equality: *see*
    Hadash
Fula, 6, 10

Galilee, 4, 5, 54
    bedouin of, 48, 52, 60
    Palestinian inhabitants of, 43,
    45, 57, 61
    Sea of, 31, 156
Galilee Centre for Social Research,
    60
Galilee Society for Health
    Research and Services, 60
Gaza, 1, 6, 38, 65
    Egyptian administration of, 33,
    82
Gaza–Jericho agreement, 122, 124
Gaza Strip, 32, 33, 40, 112, 148
    closure of, 116, 124

economy of, 88-89, 92, 101, 109, 132, 141-43, 144
education in, 135
financial assistance for, 143, 145
indigenous population of, 32, 33, 65
Israeli military occupation of, 38, 83, 84, 93, 134
Jewish settlements in, 84, 85, 87, 124, 156
land seizures in, 85, 155
Muslim Brotherhood in, 103
and Palestinian state, 76, 94, 120
population growth rate, 125
protest demonstrations in, 99
raids from, 38, 93
refugees of, 1, 32, 33, 65, 108
resistance in, 81, 84, 93, 97
self-government for, 118-20, 124
social cohesion in, 145-45
water resources of, 157
Gemayel, Bashir, 75
General Union of Palestinian Students (GUPS), 69
General Union of Palestinian Workers, 69
Geneva Conventions, 82, 84, 85, 94, 111, 114, 162, 164
gentiles, 51
Germany, 20
Nazi, 50
Glubb Pasha, 35
Golan, 39
Goldstein, Baruch, 123
Gramsci, Antonio, 96
Grand Mufti, position of, 18
Grand Vizier, position of, 11
Great Britain, 15, 21, 26
Balfour Declaration, 15, 164
and Jewish immigration, 21
Palestine mandate, 3, 5, 13-21, 26, 28, 46, 50-51, 82, 84
and Palestinian people, 161-62
and Suez, 38
and Zionists, 13-15, 16, 17
Great Powers, 11, 14
Greater Israel, 118, 151
Greater Syria, 3, 15, 23

Grossman, David, 83
guerrilla warfare, 21, 38, 39, 69
and Hamas, 128
guerrilla fighters, 38, 70, 71-72: *see also fidayin*
Gulf war, 90, 107-10, 144
Gulf states, 96, 108-9, 111
Palestinian workers in, 67, 90, 108
Gush Emunim (Bloc of the Faithful), 87

Habash, George, 71
Hadash party, 58
Haganah, 25, 26, 29
Hague Regulations (1907), 82
Haifa, 5, 18, 53, 69
Hamas, 96, 104, 121, 137
attacks by, 122, 123, 124, 128
expulsion of supporters of, 114-15
negotiations by, 123-24
organizations of, 128-29, 145
and women, 131, 132
*hamulas*, 5, 16, 48-49, 58
al-Haq, 120-22, 146
al-Harakat al-Islamiya (Islamic movement), 59
Harakat Tahrir Filastin (Palestine Liberation Movement): *see* Fatah
Haram al-Sharif, 18, 111
Hashemite family, 15, 93
monarchy of, 33-34, 66, 72
Hawatma, Naif, 71
health care, 57, 50, 72, 119
of children, 133
and disability, 137-39
networks for, 97-98, 100, 101, 103, 138-39
Hebrew language, 19, 60
Hebrew tribes, 3
Hebron, 4, 6, 33, 99
expulsions of Arabs from, 31
Jordanian control of, 34
massacre of Jews in, 17
massacre of Palestinians in, 50, 123
religious importance of, 122
Hellenization, 4
Herzl, Theodor, 8, 9, 10, 28

Higher Women's Committee, 129
hijacking, 76, 77
Histadrut (General Labour Federation), 53-54
Hitler, Adolf, 21
Holocaust, the, 20, 21, 161
Holy Land, the, 4, 6: *see also* Israel, Palestine
house demolitions, 56-57, 82, 99, 101, 115, 164
house searches, 134
housing, 49, 51, 56-57, 152
Hovevei Zion (Lovers of Zion), 8, 9
Hula, Lake, 45
human rights, 60, 113, 120, 162, 164
al-Husayni, Faysal, 124
Hussein, King of Jordan, 34, 78
Hussein, Saddam, 108
al-Husseini, Hajj Amin, 16, 18
Husseini family, 16

IDF (Israeli Defence Forces), 1, 29, 36, 54, 124
  and Arab Israelis, 45-46
  border guards of, 49-50, 81
  brutality of, 49-50, 77, 84, 100-1, 115-16, 124
  and *intifada*, 99-100, 102, 114
  in Lebanon, 75, 156
  in Occupied Territories, 38, 84, 99-100, 123
  reservists killed, 114, 122, 124
  strength of, 34
Ikhwan al-Muslimin (Muslim Brotherhood), 103-4, 129
immigration: *see* Jewish immigration
imperialism, 71, 161
industry, 53-54
  polluting, 54
infant mortality, 138
infiltrators, 35-36
international community, 79, 80, 116
  and *intifada*, 100, 102
  and partition, 31
  and rights of Palestinian people, 154, 162-66
international law, 83, 107, 162

human rights, 164
  Israeli contravention of, 82, 84, 85, 100-1, 114, 124
international trade, 6
*intifada*, 60, 80, 99-100, 138-39
  control of, 102
  economic cost of, 109, 117, 144
  Hamas joins, 104, 114
  reprisals against, 100-1, 111, 113, 115-16, 134, 136
  women's committees, 130-31
  youth participation in, 102, 133, 134
Iqrit, 46
Iraq, 19, 40, 72, 110, 111, 152
  invasion of Kuwait, 107, 108-9
Irgun Zvai Leumi (IZL), 28
Islam, 3, 4
  and Jerusalem, 152-54
  militant, 129, 131
  revival of, 103, 104, 128-29
  and Palestine, 4-5, 18
  and women, 129-30. 131-32
Islamic Empire, 5
Islamic Jihad, 101, 104
Islamic Movement, 59, 128
Islamic state, 129
Israel, 3, 10, 25, 138
  and Arab governments, 34-35
  and Arab labour, 53, 89-90, 101, 142-43
  attitude to Arabs, 26, 31, 43-46, 50-51, 54, 61, 135, 158-59, 162
  borders of, 23-24, 34-35, 39, 46, 120
  Camp David agreement and, 94
  citizenship of, 24, 44
  declaration of independence, 43
  economic development of, 53-56, 88-89, 117, 140
  establishment of, 24-27
  expulsion of Palestinians from, 24-25, 26-31, 39, 43, 45, 63, 75-76, 99, 114-15
  government of, 27, 40, 44-45
  guerrilla raids into, 36, 38, 71, 73
  and Hamas, 105, 124, 128
  human rights abuse by, 60, 113, 120, 162

immigration policies, 43-44, 45, 114, 117, 158
as Jewish state, 43-44, 76, 113, 117, 154-55, 164
and Jordan, 34, 38, 39, 41, 81-82, 93, 95, 99
land seizure by, 46-48, 51-55, 57, 58, 85, 111, 134, 154, 164, 165
and Law of Return to, 43, 60, 164
Lebanon invaded by, 73, 74-75, 78
markets of, 89, 90-91, 101, 142
military strength of, 25-26, 34, 154
1973 war, 41
and Occupied Territories, 39, 40-41, 76, 81-90, 96, 102, 113, 117, 122-23, 140, 158
and Palestinian popular protest, 95, 98, 99-100
peace process, 112, 113, 117-22, 147, 152-54
and PLO, 1, 61, 76, 78, 95, 117-18, 142
and refugees, 27-28, 31-32, 35-40, 41, 43-44, 68, 148-51
repressive measures by, 56-57, 82, 84, 99-101, 111, 113, 114-16, 122, 134, 144, 161
security of, 154-55
settlement policy, 85-87, 110-11, 113, 155-6, 162
territorial claims of, 39, 41, 76, 85-87, 120, 155-56
and the USA, 31, 32, 38, 41, 74, 77, 91, 107, 108, 114
water resources for, 85, 88, 140, 156-57, 162
Israeli Palestinians, 24-25, 43, 147
birth rate of, 44, 61, 125-26, 158
Christian, 46, 127
cultural and political rights, 50, 58, 61
discrimination against, 43-45, 49, 54-55, 60, 113, 157-58, 163
Druze, 47-48
electoral power, 57-59, 158

economic situation, 54-55, 58
employment of, 51, 53, 158, 163
internally displaced, 43, 46, 65
land of, 46-48, 50, 53, 56, 164
living conditions of, 54-57, 59-60
Muslim, 127
military control of, 45-46, 47, 51, 57
political activism of, 59-61
state services to, 47, 164
water rights of, 53
Israel Defence Forces: *see* IDF
Israeli military intelligence, 29
Israeli paramilitary forces, 30
Istanbul, 5, 11
IZL (Irgun Zvai Leumi), 28

Jabal Amil, 79
Jaffa, 5, 6, 8, 17, 18, 53
Arabs flee from, 28
women's associations in, 96
Jami'at In'ash al-Usra (Family Revival Society), 96-97
Jenin, 6
Jericho, 143
self-government for, 118-22, 124
Jerisi Commission, 55
Jerusalem, 3-4, 8, 13, 16, 33, 34, 87, 111, 152-4
Arabs expelled from, 28, 113
East, 41, 85, 88, 112, 113, 114, 120-22, 135, 147, 152-4, 162
holy places of, 5, 6, 18, 116, 152-54
*intifada* in, 111
massacre of Jews in, 17
Mufti of, 16
status of, 112, 117, 120, 147, 151-52, 165
women's associations in, 96
Jezreel, Plain of, 6
Jewish Agency, 15-16, 23, 24, 26, 57
Executive of, 24
Jewish Agency (Status) Law (1952), 44
Jewish brigades, 21
Jewish immigration, 8, 9

absorbtion of, 27, 31, 32, 43-44,
45
from Africa and Asia, 51
British encouragement of, 13,
15, 17
and Holocaust, 20, 21, 161
and land purchase, 10-11, 19
opposition to, 11-12, 16-17
restriction of, 18, 19-20, 21
Russian, 31, 52, 61, 110, 114,
117, 158
Jewish Law of Return, 43, 60, 164
Jewish Lawyers' Association, 50
Jewish National Fund (JNF), 10, 24
land administered by, 47, 53,
163
land purchase by, 11, 18
Jewish nationalism: *see* Zionism
Jewish settlements, 8, 9, 10-12,
15-18, 61, 111, 120
attacks on, 11, 17, 18
freeze on, 113, 121, 152
in Occupied Territories, 52, 83-
88, 90, 100, 110, 113-14,
124, 147, 156, 162, 164
water use by, 88:
*see also kibbutzim, moshavim*
Jewish settlers, 120, 156
attacks on, 115, 122
violence by, 84, 95, 100, 116,
122-23, 134
Jewish state, 24
idea of, 9-10, 14
recognition of, 23: *see also*
Israel
Jews, 5, 6, 13, 23
assimilated, 8
attacks on, 11, 17-18, 25, 35,
36, 76, 111
birth rate of, 125
civil and political rights of, 19,
82
cultural identity of, 4, 8, 10,
158
expulsion of, 21, 150
history of, 3-4
and Holocaust, 20, 21, 155, 161
ideological, 12
European, 4, 8, 11, 17, 150
and Law of Return, 43, 60, 164
non-Zionist, 18

of Palestine, 4, 8, 17
Jibril, Ahmad, 70
*jihad* (holy war), 103, 104
Jordan, 33, 76, 77, 104, 110, 129,
135, 155
and Israel, 34, 38, 39, 41, 81-82,
93, 95, 99
laws of, 82, 83
Palestinian struggle with, 71-72
and PLO, 70, 72, 78, 95, 98, 111
refugees in, 33-34, 65, 66, 68,
69, 108, 134, 150
West Bank sovereignty, 33-34,
45, 65, 93-94, 95, 96
Jordan River, 3, 5, 34, 40
East Bank of, 70
water of, 39, 156
Jordan valley, 5, 39, 81, 85
Jordanian troops, 72
Judaea, 9
kingdom of, 3, 4
Judaism, 4

Kafr Bir'im, 46
Kafr Qasim, 45
massacre at, 49-50
Karama, 70
*al-Karmil* journal, 12
Khalil, Samiha, 96
Khan Yunis, 38
*kibbutzim*, 36, 46
Klinghoffer, Leon, 77
Knesset, 44, 51, 58-59
Kurds, 152
Kuwait, 69, 162
Gulf war over, 90, 107-10, 144
Iraqi invasion of, 90, 107, 108-9
Palestinian workforce in, 69,
108-9

Labour party (Mapai), 45, 58, 94,
118, 147, 155
Land Code (1858), 7
land acquisition, 12
Zionist, 10-11, 18, 19
Land Acquisition (Validation of
Acts and Compensation) Law
(1953), 46
Land Day, 50
land deeds, 46
land ownership, 6, 8, 46

foreign, 7
  state control of, 46, 83, 85
land registration, 7
  under British mandate, 46
Land Registration Law (1871), 7
land seizure, 46-48, 51-55, 57, 58,
    165
  in Occupied Territories, 85, 111,
    134, 154, 164, 165
land tenure, 12
landlords, 7, 98
  absentee, 7, 10, 11
landowning families, 6
Landau Commission, 84, 113
Latrun Salient, 154, 155
Lausanne, Treaty of, 150
Law of Citizenship (1952), 44
League of Nations, 15, 16, 21
League of Palestinian Women, 69
Lebanese army, 73, 78
Lebanese Christian Militia, 74
Lebanon, 3, 145, 156
  civil war in, 73, 74, 145
  Israeli invasions of, 73, 74-75,
    77, 95, 116
  Marj al-Zuhur, 114-15
  Palestinian refugees in, 63-65,
    67, 69, 74-75, 108, 109, 119,
    134, 149-50
  PLO influence, 70, 72-73, 79,
    111
  PLO expulsion from, 74-75, 78
  Syrian influence in, 78, 79, 111
LEHI (Lohamei Herut Israel), 27,
    28
Likud party, 58, 85, 94, 110, 112,
    114, 147, 155
Litani River, 156
'Little Triangle', 43, 45, 49, 61
local councils, 55, 56, 58
  political mobilization through,
    59-60
Lod, 154
Lydda, 29, 34

Maale Abrakim, 38
Ma'alot, 54
  DFLP attack on, 76
Madrid conference, 112, 120, 148
Majdal, 6, 31, 118
Mamluk dynasty, 5

*al-Manar*, 12
Mapai: *see* Labour party
Mapam party, 28
Marj al-Zuhur, 112-13
Markovitch Report, 56-57
Maronite Christian community,
    65, 72
medical professionals: *see* health
    care
merchants, 6
Middle East, 67, 102
military courts, 83
military regulations, 82, 120
military service, 44
  by Druzes, 47
Misgav Regional Council, 56
missionaries, Christian, 7
modernization, 8
monotheism, 3
Morris, Benny, 30, 36
*moshavim*, 46, 52
mosque building, 103
Mufti of Jerusalem, 16
al-Mujamma' al-Harakat al-
    Muqawana al-Islamiya: *see*
    Hamas
al-Mujamma' al-Islami (Islamic
    Association), 103-4, 128
*mukhtars* (government-appointed
    headmen), 6
Multilateral Refugee Working
    Group, 150
Munich, 76
Muslim Brotherhood, 103-4, 129
Muslims, 1, 11, 73
  conquest of Palestine by, 4-5
  ideological, 122
  Palestinian, 15, 16, 47, 127
  secular, 129
Muslim clerics, 6
Muslim world, 18

Nablus, 5, 6, 99
  Israeli control of, 84
  Jordanian control of, 34
Nashashibi family, 16
Nasser, Gamal Abdel, 38
National Guidance Committee,
    94, 95
National Salvation Front, 78
nationalism, 13

Arab, 11, 34, 59, 71, 73
Jewish: *see* Zionism
and national identity, 159
Palestinian, 94, 143
Nazareth, 5, 43, 54, 55, 60
Nazareth Illit, 54
Nazis, 30, 36, 50, 149
Naqab: *see* Negev dessert, 5
National Insurance Law (1953), 44
National Planning and Building
  Law (1965), 47
Negev desert, 5, 29, 35, 52, 54, 57
  bedouin of, 43, 46-47, 48, 60
1948 war, 25-26
  Armistice of, 27, 31, 33, 34, 43,
    45, 154
  expulsion of Palestinians, 26-
    31, 63, 118, 148
1967 war, 38-40, 60
  and PLO, 70
  refugees from, 39-41, 81, 148
  territory captured in, 39, 41, 76:
    *see also* Occupied Territories
nomads, 5: *see* bedouin
non-violent resistence, 50
Norwegian government, 117

Occupied Territories, 48, 58, 60,
    155
  autonomy plan for, 1, 85, 94,
    117, 120, 146
  capture of, 39, 41, 76
  children in, 133-35
  Christian community in, 127
  economy of, 88-92, 108, 109,
    111, 120
  health provision in, 137-39,
    140
  human rights in, 113
  infrastructure of, 140-41
  *intifada* in, 81, 99-103, 109
  Islamic revival in, 103, 104
  Israeli administration of, 81-82,
    84, 89, 111, 123, 142, 158
  Jewish settlements in, 52, 61,
    84-88, 90, 100, 110, 113-14,
    116, 122-23, 124, 147, 156,
    162, 164
  labour force of, 89-90, 101
  notable class in, 93, 94, 95, 98,
    99

and peace accord, 119-22, 124,
    162
  PLO influence in, 76, 93-95,
    112, 139
  popular movement in, 96, 102,
    116-17
  protest demonstrations in, 94,
    99, 101, 111
  self-determination hopes for,
    76, 77, 78, 94, 95, 120
  social cohesion in, 143-46
  steadfastness fund for, 94-95
  support for Saddam Hussein,
    108
  water resources of, 85, 88, 140,
    157, 161
  withdrawal plans, 119, 154-55,
    164
  women's committees in, 97, 98
Office for Arab Affairs, 49
oil industry, 69
Operation Hafarfaret, 45, 49
Orthodox Christianity, 4, 7
Oslo, 122
Ottoman empire, 9, 12
  administration of, 5, 6, 11, 15
  land registration under, 7, 47
  laws of, 82
  rule of Palestine, 5-7, 9, 11-13

Palestine, 1, 3, 10, 12, 41, 70
  Arab rule of, 3, 4-5
  and Arab states, 21-23, 24, 25,
    26
  British mandate in, 3, 5, 13-21,
    26, 28, 46, 50-51, 82
  Christian community, 1, 4, 7,
    15, 16
  economy of, 7-8, 15
  European penetration of, 6-7,
    11
  extinction of, 31, 34, 164
  Jewish community of, 4, 8, 17
  Jewish settlement in, 8, 9, 10-
    12, 15-18
  Jewish state and, 9-10, 14, 23-
    24, 113, 120
  liberation of, 69, 71
  and Jordan, 34
  Muslim communities, 1, 15, 16,
    18

new state of, 119, 125, 141: *see* Palestinian state
1948 war in, 25-31
Ottoman rule of, 5-8, 9, 11-13
partition of, 19, 20, 23-24, 26, 31, 51, 148, 154
Roman domination of, 3-4
society, 4, 5-6, 7-8, 12,
Zionist colonization of, 9-11, 13-15, 18, 161
Palestine Communist Party, 78, 101
Palestine Conciliation Commission (PCC), 31, 32
Palestine Economic Council for Development and Rehabilitation (PECDAR), 126, 143, 145
Palestine Liberation Army (PLA), 69
Palestine Liberation Organization: *see* PLO
Palestine National Charter, 73-74
Palestine National Council, 75, 77, 104
    reconciliation at, 98
Palestine People's Party, 95-96
Palestine Red Crescent Society, 72, 139
Palestinian children, 133-35
Palestinian emigration, 25
Palestinian National Authority (PNA), 118, 137, 145, 154
    accountability of, 166
Palestinian nationalism, 94, 143
Palestinian police, 119
Palestinian population centres, 84, 85, 140
Palestinian refugees, 1, 4, 31, 63-64, 119, 158
    child, 134
    citizenship of, 66, 149, 150
    distribution of, 32, 33, 34, 45, 64
    education of, 67, 69, 79, 133-34, 135-36
    employment of, 67, 69, 73, 108, 109
    expulsions of, 26-31, 63, 118, 148, 150
    family reunion and, 134, 148

health of, 137-38
infiltration by, 35-36, 81
internally displaced, 39-41, 43, 46, 52, 64, 81, 148, 149
Israeli policy towards, 27-28, 31-32, 39-40, 148-51
Jordanian conflict, 72
Lebanese civil war and, 71-75, 78
national identity and, 68-70, 134-35, 149
and peace accord, 120, 147
political activity by, 65, 69
psychological impact on, 65-66, 69
right of return of, 31-32, 60, 68, 148-51, 163, 164
resettlement of, 32, 40, 68, 158
Sabra/Shatila massacre of, 75, 79
social institutions of, 72-73, 79
Palestinian state, 119, 125, 147, 157
    boundaries of, 147, 154-55
    democracy and, 144-46, 166
    draft constitution of, 132-3
    economic development of, 141-43, 165
    financial aid for, 143, 165
    free elections for, 118, 146, 166
    infrastructure of, 140-41, 144, 165
    legal protections in, 164, 166
    as Muslim endowment, 104
    population growth of, 125-26
    two-state solution of, 76
    water resources of, 157, 165
Palestinian villages: *see* villages
Palestinian women, 96-97, 98, 129-33, 145
Palestinians, 20, 161
    civil rights of, 14, 50, 82, 108, 109, 112, 124, 163-66
    Christian, 1, 4, 7, 15, 16, 46, 127
    discrimination against, 43-45, 49, 54-55, 60, 87, 113, 157-58, 163
    emigration of, 127
    factionalism of, 16, 21, 25, 26, 47-48, 144-45

education of, 135-37
expulsion of, 24-25, 26-31, 39,
  43, 45, 63, 75-76, 99, 114-15,
  148, 161
family rivalries, 16
flight of, 27-31
guerrilla warfare, 21, 36, 38, 39
and Gulf crisis, 108-10
Hamas popularity, 124, 128-29
health of, 137-39
identity of, 5, 8, 10, 13, 34, 68,
  125, 149
infiltration of, 35-36
Islamic movements, 59, 99, 104
Islamic revival among, 127-29,
  131
labour of, 52-53, 66, 89-90, 101
land of, 7, 46
leaders of, 16, 19, 21, 28, 83,
  95, 101, 137, 145-46
opposition to Zionism, 11-12,
  15-17, 129
peace negotiations, 112-13,
  119-20
political demands of, 15, 18,
  23, 112, 128-29
population growth of, 44, 61,
  125-26
professional, 90, 96, 97, 114,
  131
resistance movement, 39, 60,
  69-75, 81, 84: *see also intifada*
self-determination and, 19, 26,
  23, 112, 120-22, 147, 159
social attitudes among, 129-30,
  131-33, 139
status of, 1, 43-45
transfer of, 9, 19, 24, 28, 45, 61,
  150
unemployed, 53, 55, 109
violence against, 28-29, 49-50,
  75, 77, 87-88, 109, 115-16,
  122-23
unemployment of, 53, 55, 109,
  129
water rights of, 53, 88
Zionist attitudes to, 9, 10-11, 17
partition, 19, 20, 23-24, 26, 31, 51
  boundaries for, 147, 154-55
partition plan, 23-4
pastoralism, 5

Patriotic Front, 93-94
peace negotiations, 110-13, 117-
  22
  refugees and, 148-49
  Palestinian Israelis and, 163-64
  Western governments and, 164,
    166
peasants, 5, 10, 47
  employed in Israel, 96
  land (registration) and, 6, 7
  loss of land of, 8, 11, 18, 52
  as refugees, 28, 29, 35-36, 65-66
  uprising by, 18-19
  women, 131
Peel Commission, 19
Peel Report (1937), 19, 23
Peres, Shimon, 99, 118
Perrin, Rabbi, 123
Petah Tikva, 8
PFLP, 70-71, 76, 93, 94, 96
  and *intifada*, 101
  women's committees of, 98
PFLP General Command, 71
Phalangists, 75
Philistines, the, 3
pilgrims, 6
Plan Dalet, 26, 28
plastic bullets, 100
PLO, 59, 71, 98
  authoritarianism of, 145
  and Arab states, 69-70, 99
  autonomy organization and,
    124, 129, 132, 141, 142
  criticism of, 94, 95, 103, 104,
    116-17, 120
  diplomacy and, 75, 76-77
  executive committee of, 71
  finances of, 70, 96, 110, 116
  and Gulf crisis, 108-10
  and Hamas, 104-5, 115, 124
  and *intifada*, 80, 101-102, 103
  and Islamic revival, 128
  and Israel, 1, 61, 74, 76, 78, 95,
    117-18, 142
  Israeli assault on, 95
  and Jordan, 71-72, 78, 95, 98
  in Lebanese civil war, 72-73, 74
  in Occupied Territories, 77, 93-
    95, 99
  peace negotiations of, 111-12,
    113, 117-22, 124, 164

Tunis headquarters of, 74, 103, 117, 137
UNSCR 242 accepted by, 102-3
violent acts by, 70, 72, 73, 74, 75-76
PNA: *see* Palestinian National Authority
pogroms, 8, 17
police force, Palestinian, 119
political prisoners, 19, 147
Popular Front for the Liberation of Palestine: *see* PFLP
Population Transfer Committee, 24, 28, 30
population transfers, 9, 19, 24, 28, 45, 61
international law and, 82
Progressive List for Peace, 58
protest demonstrations, 84, 94, 99, 101, 111
Protestant Christianity, 7
public health, 57, 50

Qalqilia, 43
Qibya, 38
Qiryat Arba, 123
Qur'an, the, 103

Rabin, Yitzhak, 40, 100, 113, 114, 116, 123
and PLO, 117, 124
racism, 60, 113, 123, 152
Rafah, 38
Rahat, 55-56
Rakah: *see* Communist Party
Ramadan, 79, 123
Ramallah, 84, 99, 139
Chamber of Commerce, 128
Ramat Hovave, 52
Ramat Rachel, 38
Ramiya, 52
Ramle, 29, 34, 154
Rashidiya, 78
Reagan, President Ronald, 77
Reelef, Rabbi Yitzhak, 9
refugee camps, 1, 31, 34, 40, 66-67, 69, 149-50
children in, 134
*intifada* in, 102, 116
in Lebanon, 72, 74, 75, 78-79, 149-50

women's committees in, 97
refugee rights, 148-49: *see also* Palestinian refugees
regional councils, 56
Rejection Front, 119-20
Ridha, Rashid, 11
right of return, 31-32, 60, 68, 148-51, 163, 164
Roman Catholicism, 4, 7
Roman empire, 3
Rothschild, Lord, 13
Roy, Sara, 144-45
rural population, 96
Russia, 7, 13
Jewish immigration from, 31, 52, 61, 110, 114, 117, 158

Sabra/Shatila massacre, 75, 79
Safed, 4, 5
massacre of Jews in, 17
*al-Sa'iqa* (The Thunderbolt), 71
Saladin, 5
SAMED, 72-73
Sanu, 39
Sea Peoples, 3
Second World War, 20, 21, 25-26
secularism, 8, 59, 103, 128 132
security services,
Israeli, 81
Lebanese, 72
and refugees, 66, 149
self-determination
service industries, 53
settlements, 82, 155-6
Shabak, 81
torture by, 84
Shafa Amr, 55
*shahabs*, 102
Shamir, Yitzhak, 99-100
and Stern Gang, 27
Shapira, Ya'acov, 50-51
sharecropping, 8
Sharett, Moshe, 27, 45
Sharon, Ariel, 152
*shari'a* law, 131-32, 133
shaykhs (tribal heads), 6
Shehadeh, Raja, 122, 124
Shia Islam, 4, 72, 78, 79
Siddon, 149
Sikki, 149
Silwan, 113

Sinai, 3, 40, 68
  Israeli withdrawal from, 52
Sinai campaign/1956 war in, 38,
  39, 45
Six Day War, 39-40
Solomon, King, 3
South America, 45
South Lebanon, 72
  Israeli occupation of, 116, 156
Soviet Jews, 61
Soviet Union, 77, 110, 161
Stern Gang, 27
stone-throwing, 84, 99, 134
Straits of Tiran, 39, 40
street fighting, 102
strikes, 101, 102
Suez Canal, 13
Suez operation, 38
Sunni Muslims, 4, 47
Superpowers, 93
Supreme Muslim Council, 18
Sursuq, Ilyas, 10
Swedish government, 141
Sykes-Picot Agreement, 13-14
Syria, 5, 11, 40, 69, 78, 156
  Greater, 3, 15, 23
  and Israel, 39, 41
  and Lebanon, 78, 79
  and Palestine, 3, 26, 32, 38
  Palestinian refugees in, 45, 64,
    65, 66, 136
  and Palestinian resistance, 71,
    75, 78, 111

Tal al-Malah, 52
taxation, 4, 6, 7, 88, 102, 141
tax collectors, 6
Tel Aviv, 8, 101, 154
Temple, destruction of, 3-4
Temple Mount, 18, 111
terrorism,
  militant settler groups, 95
  Palestinian, 36, 76, 77
  PLO, 102, 103
  Zionist, 21, 28, 77
textile industry, 7
Third Reich, 149
Tiberias, 4, 5
Tiyaha confederation, 48
torture, 84, 98, 107
town-dwellers, 4, 6, 49

toxic waste, 53
trade union movement, 98: *see
  also* Histadrut
traders, 4
Transjordan, 26, 31, 32
travel permits, 49, 66
travel restrictions, 46
treaty law, 82
Tunis, 74, 103, 117, 137
Turkey, Ottoman, 13, 14
Turki, Fawaz, 68-69
two-state solution, 76
Tyre, 79

Umm al-Fahm, 43, 59
unemployment,
  Palestinian, 53, 55, 109, 129
Unified National Leadership of
  the Uprising: *see* UNLU
Union of Arab Women, 96-97
Union of Palestinian Medical
  Relief Committees: *see*
  UPMRC
United Arab Republic, 69
United Nations, 21
  and Palestinians, 38, 40, 51,
    111
  and Palestinian refugees, 27,
    31-32, 41, 64
  recognition of PLO, 94, 110-11
  sanctions, 38
United Nations General Assembly
  Resolutions, (UNGAR 181),
    23, 24, 25, 156, 154
  (UNGAR 194), 27, 41, 68,
    150-1, 154, 163
  (UNGAR 3379), 113
United Nations High Commission
  for Refugees (UNHCR), 66
United Nations Interim Force in
  Lebanon (UNIFIL), 74
United Nations Relief and Works
  Agency (UNRWA), 63, 64,
    66-68, 69, 132, 135, 137-38,
    139
United Nations Security Council,
  78
  Resolution 242, 40-41, 77, 78,
    94, 102, 118-19, 148, 154,
    161, 162
  Resolution 338, 41

Resolution 425, 74, 116
Resolution 779, 115
United Nations Special Commit-
    tee on Palestine (UNSCOP),
    23
United States of America, 23
    and Camp David, 94
    and Gulf war, 107, 109, 110
    and Israel, 21, 31, 32, 38, 41,
        74, 91, 107, 108, 114, 162
    and Palestinian people, 67-68,
        75, 148, 161, 162
    peace negotiations and, 110,
        111-12
    and PLO, 77, 78, 99, 103
UNLU, 101-3
unskilled labour, 51, 53, 54, 66, 91
UPMRC, 97-98, 100, 138

Village Leagues, 95
villages, 6, 35, 39, 46, 108, 133
    collective, 52
    destruction of, 27, 29
    land loss, 47, 51-52
    Israeli administration of of, 55-
        57
    organization of, 5, 48-49
    urbanised villages, 55
Villayet Law (1864), 7
voluntary agencies, 95, 99, 139,
    145-46, 166

*waaf* property, 47
wage labourers, 8, 10, 18, 52, 53
    low-paid, 51
wages, 58
Wailing Wall: *see* Western Wall
Washington, DC, 112-13, 114,
    118, 120
water resources, 52, 88, 140, 147
    agricultural irrigation, 88, 142
    reserves of, 156-57
Weitz, Josef, 24
Weizmann, Chaim, 14-15, 16, 28,
    150
West Bank, 31, 38, 39, 40, 43, 51,
    84, 94, 120
    closure of, 116
    economy of, 144
    education in, 136
    family reunion, 148

and Gulf crisis, 109
Hamas activism in, 104
health in, 138
Israeli military occupation of,
    82-83, 92, 134
Jewish settlements in, 84, 87-
    88, 156
Jordanian annexation of, 33-34,
    45, 65, 78
land seizures in, 85-87, 111
Palestinian refugees in, 33-34,
    45, 64, 65, 108
PLO foothold in, 119
return of refugees to, 150-51
self-government for, 119
social cohesion in, 144, 145
water resources of, 87, 140, 157
workforce of, 132
West Bank mayors, 94
    expuslsion of, 95
West Beirut, 74, 78, 95
western Europe, 89
western Gallilee, 54-55
Western governments, 1
    and Arab–Israeli conflict, 37-38,
        76, 77, 161-63, 166
    and PLO, 77, 78, 99
Western (Wailing) Wall, 17-18
women's movement, 69, 96-97,
    98, 129, 130-33, 145-46
work permits, 49, 66, 90
World Bank, 143
World War I, 13, 14
World War II, 20, 21, 25-26
World Zionist Organization, 44

Yamit, 52
Yarmuk–Jordan valley develop-
    ment, 68
Yasin, Shaykh, 101, 126
*Yellow Wind, The* (Grossman), 83
Yishuv, the, 9, 10, 11, 17
    leadership of, 21
    strength of, 23
Young Turks, 12

Za'im, Husni, 32
Zangwill, Israel, 9-10, 14
Zionism, 3, 4, 14, 44, 60, 129, 149
    and colonization, 9-11, 13-15,
        18, 161

early, 8-11
'Greater Israel' ideology and,
    118, 151
opposition to, 11-12, 15-18, 57,
    71, 76
territorial claims of, 23, 26, 43-
    44, 76, 113, 117
Zionist Congress, 8-9
Zionist political parties, 58
Zionists, 11
    attitudes to Arabs, 9, 10-11, 17,
        19, 28
    land purchase by, 10, 11, 18, 19
    leaders of, 9, 17, 19
    terrorist organizations of, 21,
        28
Zisling, Aharon, 30

## About Minority Rights Group Reports

Minority Rights Group began publishing in 1970. Over two decades and ninety titles later, MRG's series of reports are widely recognized internationally as authoritative, accurate and objective documents on the rights of minorities worldwide.

Over the years, subscribers to the series have received a wealth of unique material on ethnic, religious, linguistic and social minorities. The reports are seen as an important reference by researchers, students, campaigners and provide readers all over the world with valuable background data on many topical issues.

Around six reports are published every year. Each title, expertly researched and written, is approximately 36 pages and 25,000 words long and covers a specific minority issue.

*Recent titles in our report series include:*

| | |
|---|---|
| Afghanistan | The Adivasis of Bangladesh |
| Land Rights | The Maya of Guatemala |
| Education Rights | |

If you have found this book informative and stimulating, and would like to learn more about minority issues, you should subscribe to our report series. It is only with the help of our supporters that we are able to pursue our aims and objectives – to secure justice for disadvantaged groups around the world.

We currently offer a reduced annual rate for individual subscribers – please ring our Subscription Desk on +44 (171) 978 9498 for details. Payment can be easily made by MasterCard or Visa by either telephone or post.

All enquiries to: Sales Department
Minority Rights Group
379 Brixton Road
London
SW9 7DE
UK